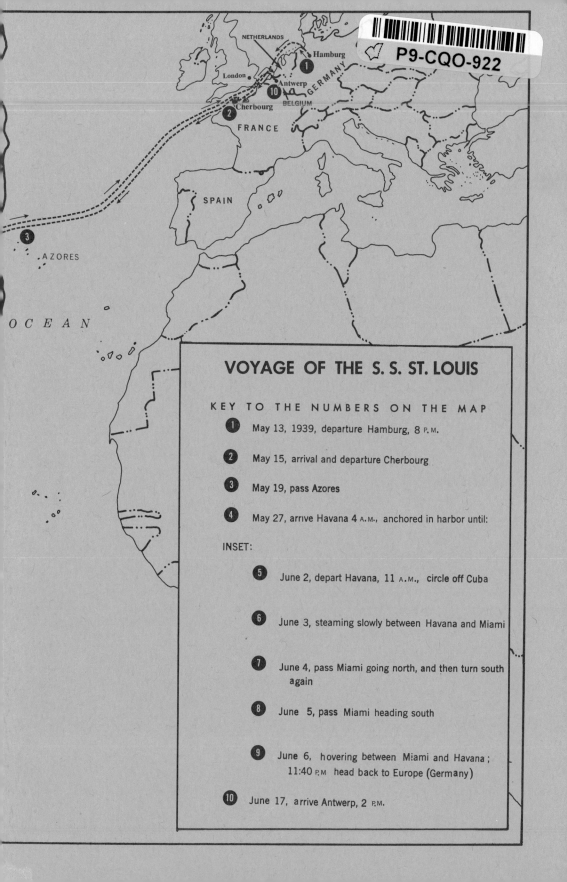

VOYAGE OF THE S. S. ST. LOUIS

KEY TO THE NUMBERS ON THE MAP

1 May 13, 1939, departure Hamburg, 8 P.M.

2 May 15, arrival and departure Cherbourg

3 May 19, pass Azores

4 May 27, arrive Havana 4 A.M., anchored in harbor until:

INSET:

5 June 2, depart Havana, 11 A.M., circle off Cuba

6 June 3, steaming slowly between Havana and Miami

7 June 4, pass Miami going north, and then turn south again

8 June 5, pass Miami heading south

9 June 6, hovering between Miami and Havana; 11:40 P.M. head back to Europe (Germany)

10 June 17, arrive Antwerp, 2 P.M.

VOYAGE
OF
THE
DAMNED

VOYAGE
OF
THE
DAMNED

Gordon Thomas AND Max Morgan Witts

STEIN AND DAY/*Publishers*/New York

First published in 1974
Copyright © 1974 by Gordon Thomas and Max Morgan Witts
Library of Congress Catalog Card No. 73-91845
All rights reserved
Designed by David Miller
Printed in the United States of America
Stein and Day/*Publishers*/Scarborough House, Briarcliff Manor, New York 10510
ISBN 0-8128-1694-3

Dedication

This book is dedicated to those who were the damned, on the *St. Louis*—not only the passengers who are alive today and told their story to us, but all on board the ship, who were caught up in events they did not understand and could not control.

Those who survived the voyage and aftermath are today scattered throughout the world—North and South America, Great Britain, Australia, Europe, and, of course, Israel. And also Germany. Some are now wealthy, a few poor. Some still live in fear.

Almost everyone we approached was willing to meet us. One or two found that when the time came they could not bring themselves to recall and relive the experience. The minds of a few, in particular those who were young and impressionable in 1939, are now so cruelly scarred by what happened to them that their mental state led us, regretfully, to conclude their testimony was untrustworthy.

A few agreed to talk to us on condition that they not be quoted. We have respected this wish, understanding their desire for anonymity; what they told us was useful as background information and corroborative evidence. But they, and those unwilling or unable to meet us, were in the minority. For most, telling a stranger things they could hardly bring themselves to discuss with their closest friends seemed therapeutic, almost as if the experience was exorcised by the telling.

Inevitably, the passage of time, the insidious influence of propaganda, a confusion between what they have read and what actually happened, led some we interviewed to mix fiction with fact. We have tried to get around this by relying on interviews with survivors, crew members, and others directly involved with the voyage of the *St. Louis*, and consulting official archives, diaries, letters, and other eyewitness accounts written at the time.

Our responsibility to those living and dead was to tell the story as impartially and truthfully as the available sources and our combined talents allowed. *Voyage of the Damned* is not meant to be a crusading book, but it is, we hope, an honest and revealing one.

We thank especially those passengers whose names are listed below. Their experience has taught most of them to revere life, and to respect time. They told us something of the first, and granted us a precious proportion of the second. Without both, this book could not have been written.

Max S. Aber
Otto Bergmann
Rosemarie Bergmann
Hildie Bockow (formerly
    Reading)
Meta Bonné
Richard Dresel
Ruth Dresel
Werner Feig
Alice Feilchenfeld
Hans Fisher
Herbert Glass
Herta Glass
Rita Goldstein
Frank Gotthelf
Herman Gronowetter

Lilly Kamin (formerly Joseph)
Carl Lenneberg
George Lenneberg
Gisela Lenneberg
Liesl Loeb (née Joseph)
Fritz Loewe
Gertrud Mendels (née
    Scheuer)
Pessla Messinger
Frank Metis
George Moss
Thea Moss
Renatta Rippe (née Aber)
Babette Spanier
Marianne Vargish
    (née Bardeleben)

Contents

Illustrations

Give me your tired, your poor,
Your huddled masses yearning to breathe free,
The wretched refuse of your teeming shore.
Send those, the homeless, tempest-tost to me.
I lift my lamp beside the golden door.

INSCRIPTION BY EMMA LAZARUS
Statue of Liberty, New York Harbor

Yet there comes a time for forgetting,
for who could live and not forget?
Now and then, however, there must also
be one who remembers.

ALBRECHT GOES,
Das Brandopfer

VOYAGE
OF
THE
DAMNED

Prologue

On January 30, 1933, Franklin Delano Roosevelt celebrated his fifty-first birthday; in little more than a month he would be president of the United States.

That same day, Adolf Hitler became chancellor of Germany; in a little less than two months, the Reichstag would make him absolute master of his country.

On taking office, the two men faced similar problems, but they chose opposite paths to a solution. Their policies would force them inexorably onto a collision course.

In Germany, the Fuehrer took over a country suffering from self-doubt and in the grip of an economic collapse so serious it seemed insoluble. His solution was to make the Jews scapegoat for all the nation's ills. Get rid of them, he maintained, and the patient would recover. Hitler never wavered from this prescription, never concealed it, and by May 1939, thousands had fled, thousands were in hiding, thousands in concentration camps. Though the gas ovens were not yet in operation, many people died daily of malnutrition and maltreatment, and what was happening in Dachau and Buchenwald was already known to the governments of the major powers.

In America, in 1933, Roosevelt had also been confronted by a critical situation. The worst economic crisis in history left banking in chaos: there were some twelve million unemployed; the nation was suffering from an acute loss of self-confidence.

In 1935, America's isolationism was strengthened with the passing of the Neutrality Act: the United States was not yet willing to take sides.

The Jews in Germany—there were some 500,000 of them when Hitler took power—were of two minds. Some viewed Hitler as a

15

temporary aberration and waited, alas in vain, for things to change. Other Jews sought to escape. They illegally crossed the borders of Switzerland, Holland, Belgium, and France; they sometimes intentionally broke laws in order to be put into prison, a safer course than being returned to Germany. A small percentage made it to America or England. But for most of those trapped in the German concentration camps, or those about to be put to death, escape could come only if they could convince the Nazis that they could book passage on a ship that would take them away from the Fatherland. There were few ships available, and precious few countries willing to accept them as passengers.

By 1939, Britain, faced with an Arab revolt in the Middle East, was about to drastically curtail the number of immigrants it would allow into Palestine. At home, there were 25,000 refugees. Britain may have been more charitable than many other nations, but His Majesty's Government was preparing for all-out war, and there was no great enthusiasm for accepting more refugees from the country Britain was about to fight.

France, overflowing with some 250,000 refugees, many from Spain's Civil War, stated that it had reached the saturation point. A trickle of German refugees was allowed into certain South American, African, and Commonwealth countries, but not nearly as many as needed a haven. Shanghai was the end of the road; 15,000 found refuge there in two years. But even Shanghai's open door was soon to be shut when the Japanese occupied the port.

President Roosevelt appealed to the world for a suitable area "to which refugees could be admitted in almost unlimited numbers." Hitler suggested Madagascar. Roosevelt wrote to Rome about Ethiopia. Mussolini replied in favor of "the open areas of Russia." The Soviet Union considered Alaska appropriate. America suggested Angola; Portugal thought other places in Africa had more to commend them. The United States then favored the Central African highlands for the German Jews, most of whom were middle-class professionals, shopkeepers, and businessmen now softened by centuries of European civilization.

The Orinoco River valley in Venezuela, Mexico, the plateaus of southwestern Africa, Tanganyika, Kenya, Northern Rhodesia, Nyasaland—the entire confusing collection of suggested sites was discussed, investigated, and dismissed, either by Jewish organizations or by national governments. Understandably, most of the refugees wanted to go to the legendary land of opportunity, America.

Throughout the thirties, America stuck rigidly to its old immigration laws. Her early settlers were mainly British, Irish, and other northern European whites. When the quota system was introduced, it had the effect of maintaining America's status quo: the number of immigrants allowed in from any one country depended on the proportion of settlers who were already in America from that country around the turn of the century. Thus a system originally introduced to stop the wholesale entry of "undesirables" of the nineteenth century was, by 1939, acting as a deterrent in a quite different situation.

The United States was prepared to accept 25,957 immigrants from Germany per year, in normal times a relatively large number, but in the critical situation of German Jews, all too few. In any case, since the Jews in Germany were hardly treated as ordinary Germans, the question remained: of the 25,957 Germans allowed into America per year, how many should be German Jews? The answer often depended on the personal inclinations of American consular officials in Germany.

Any applicants "likely to become a public charge" were refused. The ten Reichsmarks—about four dollars—Germany allowed refugees to take with them was insufficient, according to many consular officials. Nor did the officials always understand it was not possible for the refugees to acquire from the Nazi government the character references required for admission to the United States.

Eleanor Roosevelt, wife of the President, was sympathetic to the plight of the refugees; she favored every move in support of refugee aid. But her husband Franklin Roosevelt was a politician who knew it was hazardous to ignore public opinion. The majority of the American electorate, then as now, wished not to be involved in the affairs of others. A large part of the populace, "middle America," the blue-collar class, was openly anti-Semitic. Many were themselves earlier emigrants from central and eastern European countries where anti-Semitism was endemic. In America, they were further influenced by men like Father Charles E. Coughlin, the Detroit priest who used his Sunday-afternoon

radio broadcasts to preach Nazi principles to an audience of
fifteen million. In Yorkville, American heart of Nazism, the
Fuehrer of the German-American Bund, Fritz Kuhn, found
especially receptive audiences for his views; large crowds
thronged to Madison Square Garden for Nazi rallies.

Roosevelt's cabinet was not generally composed of men
inclined to confront the issue. Some senior members, such as
Secretary of State Cordell Hull, seemed to have been chosen more
for their usefulness as a bridge between the President and the
conservative senators than for their energy or diplomatic and
intellectual abilities. And most congressmen were rigidly isolationist.

In 1939, with an election pending, an opinion poll showed
that 83 per cent of the electorate was against increasing the
number of refugees allowed into the country. The message was
clear: any president would change the American immigration
laws at his peril.

Refugees from Germany, who wished to enter the United
States, if they were able to satisfy all the requirements, were put
on the quota. This gave them a place on the increasingly long
waiting list; when their number came up in the queue, they would
be allowed in. In 1939, many on the quota were told the waiting
time for them would be years. They knew they would not survive
the delay; they had to find somewhere outside Germany where
they could wait safely until their numbers came up and they could
then enter America. There were few friendly countries who
offered this essential temporary refuge.

Cuba was the only country close to the United States willing to
accept refugees in large numbers—for a price. But the question
was, Which Cuban politicians would get the money?

By early May 1939, the cast for the drama was beginning to
assemble. They were 937 men, women, and children. Some had
been on the run, some in concentration camps, some had been
waiting to be imprisoned; all were seeking an opportunity to
escape.

The decision that they would be allowed to leave Germany
was approved during a working luncheon in a private dining room
of the Hotel Adlon in Berlin, in April 1939.

For Reichsmarschal Hermann Goering the decision was a practical temporary solution. He accepted the Fuehrer's directive that there must be a final solution to the Jewish Problem, but until it could be implemented, he was in favor of letting Jews go. Naturally the Reich would extract as high a price as possible: confiscation of all goods and property except personal clothing, or the imposition of prohibitively high taxes—payable preferably in the foreign currency needed to boost Germany's faltering economy and to purchase raw materials for a war to come.

What most interested the Nazis was the use that could be made of the ship and its passengers once it had left Germany. Dr. Joseph Goebbels, Minister of Propaganda, spoke openly at the luncheon. The voyage could be exploited to the full for propaganda purposes: the German nation could be told that it was part of the general "housecleaning" operation; the world at large could be told that here was clear evidence that Germany was allowing Jews to leave unharmed and unimpeded. The host, Admiral Wilhelm Canaris, head of German Military Intelligence —the Abwehr—laid his plans quietly. By the time he returned to his second-floor office at 72-76 Tirpitz Ufer, he had begun to work out a scheme. The ship would be used for an important espionage mission. And so it was that in May 1939, the S.S. *St. Louis* sailed into a sea of uncertainty, one of the last ships to leave Nazi Germany before Europe was engulfed in war.

I

A Chance
To Live

WEDNESDAY, MAY 3, 1939

The captain of the Hamburg-America Line passenger ship *St. Louis* did not look forward to the meeting that cool Wednesday morning of May 3, 1939. For the first time in his thirty-seven years at sea Gustav Schroeder was uncertain and uneasy about a voyage.

The newly pressed blue serge trousers and high-buttoning jacket were, for him, a reminder that his meeting with line director Claus-Gottfried Holthusen was to be an important one; usually Schroeder slipped into his favorite gray suit to go ashore for his end-of-voyage report to the marine superintendent in Hapag House, a few blocks away from shed 76, where the *St. Louis* was now tied up on the Hamburg waterfront.

But this morning, when the liner berthed after another voyage from New York, Schroeder had been ordered to report personally to Holthusen.

After he dressed, slowly and carefully, Schroeder once more opened the wall safe in his day cabin to read the cable again to seek a clue in its content.

The message had come during dinner some eight hundred miles out of New York when his steward discreetly handed him the radiogram. It gave him an excuse to leave the tedious table talk about Hitler and Nazi dreams of expansion in the half-empty first-class dining room.

The absence of passengers—the liner was less than a third full—was depressing evidence of the deepening world crisis. The majority on board were Germans returning from the United States. Some of them wore party badges and were pleased to see that many of the crew also displayed the Nazi emblem on their uniforms. The fact that the captain did not caused much comment, but no one dared raise the matter with him.

He was reputed to be precise, studious, and correct in all
details. To his deck officers he seemed to be of the courtly nineteenth century, not of the twentieth. But when Schroeder was
roused by something that displeased him, his language was so
forceful and salty that it stunned those he addressed. He was also
said to be "the smallest officer in the German merchant navy,"
and "the *Graf* on the bridge." Captain Schroeder *was* only five
feet, four inches tall, but although he was small, it seemed im-
material. His body had hardly an ounce of surplus fat; he practiced calisthenics for twenty minutes each day without fail. The
only wrinkles on his face were tiny crow's feet fencing his clear,
blue eyes; he had the look of a man who had measured distant
horizons all his life. His hair was gray, clipped short at the
temples. He had it trimmed once a week by his steward. His skin
was tanned from almost a lifetime at sea. Gustav Schroeder
looked what he was—an energetic, experienced, and capable
captain.

After the cable came, Schroeder had deciphered the apparently meaningless numbers. The code had been introduced by
the line to communicate confidential information to its captains
at sea. In the four months he had commanded the 16,732-ton
liner, Schroeder had never before received a coded message.

The coded cable was typical of the nagging pressures now
intruding on his orderly life. Recently such pressures had exceeded the bounds of what Schroeder believed were proper
company demands. He was increasingly aware of the intrusion of
Nazi influence on his ship, and did not like it. There had been the
compulsory signing on of six Gestapo agents as firemen officially
on board to check sabotage attempts. A few voyages before, in
New York, a bomb threat had been made against the *St. Louis*. No
bomb was found, but the rumor made it difficult for Schroeder to
argue that the firemen were not needed. The Gestapo agents had
tightened security precautions and made attempts to spread
party doctrines to all sections of the crew. Schroeder ordered
them to stop such blatant propaganda, but he knew it was impossible to enforce such an order. He personally loathed the Nazi
ideology; he had steadfastly maintained to his few close friends
that as long as he believed in Germany's future as he did in the
company's destiny, he would continue to oppose Hitler's doctrines. But he must do so circumspectly.

The most serious interference with the captain's command was the presence of a second-class steward he had inherited when he took command of the *St. Louis* in February 1939. Otto Schiendick had established himself as the ship's *Ortsgruppenleiter,* but his powers went beyond those of mere party political shop steward. He had arranged for at least two members of the crew to be forcibly removed from the ship for expressing attitudes not in keeping with Nazi policy. His greatest coup had been the dismissal of Captain Friedrich Buch, master of the *St. Louis* since its maiden voyage in 1929; Buch had been escorted from the ship by Gestapo agents under Schiendick's guidance.

Captain Schroeder took over from Buch, and during the short time he had been in command, tension had grown between him and Schiendick. Each man tested the other's strengths and weaknesses, waiting for a chance to make one swift, decisive thrust that would resolve the conflict. By simply not wearing the party badge Captain Schroeder knew he had made himself vulnerable; in the end, either he or Schiendick and the Gestapo "firemen" would have to go.

For six years Schroeder had resisted requests to join the Nazi party. Before the last voyage, a line official called on him as the ship was about to sail and warned him that refusal to join the party might mean loss of command. Schroeder was shaken, but he ordered the man off the ship.

Perhaps the radiogram was retribution for that action. The message he found was simple but mysterious: his next voyage was to be an unscheduled, "special" trip. He was filled with apprehension.

Schroeder knew his meeting with Holthusen was linked with that message; he had remembered that the director had responsibility within the company for all "special" ventures. Claus-Gottfried Holthusen was one of the most powerful men in German shipping. Schroeder had met him only once, some four months earlier, shortly after taking command of the *St. Louis.* At a lunch given by the company for its captains, Schroeder had sat opposite Holthusen. The director was expansive, suave, and charming; Schroeder was shocked that he so easily accepted Nazi domination of the line.

Holthusen's optimistic predictions at that luncheon had not come true: Hamburg-America, Hapag, was in deeper financial difficulties. Schroeder hoped Holthusen would reassure him that the line was in good health; he trusted the line would return "to the old ways."

In 1934, the Reich had become the majority shareholder, and the company had lost the independence it had successfully defended for ninety years. The swastika flying over the portal of the somber Hapag House represented a major upheaval involving both the Gestapo and German Military Intelligence, the Abwehr. Many of the line's ships now carried espionage couriers as crew members; the Gestapo had a number of agents constantly watching the staff.

Schroeder walked into Hapag House, a place that seemed to him to have little to do with the sea, filled with its clerks perched on high stools, concerned with profits and apparently little else. As he reached Holthusen's office he wondered whether the time had come for him to present his resignation; if not immediately, then he would do so soon.

Holthusen was in no hurry to come to the point. He discussed the last voyage. Had there been any problems? It was the opening Gustav Schroeder wanted. He told him bluntly that there were "disruptive elements" on board. He described "the intrusion of politically motivated persons."

Holthusen was silent.

Then, in the loud, confident voice Schroeder remembered and disliked, Holthusen said: "There are some things which are better left alone. For your own good, and the good of the company."

Schroeder was too disappointed to speak. He could expect no support to rid the *St. Louis* of its Nazi elements.

Holthusen was speaking again, this time about the "special" voyage. The *St. Louis* was to carry nearly 1000 refugees from Germany to Cuba. The trip would require "the greatest tact" on Schroeder's part. Though he was new to command, it had been decided that only Schroeder had the necessary qualities for such a voyage.

"Most important of all, Captain," the director continued, "this trip will ensure that your ship is fully booked at a time when our financial resources are at a low ebb."

Captain Schroeder responded to this appeal to his company loyalty. He had one question: Who were the refugees?

"Jews. But nothing out of the ordinary. Only people wanting to leave Germany," Holthusen replied.

Schroeder knew now that he must not resign until he had delivered the refugees to Cuba. But as he was driven back to the ship, he felt deeply perturbed by a conviction that the director had not been totally frank about the voyage.

His first action aboard was to muster the entire ship's complement in the first-class social hall. He briefed them on the forthcoming voyage and its passengers, then took the first deliberate step toward a confrontation with Otto Schiendick and the Gestapo "firemen," as he announced: "Any of you who do not want to accompany these people to Cuba can sign off now."

Neither Schiendick, the Gestapo agents, nor anyone else said a word. Gustav Schroeder returned to his cabin aware that he would have to take with him to Cuba members of a crew who actively hated the passengers for whom he would be responsible.

The first of those passengers—the Spanier family—arrived in Hamburg late that same evening of May 3, ten days before the *St. Louis* was due to sail. They came in a car flying a swastika and driven by a young S.S. officer.

On the long drive from Berlin, Dr. Fritz Spanier repeatedly whispered to his wife that this was the most bizarre twist of fate they had experienced in six years of increasing persecution; the memory of his remark remains with Babette Spanier to this day.

In April 1933, a Nazi decree barred Jews from working in state hospitals or clinics. Within a year, Dr. Spanier had to move his wife and seven-year-old twin daughters, Renee and Ines, from his comfortable home in the fashionable Berlin suburb of Dahlem, to a more predominantly Jewish quarter of the city. He found work in private practice, Babette Spanier was still able to dress fashionably in the Paris models offered by the Kurfuerstendamm shops. The family continued to go sailing at weekends on the Wansee; they could still buy lox and matzo. Dr. Spanier avoided those who said there were only two alternatives to the worsening situation: arm and fight, or leave Germany. The majority of his friends and relatives, anchored by their possessions and inured to the prospect of suffering, also stayed on.

Once, out of curiosity, he had attended a meeting of an underground Zionist organization. The twenty present had listened to a young man arguing that if each Jew in Germany was prepared to kill one Nazi before being taken to the camps, the wave of arrests would end. Hitler would realize he could not continue such persecution. It might take hundreds, even thousands, of lives, but it would happen.

Dr. Spanier had been shocked by the crudity of the plan. He could not accept that argument that those who had already gone so meekly to the concentration camps had doomed the rest. He had never attended another meeting. He ignored all the signs until July 25, 1939, when a decree drove Jewish doctors even from private practice. A few were authorized to serve their own community; Dr. Spanier was one of them.

Four months later had come the *Kristallnacht*. On that "night of broken glass," November 9/10, 1938, the Nazis committed a national act of vengeance against all German Jews in the Third Reich: 191 synagogues were desecrated, 171 Jewish-owned apartment houses set on fire, 7500 Jewish shops looted; 20,000 Jews were taken into "protective custody," half of them being shipped to Buchenwald camp. The police made only 117 arrests of non-Jewish Germans; not one was ever brought to trial.

The Spaniers escaped unhurt, but soon afterward they were forced to escape from their rented apartment to a garret owned by a widow. Her son was a medical student, and Dr. Spanier befriended and helped tutor him, not knowing the youth was a member of the S.S. When the student heard that the Spaniers were due to be arrested in the next roundup of Jews, he offered to drive the family to Hamburg.

Some time before that Dr. Spanier had spent 3000 Reichsmarks on permits for the family to enter Cuba and later, hopefully, the United States; he had kept to himself the knowledge that the permits were worthless unless the family obtained passage to Cuba. For weeks he had haunted the Berlin travel agencies that specialized—and grew fat—on "facilitating" the departure of refugees.

When he was informed of the impending arrest, he tried again, and fortunately, found one agency that was selling tickets for the *St. Louis*. He bought four first-class berths for 3200 Reichsmarks.

He paid an extra 1000 Reichsmarks for permission to take his surgical instruments out of the country. All the money had come from a relative in Canada. The family were assigned to cabins 111 and 113 on B Deck. By midafternoon of May 3, they held the papers that could keep them from Dachau, or Sachsenhausen, or Buchenwald.

Babette Spanier had spent a busy morning selling off what remained of her household goods to buy more clothes for the twins; Renee and Ines now had enough dresses to last them for the next five years. She bought a topcoat for her husband and a fur wrap for herself, and packed the family's remaining possessions into trunks.

Babette Spanier had been reluctant to leave Berlin. In spite of the insults, the taunts, the jostling on the pavements, the shops, theaters, and cinemas proscribed to her and her family, she wished to stay, because, as she explained later, she was a Seidemann, and there had been Seidemanns in the Ruhr for more than four hundred years: "We regarded ourselves as German through and through. We spoke German, we thought in German, we *were* German. The very idea of leaving the country where our roots were was heartbreaking."

There was another, and more personal, reason why Babette Spanier did not wish to emigrate. Her marriage was in difficulty; she feared that it could not survive a move halfway across the world, that her handsome husband might divorce her once they reached his ultimate goal, America. But, faced with the sailing tickets, the specter of the Gestapo, and her husband's promise of a "wonderful new life ahead," she, with the children, left Berlin; she was comforted by her husband's hand in hers throughout the journey.

That evening, in Hamburg, near the railway station, their car was forced to a halt by men and youths from a big Nazi rally who surrounded it. Many carried party banners on their shoulders, like rifles, rolled tight around the staves. Suddenly a squad of storm-troopers surged toward a man coming out of the railway station, carrying a cheap suitcase. He tried to flee, but the soldiers were too quick. They rammed him against the wall, kicking and jabbing him with their staves. In moments the storm troopers stepped back, leaving him crumpled on the sidewalk.

In the back of the car the twins whimpered; their mother
calmed them with a lullaby. Only later did she realize she had
crooned a Jewish lament her mother had sung to her. As the car
drove on, protected by its swastika flag and uniformed S.S. driver,
Dr. Spanier noticed dozens of people staring at the figure on the
ground. Not fifty yards away a squad of armed policemen ignored
the whole incident. The Spaniers saw the man crawling away,
shaking his shaved head, dragging his suitcase behind him.
Though they did not know it, he had also come to Hamburg to
board the St. Louis.

That night the young S.S. officer drove them to a small hotel in
the old quarter of Hamburg. Inside, a sign over the desk stated:
"Jews forbidden." Dr. Spanier booked two adjoining rooms, and
then the family shook hands with the benefactor who gave each of
the children ten Reichsmarks and wished them all a safe journey.

Shortly afterward two Gestapo officers arrived at the hotel.

About a mile from the hotel, Aaron Pozner, the man who had
been beaten, finally found a hiding place that even the Gestapo
would have little stomach to stand. He had dragged himself down
to the waterfront and there, a few cable lengths from the St. Louis,
he discovered a yard stacked with animal hides from an adjoining
slaughterhouse. Born and raised in a farming community, he knew
the skins would be left undisturbed for weeks to cure. So, tying a
handkerchief across his nose and mouth, he burrowed into the pile
of skins, ignoring the dried blood and pieces of flesh, the flies, and
the stench. For a man who had survived Dachau, it was not hard to
bear.

On Kristallnacht, 178 days ago, Pozner, a Hebrew teacher, had
been dragged from his home by the Gestapo and shipped to
Dachau, one of some 8000 Jews brought to the camp during that
November night. His head had been shaved, and his clothes
exchanged for a coarse linen suit with a yellow star stamped on it;
it became his badge of shame, an excuse for the guards to beat him
at every opportunity. His only link with the outside world—a
snapshot of his wife, Rachel, and his small children, Simon and
Ruth—was snatched from him by a guard, who urinated over it.

He wrote in his diary of the public hangings after morning roll
call which he was forced to witness, the public floggings before
afternoon roll call, and the drownings in vats after the evening

count. In between there were crucifixions, garrotings, and, the speciality of one guard, castration by bayonet. Men died and their bodies were barrowed away by their brothers to quicklime pits; across on the far side of the vast Dachau complex the foundations were being laid for what would become the crematoria.

Then, suddenly, incredibly, he and a group of other men were released on condition they all leave Germany within fourteen days. They were driven out of the camp and dumped at Nuremberg's station. There, waiting for him, aged and drawn but smiling was Rachel, with the children. She held a shabby suitcase filled with his clothes. She explained that her family had raised the money to buy him a Cuban visa and tourist-class ticket on the *St. Louis;* he wept as she said that she and the children would follow, later, on another boat.

"The important thing, Aaron," Rachel insisted, "is for you to go and prepare a new life for us."

Moments later he had boarded the train to Hamburg. Aaron Pozner knew his wife's parents would never be able to raise the money to send his family after him; that unless he was able to do so, he would never see any of them again.

As the train had steamed northward, despair over leaving his family so overwhelmed him that he decided to return to them, but as he tried to leave his compartment with its "J" labels plastered on the window and door, at the Cologne station, a Gestapo official drove him back with a flurry of blows. In Hamburg had come that second beating outside the railway station.

Others, too, ran the gauntlet of storm troopers at the station. But the Loewe family were lucky; they had arrived in Hamburg at an hour when the Nazis' bullyboys were diverting themselves by hounding Jews out of the city parks. Max Loewe, with a cunning that surprised his family, swiftly ushered them out of the station to wait in a safe place for the moment they could board the ship.

For the past three weeks, waiting, hiding, and running had become second nature. He knew that neither his wife, Elise, nor Ruth, seventeen, or Fritz, twelve, would ever really understand his fear. Unlike him, they had not been on the Gestapo's wanted list, prepared at a moment's notice to move from one place to another to avoid being caught and sent to a concentration camp.

Max Loewe had been a successful attorney until a Reich act removed him from practice in September 1938. He had wanted to leave then and obtained visas to take the family to England. But war was coming, and even Britain had not seemed safe. He bought permits for Cuba.

Still, Elise Loewe had not wanted to leave Germany, and they waited. Max Loewe made a living as an "economic adviser," discreetly preparing briefs for trials, and then handing them over to a friendly German lawyer to present in court. It was unsatisfying, and it was illegal. In April 1939, he learned the Gestapo had discovered his ruse. He was forced into hiding.

In these past weeks he had been pushed almost beyond terror as he waited for the day when he could surface long enough to join his family and make a train dash to Hamburg and board the *St. Louis* before the Gestapo were aware he had slipped through their net.

When he had reappeared, Ruth and Fritz were shocked by the change. He was older, more nervous, irritable. His world had crumbled; he stood outside himself and could never return to his past life. His wife and children had tried to cheer him up on the journey to Hamburg. He had not responded, sitting in the train, smaller, shrunken, huddled in his clothes, looking much older than his forty-eight years.

But when he arrived in Hamburg, he guided his family on a dangerous and deadly game of hide and seek, now alert and watchful, darting out of the way of any uniformed official, convinced each was a Gestapo officer waiting to take him.

That same night, Otto Schiendick, the acknowledged ringleader of the Nazi cabal on board the *St. Louis*, hurried ashore with the Gestapo "firemen." Like other members of the crew, they had been granted shore leave. But Schiendick and the Gestapo men did not follow their custom of spending time around the bars and brothels of Hamburg's Reeperbahn. Instead they made their way to Gestapo headquarters. Afterward Schiendick went to the local office of the Abwehr. The crewmen who saw him enter the building did not realize until years later that this was a further indication that Schiendick was what nobody on the *St. Louis* except the Gestapo "firemen" knew at the time—a courier of the German Secret Service. His position as party *Leiter* on the ship provided the perfect cover for this far more important role.

Schiendick had been recruited by the Abwehr in 1935, and within months shown himself highly adept at smuggling out classified material from German spy rings operating within the United States. By 1937 his name and reputation had even reached the ears of Admiral Canaris, head of the Abwehr; he looked on Schiendick as one of his important links in the Nazi espionage chain extending across America.

By 1939, the Abwehr had more spies in the United States than almost anywhere else in the world. The agents channeled their information to New York, to the Times Square area, close to the piers of the German shipping lines on the Hudson River.

Before almost every voyage out of New York for many months past, Schiendick attended a *Treff*—a secret meeting—in one or more of the cafes or beer cellars on East Eighty-sixth Street, the stronghold of German, and often Nazi, sympathies in New York. There he received documents and blueprints, exchanging them for equally secret orders he brought from Hamburg.

For star runners in its stable of couriers, the Abwehr was generous with expenses, and Schiendick, a dumpy, unattractive man, found that the money bought him female company of a kind in both New York and Hamburg. Then, in the spring of 1939, in one swoop after another, the F.B.I. broke link after link in the Abwehr spy chain; stewards from a number of German ships were arrested, spies were picked up in many American cities and indicted before grand juries. Before this last voyage out of New York, the Hapag pier had teemed with F.B.I. agents, police, and customs men, who subjected the crew to a thorough search. They failed to find the hiding place Otto Schiendick used to carry his information—almost certainly a sealed tube inserted in his anus, a means long favored by Abwehr agents.

Now, in the Abwehr office in midtown Hamburg, Schiendick gave the information to his debriefing officer. Exactly what followed cannot be known in precise detail, but enough clues exist in surviving German intelligence records and the recall of crewmen to confirm that the meeting Schiendick had with Commander Udo von Bonin, head of the Abwehr section responsible for all espionage activities in America, was to affect, in varying degrees, the refugees on the *St. Louis*, the ship's captain, his crew, and the intelligence services of the United States.

Although German intelligence had suffered severe blows in

America, the need for updated information was greater than ever; with war drawing closer it was vital for Germany to know the hidden strengths and weaknesses of the United States. The Abwehr had forged a new and elaborate chain to get secret information out of America to Havana, Cuba. There they maintained a highly organized espionage ring which had stockpiled American secrets, awaiting a safe means of bringing them to Germany. The material included blueprints of several American destroyers, and specifications for an underwater sound detector which could be used against submarines.

Otto Schiendick and the *St. Louis* had been selected by von Bonin as the safest and fastest method of bringing those secrets to Germany. The plan, code-named Operation Sunshine, was bold and simple: Schiendick would go ashore in Havana, pick up the material, and return to the ship, which was scheduled to sail for Europe after only a day's stopover.

Schiendick was given $500, which he could use to bribe any inquisitive Cuban official. His contact was to be Robert Hoffman, assistant manager of the local Hapag office in Havana—the very office Captain Schroeder would have to rely on for help should he run into difficulties in Cuba.

THURSDAY, MAY 4, 1939

In Havana, Robert Hoffman was already being watched by members of four separate American intelligence agencies—the secret service of the U.S. Immigration Department, the F.B.I., and Naval and Military Intelligence. The most active of these was Colonel Ross E. Rowell, of Naval Intelligence, who had been in Cuba for only a month, but whose secret reports to Washington were already being studied with special interest.

Now, on May 4, he returned to his small office in the American Embassy on the Avenida de Mislones to draft another communiqué; its subject was a known Nazi woman courier who had arrived from the Panama Canal Zone to keep a *Treff* with Hoffman.

Neither Rowell nor any of the other American intelligence officers in Cuba had authority to search or arrest a suspect. There was little point in enlisting the help of the indolent Cuban police. Bribery and persuasion allowed the Abwehr an almost free hand to use Havana as the center of their activities throughout North and South America.

Virtually all Rowell could do was watch, listen, and report, but his reports left no doubts about the power of the Nazi spy ring on the island. Report S/N R-233-39 identified the Abwehr strength in Havana as "about sixty agents." Report R-304-39, prefaced, *"Source of information : semi-reliable : Subject : Germany, intelligence ashore,"* contained an insight into Hoffman and his methods. The Nazi spy emerged as a cold man, well-versed in bribery and blackmail. Report R-236-39, "reliable," identified a key Abwehr agent as:

"Julius Otto Ott, owner of the Swiss Home Restaurant in Havana. It is not known whether he is a Swiss or a German. He resides at Edificio Carreno, Apartment 39. Ott is between 35 and 40 years of age and is a hump-backed dwarf, being not more than four feet five inches in height. He has a sandy complexion, is freckled, and sometimes wears glasses."

Rowell knew that the woman courier who had delivered a packet to Hoffman was staying in Ott's apartment. She posed as a tourist and, as such, could move about freely without restriction. On previous visits to Havana, Rowell had tailed her to Ott's restaurant, a meeting place for European immigrants. He had identified, in the words of his Report R-237-39, again "reliable," many of the diners as "high-powered Nazi agents, camouflaged under the guise of Jewish refugees."

He had also unearthed a nest of such spies living nearby in the Hotel Nacional and the Hotel Sevilla. Rowell had tapped their mail. Among other things, he discovered an Abwehr plot to buy 100 tons of glycerine in New York for sabotaging key American plants in the event of war. His tip resulted in the Abwehr men in New York being arrested.

But the agents living in the Nacional and the Sevilla were immune from arrest, living out their cover as refugees—even to the point of seeking welfare aid from the local Joint Relief Committee. Rowell had cultivated the organization to build up a file on each bogus refugee waiting for his American quota number to come through; once they entered the United States they would be arrested.

What Rowell did not know on this humid May evening as he drafted his latest report to Washington was what the package the woman delivered to Hoffman contained. Years later, an Abwehr source claimed the package held detailed drawings of the dams at Lakes Gatun and Pedro Miguel, source of all the water from the Panama Canal locks, plus a wealth of information about secret military installations that rendered them vulnerable to sabotage; that package the source claimed, represented the most telling single blow the Abwehr had yet struck against the United States. The documents were to get to Germany by courier on the next Hapag ship, the *St. Louis*.

In Hamburg, on the afternoon of May 4, Claus-Gottfried Holthusen waited with some anticipation for the telephone connection to Paris. He would have to choose his words carefully, for as a result of the call, the voyage of the *St. Louis* would become public knowledge. How much of the background to the trip would it be wise to divulge?

Holthusen had received permission for the *St. Louis* "special voyage" from the *Reichssicherheitshauptamt*, R.S.H.A., a powerful government division destined to spawn the notorious Department IVB4, which, under the leadership of a thirty-three-year-old up-and-coming bureaucrat, Adolf Eichmann, would soon be responsible for the concentration, deportation, and extermination of Jews within the Reich and its occupied countries.

Since early 1938, four Hapag ships had regularly carried to Shanghai and South American ports those allowed or forced out of Germany. The profits were considerable; passengers had to pay for a return ticket to cover unforeseen "eventualities." Once ashore in Chile or China, if they were lucky, they received a credit note stating that the return portion of their fares was lodged in a "special" account in Germany which could be redeemed if they ever returned to the Fatherland. Hapag did not expect to be required to repay the money.

As his telephone rang to connect him with Paris, Holthusen decided to say as little as necessary to the man at the other end, Morris Troper, the European director of the American Jewish Joint Distribution Committee—the Joint—one of the organizations responsible for helping the victims of Nazism.

Holthusen was wary of the American, whom he had never met but knew to have considerable connections in the United States, and listening posts in a dozen European countries. More than anyone else Holthusen knew, Troper was exceptionally well informed on events in Germany, and that, above all, made Holthusen uneasy in his dealings with him.

Holthusen explained the "special voyage" to Cuba, adding that the *St. Louis* had been chosen simply because of her availability. She would carry, he continued, nearly 400 first-class passengers at 800 Reichsmarks a head, and more than 500 tourist-class at 600 Reichsmarks. All would be required to pay the "customary contingency fee" of 230 Reichsmarks for the return voyage in case of "circumstances beyond Hapag's control." Tickets were being issued on a first-come, first-served basis.

Troper had only one question for Holthusen: *Was the line sure Cuba would accept such a large single consignment?*

The question alarmed Holthusen: *Had Troper heard something?*

He had not. The remark simply stemmed from the fact that nearly 1000 emigrants on the *St. Louis* would be the largest number ever of refugees to land in Cuba at one time.

Holthusen insisted there was no cause for alarm, provided the "usual precautions" were enforced: no publicity, no violation of any Third Reich decree applying to emigrants. In practice that meant each passenger would be allowed to leave Germany with only ten Reichsmarks in cash—about four dollars—plus "shipboard money," which they could purchase from Hapag up to the value of 230 Reichsmarks. This money could be spent only at sea and could not be converted back into Reichsmarks.

Troper realized Holthusen had sidestepped his question, but he decided not to press the matter. Theirs was a strictly working relationship, born out of the need of one of them to advance company profits and the desire of the other to save lives.

Holthusen ended the conversation with the words, "You know our motto: 'You travel well with the Hamburg-America Line.' "

Morris Troper was both elated and depressed by news of the voyage. There would be no problem in filling the *St. Louis* with those who were financed by hidden money, contributions sent from relatives outside Germany, and even help from ordinary Germans. But it would require Hapag's entire fleet to satisfy the demands of all those desperate to get out of Germany. Yet the majority would be prevented from leaving by the simple need of money. After six years of being crowded into ghettos and charged exorbitant rents, their profits confiscated by the state, their professional services rejected, the resources of most were exhausted. They could not even raise the basic passage money, let alone the cash for all the other "dues."

Morris Troper cabled the head office of the American Jewish Joint Distribution Committee in New York. The Joint would undoubtedly help the emigrants find their way in the New World. News of the forthcoming voyage was received with satisfaction, and the Joint immediately made it known to a number of

interested American organizations, among them the President's
Advisory Committee on Refugees. It would ensure that the
voyage did not come as a surprise to President Franklin
Roosevelt.

In London, Sir Herbert Emerson, newly appointed director of
the International Committee on Political Refugees, also learned
of the voyage from Morris Troper.

Emerson's committee was virtually the only positive outcome
of the much-mooted Evian Conference of almost a year earlier.
The initiative for the conference had come from President
Roosevelt himself. Its purpose was to coordinate emigration from
Europe. The hope was that the thirty-two countries attending
would be willing to relax their immigration policies, but the
United States, to whom the world looked for leadership, had
shown itself unwilling to put into practice the principles which
had led Roosevelt to suggest the conference in the first place.
America would allow all the places on its German quota to be
used; the "concession," which required no change in existing
United States laws, meant that the entire German quota of 25,957
could be made use of each year, but that still did not mean they
would all be German Jews.

The Intergovernmental Committee had first established its
offices in London under an elderly American director, with a
mandate to negotiate with Germany. In late 1938, the president
of the Reichsbank, Germany's "financial wizard," visited London
with a plan: during three years, 150,000 refugees would be
allowed to emigrate in return for a loan of one and a half billion
Reichsmarks, to be provided in foreign currency by a corporation
financed by "international Jewry."

Negotiations were prolonged. Hitler became disenchanted
with the Reichsbank president and dismissed him. Goering appointed his own nominee to negotiate. In February 1939, the
American director of the Intergovernmental Committee ten-
dered his resignation, and in April Sir Herbert Emerson had taken
his place.

One of the first delegations with whom Emerson had to deal
came from Germany with a message from the Gestapo: "Unless a
settlement for the proposed 150,000 was established quickly,
German authorities would return to the 'shock' tactics so suc-

cessful in ridding Germany of Jews in the past." Emerson replied
that he would not allow the Gestapo to "dictate what my committee will, or will not, do." The delegation returned to Germany
emptyhanded.

Now, as Emerson considered the news of the *St. Louis* voyage,
he came to the conclusion that it could do little but complicate
the delicate negotiations he was conducting. While the trip
would provide respite for a few, it might well boomerang against
the many remaining in Germany.

This view was confirmed when Emerson took a phone call
from the principal private secretary to the British Foreign
Secretary. The secretary read to the director a message recently
received from the British consul in Havana. If the contents were
correct, the *St. Louis* and its passengers would become the excuse
for a Nazi propaganda campaign.

Sir Herbert Emerson decided the matter could not be left to
run its course.

FRIDAY, MAY 5, 1939

Captain Schroeder had learned of the allegations Schiendick had made against him at police headquarters when a Gestapo officer arrived on board to question him about his offer to crew members to sign off instead of accompanying the refugees to Cuba. Schroeder had explained that, for "this delicate trip," he had made the suggestion for the good of the crew, the line, and the passengers. Over schnapps, he convinced the officer there was no need to probe further.

Afterward, the captain prepared his ground meticulously for a showdown with the steward. First he studied Schiendick's personal file, then he consulted a manual on marine law, and finally he created a "trial atmosphere" in his day cabin by removing all personal effects and clearing his desktop of everything apart from the law book. The final touch was to flank himself at one end of the desk with the ship's first officer, Klaus Ostermeyer, and with the purser, Ferdinand Mueller, at the other. He liked and trusted both men. At nine o'clock sharp, his traditional hour for dealing with defaulters, Captain Schroeder ordered Schiendick to be marched in to stand before the desk.

If the steward was nervous, he managed to conceal it until the captain began to speak. He was reminded of his legal right to remain silent. If he did, however, the case would be referred to a higher authority. The steward stirred uneasily and then began to bluster that he had no idea why he had been marched before the captain.

Schroeder cut him short: "You are here to explain why you have tried to create a mutinous atmosphere on my ship. I must further tell you that under the penal code you could be sentenced to death by a court if found guilty of such a charge."

41

For the first time, the captain saw fear in Schiendick's eyes. Quietly and incisively, he hammered away at the charge of "mutinous behavior"; that the Gestapo had found the steward's accusations to be baseless; that his record of service was peppered with complaints from passengers; that, in short, he owed his seaman's ticket solely to his position as party *Leiter*—and even that would not save him from punishment in a court of law.

The silence in the cabin stretched between the two men. Schroeder waited, wondering if he had pressed his luck too far, wondering whether Schiendick would realize that much of what he had said was little more than bluff; that, if pressed, it was very likely the party would back the steward.

But still Otto Schiendick made no reply.

The captain seized his advantage. He told the steward his behavior was enough to have him dismissed from the ship at the very least. The steward began to plead it had all been a misunderstanding and that such behavior would not happen again. He talked on and on.

"Enough!"

Schroeder pronounced "sentence" in a cold and distinct voice.

"One more 'misunderstanding,' and I will personally see that you will regret it all your life. Now get out of here, and get back to your real job of trying to be a credit to this ship!"

Afterward the captain, first officer, and purser debated why the steward had appeared so fearful of being put ashore, and finally agreed that it was probably the reaction of a man desperate to cling to his iota of power. Schroeder believed that the steward would now subside.

The captain was wrong.

Schiendick feared being put ashore because if he was his Abwehr mission would be aborted. Now he summoned the Gestapo "firemen," told them what had happened, and vowed revenge on the captain. As soon as the Jews boarded, they would have a chance to retaliate.

The Spaniers had already witnessed how harsh Gestapo methods could be. After they had checked into their hotel room, two Gestapo men had dragged a terrified man out of a nearby bedroom. Dr. Spanier had inched open his own bedroom door in time to see the Gestapo officers kicking the man down the stairs, while the desk clerk hovered in the background, pleading that he had no idea the guest was on a "wanted list."

Babette Spanier urged that they check out before the Gestapo went further. They might not be able to find another hotel easily, her husband said; besides, the fact that they had arrived in the company of their S.S. benefactor would protect them.

"You are always saying we are German to the core," he chided gently. "So we shall behave like ordinary Germans."

All the same it seemed prudent to avoid the hotel as much as possible, and they spent long hours trudging Hamburg's streets. The city was decorated for the city's 750th anniversary celebrations with bunting and gay lanterns, yet an air of menace, of violence, was everywhere. Serried rows of swastikas lined the main streets; the streets were filled with military traffic, S.S. men, police, and troops.

The twins were frightened and their mother did her best to soothe them. Once they were caught up in a mob of banner-waving youths. Only Dr. Spanier's explanation that they had left their party badges back at their hotel averted the gang's suspicions, and they were allowed to pass.

"You see," Fritz Spanier told his wife, "we *look* so German."

Babette replied that for the first time in her life she hated the thought that she was German.

SUNDAY, MAY 7, 1939

By May 7, the last of the tickets for the voyage were sold. Many of the passengers, too frightened to remain in their home or in hiding, had made the trip to Hamburg well in advance of sailing. Many found the delay bearable; they were nearer their destination, and somehow safer.

A few of the passengers, those who had managed to retain some wealth, came to Hamburg by plane. They were so sure of their position that they did not mind rubbing shoulders with Nazi officers. But most traveled third-class on trains, terrified that they would be recognized.

Leo Jockl had buried his face in a newspaper ever since leaving Berlin. He spoke to no one, but from time to time glanced up at other passengers on the train, wondering if they too were heading for the *St. Louis*. Once, after a Gestapo officer passed, he went to the washroom and examined his face in the mirror. The tiredness showed in his eyes: they had an expression of almost perpetual sadness, as if he were close to tears. But Jockl was concerned about one disturbing feature; his nose was slightly large. He had come to fear it was enough to give away the fact that he was half Jewish.

For six difficult years he had successfully concealed the knowledge from all but a few trusted friends. Until 1933, Jockl had been only vaguely aware of the anti-Semitism in the Vienna of his childhood. Even later, he was cosseted by living in a predominantly Protestant area. Before the *Anschluss* of 1938, when 45,000 Jews were forced to leave Austria within eight months and suicides rose to two hundred a day, Leo Jockl, then twenty-four, had slipped into Germany and assumed a new background. Since then he had lived in terror of discovery.

44

He stayed in the train's washroom as long as he dared. When he returned to his seat, as the train neared Hamburg, he, like the other Jews on the train, believed everyone was looking at him. Leo Jockl was the captain's steward on the ship. And that night of May 7, when he boarded the *St. Louis,* returning from shore leave, Schiendick sought him out. Schiendick had chosen Leo deliberately as a means of revenge against the captain, not only because Jockl was in a position to observe the captain closely, but because it gave him keen pleasure to pit the steward against the captain. He was jealous of Jockl's good manners, his general popularity on board, and his coveted place in the captain's life.

If Schiendick had suspected how close the relationship between Jockl and Schroeder really was, he would likely have made sure the senior steward was dispatched to a concentration camp. If he had known he was half a Jew, Jockl would have been in grave danger. So would the captain, for knowingly concealing a person of Jewish blood was enough to destroy Gustav Schroeder.

The captain had inherited Jockl when he assumed command of the *St. Louis,* and he liked him immediately. Over many voyages, they had come to know each other better, and a mutual affection, something not unlike the relationship between a stern but just father and a happy-go-lucky son, had developed. The natural barrier of rank and background which kept them apart ashore did not matter in the privacy of the captain's day cabin. But men realized that such a close relationship must remain unknown to the rest of the crew; it could only give rise to speculation and jealousy.

Jockl had confided that he was half Jewish. Schroeder had listened attentively and given a firm promise that his steward's secret was safe with him. The matter was never referred to again.

Now, as Jockl listened to Schiendick's demands that he should spy on the captain, he felt almost ill. For a moment he considered striking out at Schiendick, but assaulting the party *Leiter* was bound to be a punishable crime; it would achieve nothing except to bring unwelcome attention.

Instead, he nodded. His instinct told him that apparent agreement was the safest strategy for himself and Captain Schroeder. Later, alone in his cabin, he decided that, if necessary, he would feed Schiendick trivia, even lies. Jockl failed to take into account the fact that Schiendick could confirm his reports through other spies, and that he would then be in greater danger than before.

Aaron Pozner had made a discovery which filled him with anxiety. Since crawling into his hiding place, he had followed a routine. Each day he slept among the animal hides, fitfully, in the middle of the busy and noisy harbor. Each night and into the early morning, when the waterfront was mostly quiet and the pier deserted except for its guards, he crept out of his hiding place to scavenge for food. There was always the odd crate of fruit from which a banana or orange could be prized; one night he had even found a half-full bottle of milk left over from a workman's lunch. After his diet at Dachau of bread and water, with only rainwater for washing, these were treasures.

On the night of Sunday, May 7, he noticed the warships in the harbor were lit up very late. He could hear the sound of voices coming from them. Peering through the hides, he saw civilians, women, walking the decks with young officers. Sunday he thought, must be the time for cocktail parties, for showing off the new-found strength of the German navy. He could see at least a dozen such warships, each with its swastika flying at the stern. There was also a passenger ship. He crawled out of his hole, crossed behind a building, and read its name. It was the *St. Louis.* He then made the discovery that sent him scurrying back to his hiding place; the *St. Louis,* like the warships in Hamburg harbor, and like the Gestapo guard's towers ringing Dachau, was flying the Nazi swastika.

The swastika symbolized the party's control over the *St. Louis.* He understood by instinct what the captain disbelieved, that the ship was a pawn of the Nazis.

The German Minister of Propaganda, Joseph Goebbels, had, a month before, laid the foundations for a part of his plan for the *St. Louis.* He authorized fourteen Nazi propaganda agents to infiltrate Cuba, and within the month they had succeeded in stirring up anti-Semitism on the island. They arranged that an intensive, inflammatory campaign be waged on the radio and in three Havana newspapers, directed against German refugees and Jews long established in Cuba. Cuban President Frederico Bru could not ignore the growing anti-Semitism.

It was just what Goebbels wanted. The Munich Agreement of September 29, 1938, had provided, for more fortunate Jews, a delay of war and time to get out of Germany, but since 1939, the repression of the Nazis, the restrictions imposed by countries of refuge, and the success of Goebbels' propaganda machine had dammed the flow. Goebbels had told his followers: "The poorer and therefore the more burdensome the immigrant to the country absorbing them, the stronger that country will react, and the more favorable will be the effect in the interests of German propaganda." He was therefore pleased at the effect of the anti-Semitic campaign in Cuba.

From the moment the *St. Louis* passengers boarded, Goebbels intended his ministry to capitalize on the ship's journey. Passengers like Pozner—shabby, dirty, "undesirable"—would be much more than anonymous refugees. Goebbels would ensure that they, and the *St. Louis,* appeared as an example to the entire world of the Jewish situation in microcosm.

MONDAY, MAY 8, 1939

By the morning of May 8, preparations for the voyage aboard the *St. Louis* had developed a steady momentum. The liner was held to the shore fore and aft by hawsers as thick as a man's leg; 575 feet long, it was streamlined with a tapering stern and raked bow, black hull and white superstructure topped with twin black, red, and white smokestacks. Five of her decks reared above the water line; three, filled with machinery, storage tanks, and compartments, plunged deep below the surface. The crew of 231 prepared to cook, scrub, clean, polish, entertain, fetch and carry, and meet the whims of both ship and passengers.

On that Monday morning, the crew had been assembled once more in the social hall to be addressed by the captain, standing on the dance-band podium. Gustav Schroeder was brief: the slightest lapse in standards, any hint of discrimination, the briefest sign of resentment toward the refugees, would be swiftly punished.

"You will all never forget for a moment that these passengers are to be treated no differently from any others we have carried," he concluded.

Schroeder walked briskly from the room, followed by Ostermeyer, the first officer, and Mueller, the purser, aware of the silence, sensing the hostility on some faces. When the trio reached the captain's day cabin Schroeder gave way to his own feelings; in spite of his warning to the crew he knew that, as far as Hapag head office was concerned, the refugees were not to be treated as other voyagers.

That morning Hapag House informed him that there would be cheaper cuts of meat, that the ship's shop must lock away its usual range of expensive cameras, binoculars, and perfumes, replacing them with shoddier goods. The economies extended everywhere: the ship's hairdressing salon was to remove its excellent range of cosmetics, the bars were to lock away a variety of drinks. There were not even to be writing pads, pencils, and free postcards in the public rooms.

After reading out the long list of banned goods and their replacements—it extended even to the quality of toilet paper—Gustav Schroeder made a major decision: wherever possible the orders were to be ignored. The purser was told to ensure that the ship was adequately and properly supplied. Schroeder did not care how it was done: "Just do it, and do it well."

Ferdinand Mueller, the ship's equivalent of a hotel manager, was a kind man, devoted to the job of keeping passengers happy. His secret, which he constantly impressed upon stewards and cabin staff, was to take pains over those they served. He himself set an excellent example in his attentiveness, respect, and keeping a proper distance. After twenty-five years at sea, he believed he had refined it to an art. Now Gustav Schroeder had given Mueller the opportunity to show another of his qualities—the ability to scrounge and juggle with way bills. The purser set off to show that when it came to such things, there was none better on the Hapag payroll.

Alone with Ostermeyer, Schroeder confided his private feelings about the voyage. It was not only the crew's attitude that concerned him, but the attitude of the passengers as well: they had been subjected to years of tyranny, and now would find themselves in a position in which they could give the orders. When the initial shock of that wore off, if they they went too far in their demands—and they both knew, Schroeder added, how demanding passengers could be—there were bound to be repercussions.

"And then," Schroder remarked, "we will be a floating time bomb."

For the rest of the morning the two senior officers on board discussed ways and means of avoiding that crisis.

Their relationship was a close and cordial one, despite their age difference—the captain was twenty years the senior of his first officer—and their outward dissimilarity. Ostermeyer towered over Schroeder by many inches and was close to eighty pounds heavier. He had an urge for social life that the captain had no desire to match; Schroeder was more interested in the collection of books on ornithology that he kept in his cabin and in his campaign for bodily fitness; it had become a running joke between them that Ostermeyer's physical exertions did not go much beyond uncorking a wine bottle. Their friendship drew its strength not from habits shared but from a common interest in seamanship and serving passengers.

By the end of the morning Gustav Schroeder had decided how best to serve the refugees. He would, he told Ostermeyer, remain aloof from the passengers, taking, as he put it, "the view from the bridge on how the voyage develops." The effective day-to-day running of the *St. Louis* would now be in the hands of the first officer.

It was the captain's first mistake—not because Ostermeyer was incapable of such responsibility, but because he had miscalculated that the view from the bridge would provide access into every corner of the *St. Louis*. He thought he could spot trouble from above. He was wrong.

In London, the director of the Intergovernmental Committee* on Political Refugees, Sir Herbert Emerson, carefully prepared the ground for a move which he hoped would halt the voyage. He had studied the reports from Cuba and elsewhere, analyzing them with the calm, unemotional mind which made some refugee organizations feel Emerson was a hard, inflexible man who would never let sentiment sway him. Then he acted. Emerson's telegram was delivered the afternoon of May 8 to Claus-Gottfried Holthusen, the Hapag director, who had previously briefed Schroeder. It read:

> I AM INFORMED THAT IT IS CONTEMPLATED TO SEND 900 REFUGEES
> TO CUBA BY YOUR STEAMER ST. LOUIS SAILING ON MAY 13. I UNDER-
> STAND THAT GREAT DIFFICULTIES ARE LIKELY TO ARISE IN REGARD
> TO THEIR ENTRY INTO CUBA AND I STRONGLY ADVISE THAT THE
> REFUGEES SHOULD NOT BE SENT THERE.

Holthusen was disturbed by the telegram. Although he had never met Emerson, he knew the Englishman was in a position to make his views known even to the Fuehrer himself. The shipping director had immediately sent a priority cable to the Hapag office in Havana asking for clarification of the situation. There, Robert

Hoffman, the Abwehr agent who doubled as assistant manager, and with whom Schiendick planned to rendezvous, discussed it with his immediate superior, Luis Clasing.

Holthusen received the reply the next morning. It stated that Hapag, Havana, had the "personal guarantee" of the Cuban director of immigration that the *St. Louis* faced no difficulties. Holthusen, reassured, decided it was unnecessary to reply to Emerson's cable or to inform the one man who should have known of the incident—Captain Gustav Schroeder.

FRIDAY, MAY 12, 1939

For nearly an hour on the afternoon of Friday, May 12, Captain Schroeder stood alone on the starboard wing of the bridge watching passengers emerge from shed 76 to climb one of the gangways. They were Orthodox Jews, anxious to board before the onset of their Sabbath at sunset; their beliefs forbade them to begin any journey during the period from Friday evening until dusk on Saturday.

The captain had visited the customs area in the cavernous shed and had been outraged at the way these early arrivals were treated. Uniformed officials jostled them, subjected them to rough body searches, and ransacked their cases and trunks.

Schroeder had remonstrated with the senior Gestapo officer present, and so forceful was the captain's language and his threat to "raise all hell" at police headquarters that the Gestapo man had reluctantly given an order for the refugees to be treated more gently. The captain despatched Ostermeyer and Mueller to make sure that this promise was honored, and then returned to keep his own station on the bridge wing.

The appearance of the passengers distressed him. They were cowed and frightened and made him all the more determined that once on his ship their faith in the "old Germany" would be restored. Now, in the fading light of Friday evening, he was gratified to see two stewards hurrying down the gangway to assist an elderly couple weighed down with baggage.

Professor Moritz Weiler and his wife, Recha, were stunned by the stewards' offer of help; it was the first act of kindness they had experienced on the long journey from Dusseldorf. Before that, there had been another, longer, train journey, a five-hundred-mile round trip to Stuttgart, to an office block on the Koenigstrasse, to obtain their visas through OBERRAT, an old and respected Jewish administrative organization.

The journey to Stuttgart had exhausted the professor, for he was in poor health, and he had been shocked at the way they were treated by railway officials and their fellow travelers, who alternately ignored and insulted them. Recha Weiler, long accustomed to such ostracism, bore the behavior stoically.

Both had been bewildered to find at OBERRAT's offices Gestapo officers working alongside Jews. The Weilers could not comprehend that they owed their visas to an extraordinary alliance between OBERRAT and the Gestapo. OBERRAT held records dating back to the seventeenth century. They contained a mass of detailed personal information on hundreds of thousands of German Jews, information of continuing interest to the Gestapo. Since 1933 the Nazis had allowed the agency to become a "servicing organization" for emigrants, and Gestapo officers were attached to OBERRAT not only to facilitate their exodus, but to consult the records when required.

OBERRAT had found the Cuban consul in Frankfurt-am-Main most willing to sell visas for the right money, and two of those permits had been obtained for Moritz and Recha Weiler. They had spent the last of their savings on tickets for a twin-bedded first-class cabin on the *St. Louis*. Then they had packed what they could, Recha taking care to include her husband's books on religion and philosophy, dressed carefully in their best clothes, taken a train to Hamburg, and finally made their way to the ship.

Now, as they climbed the gangway, Recha Weiler wondered if they had left it until too late to leave Germany, whether her ailing husband would ever recover from the terrible blows to his pride and health. For many months she had realized that his intellectual assessment of the situation had not taken into account the emotional strain it placed him under. When the Nazis took office, Moritz Weiler had told his friends it was important to view the situation coolly. He had argued that the wave of hatred rolling across Germany was a passing phenomenon that would peak and die away. He had even predicted that the climax would come in 1936, and that afterward life would revert to normal.

In that year he lost his teaching post at the university, he was first spat upon in public, a youth threw dung at him, and this gentle and courteous old man was called a dirty Jew.

Now, alone in their cabin, B-108, Moritz Weiler clung to his wife, happy that there still seemed a Germany where people were human.

Ever since he had noticed the swastika on the *St. Louis*, Aaron Pozner had spent his waking hours watching the ship, looking for any sign of something untoward. There had been none. Even so, the *St. Louis*, flying that flag, had come to him to look like a floating prison On Friday evening, as he observed a number of passengers going aboard, he decided to leave his hiding place and chance boarding himself.

Pozner eased his way past the animal hides, pushing his suitcase in front of him, and went to a public lavatory outside shed 76. He splashed water over the stubble on his bruised face and shaven head, and washed his hands. He and his clothes reeked with the smell of stale perspiration, but he was unaware of it. He got out his papers from his suitcase, and then strode hesitantly, but as confidently as possible, into shed 76.

Inside the customs area, he was promptly surrounded by uniformed officials. They looked carefully at him, at his papers, and cursorily into his suitcase, then stood back, and motioned him toward the ship.

From a vantage point on the promenade deck, Otto Schiendick watched Pozner slowly climbing the tourist gangway. To him, as to others, the man looked a vagrant, not like the teacher of Hebrew he was. But to Leo Jockl, also watching, the suffering and courage were clear. He was filled with pity for the figure who hesitated at the top of the gangway.

A steward stepped forward and offered to take his case. Pozner instinctively drew back, pulling the case closer to him. Another steward told him an evening meal was available. He could hardly believe his ears; it had been years since a German had spoken to him politely. A third steward asked to see his boarding card and offered to direct him to his cabin. Confused, but determined to maintain some independence, he shook his head and walked away down the deck.

Otto Schiendick had viewed the scene with contempt, confirmed in his belief that all Jews were ill-mannered. As the shabby figure approached him, he placed himself in his way so that Pozner had to walk around him. Schiendick reported to the small group of stewards nearby that there went positive proof that *Der Stuermer,* the party's scandal sheet, was right—"Jews give off a peculiar aroma."

Pozner eventually found his way down to cabin 373 on D deck, and closed the door behind him. Everything was so different from what he had expected: a young cabin steward had called him Herr Pozner, an officer had actually wished him a pleasant voyage. His cabin surprised him further. Though small, it was comfortable and spotlessly clean. The pillowcase and bed linen were crisply laundered; even the hand towels were pressed and neatly folded.

Some *German* had taken the trouble to do all this for him. As he looked at his face in the mirror, he could not believe he was seeing the same person who, for the past nine days and nights, had spent his time in a hideout reeking of animal hides.

SATURDAY, MAY 13, 1939

On Saturday, May 13, the day of departure, from morning to late afternoon, nearly 900 passengers would board the *St. Louis*. The queues stretched from shed 76 to the gangways and into the ship. Almost half the refugees were women and children. Many men, like Aaron Pozner, released from concentration camps on condition they left Germany immediately, had to travel alone, leaving their families behind to follow later. Many women traveled alone or with their children; their husbands were either still trapped in concentration camps or already in Cuba waiting for them. And two young children were to make the long sea voyage alone.

Seven-year-old Renatta and her five-year-old sister Evelyne entered shed 76 early in the morning, the culmination of months of argument, planning, and scheming by their parents.

Their father, Max Aber, had been a respected and fashionable doctor in the Berlin of the thirties. Despite the Nazis, he and his wife, Lucie, had managed to lead an almost carefree life. But gradually they realized it could not last. Legally, Dr. Aber, like Dr. Spanier, had been allowed to treat only Jews, but because of his reputation, by 1938, S.S. and S.A. officers began to seek his skill as a dermatologist to cure their venereal diseases. They knew he was a Jew, and he knew it was only a matter of time before one of them returned to escort him to Buchenwald or Dachau. In the meantime, they paid well to have their syphilis and gonorrhea treated.

Dr. Aber saved those fees in preparation for an escape. He had handed the money over to a trusted friend, a Berlin lawyer, who passed on the cash to the Brazilian ambassador in Berlin in exchange for American dollars. The lawyer smuggled the dollars to Paris and deposited them in an account in Dr. Aber's name. But after several successful runs, the lawyer was caught by the

Gestapo and sent to a concentration camp, where he would die.

When Dr. Aber realized that his house was being watched, he fled. He went to New York, where he spent $500 of the $800 that had been deposited in Paris, on a U.S. Immigration Department bond that guaranteed him a place on the American quota. But until his number came up, the United States ordered, he must leave the country. With his remaining money, he traveled to Cuba to wait along with all the other refugees.

Dr. Aber had discussed the question of how to get his family out of Germany with two fellow immigrants with the same problem, who had arrived in Havana at about the same time. Dr. Bardeleben was a physician from Berlin, and Hans Fischer had managed a Breslau factory until he was thrown into Buchenwald and later given two weeks to leave Germany. Of similar ages and background, the three men became increasingly anxious about the safety of their wives and children.

But Max Aber had a worry the other two did not have. Like them, he had bombarded his wife with cables and letters about her coming to Cuba, but Lucie Aber's replies had been cool. Finally he had accepted the truth: his marriage was over and his wife loved another man. He did not altogether blame her. A busy doctor in Berlin had many demands on his time; his wife had not always understood the pressures. On occasion he had found solace in other beds. In turn, his wife had also looked elsewhere. Soon after he had left Germany, she had taken up with a German of influence and charm, and with him, she, a gentile, would need no longer face years of humiliation that came from marriage to a non-Aryan.

For Renatta and Evelyne Aber, their father's absence was hard enough to accept, but in late 1938 there had come an even harsher blow. Their mother had packed them away to a children's home outside Berlin, explaining that it was best for the youngsters. From the outset, Renatta hated the home, with its tasteless food, faded linen, and cold corridors, but she put on a brave front for her younger sister.

Her resolve had failed her only on *Kristallnacht;* now, seven months later, she still remembered the terror she felt on seeing burning synagogues, black-booted men with guns, broken glass, shops smashed, and white paint daubed on buildings.

Dr. Aber had been even more concerned about his daughters when he had learned where they were. He had pondered how to get his wife to agree to their leaving the home, and how to get them to Cuba.

"First you must have permits," a young divorcée had insisted to him one afternoon. "Go and see my former husband. He's got connections."

Dr. Aber had been long enough in Havana to know that on every street corner, besides the pimps offering girls and dirty postcards, there were men claiming to have connections. But he went. The rendezvous was in a shabby sidewalk cafe. The ex-husband was uncouth, uneducated. With paper and pencil provided by the bartender, he wrote out a message to show his "connection." Aber looked at it skeptically. His contact was claiming to know one of the most powerful men in Cuba, José Estedes.

To save the ten-cent trolley fare, Dr. Aber walked to Estedes' home. When he presented the slip of paper, to his astonishment he was immediately ushered into the presence of Estedes, who, after hearing of his plight, drove him to the office of Cuba's director of immigration. When he left the office, he had landing permits for Cuba for his wife and children.

Late in February 1939, Max Aber had sent the papers to Lucie, pleading that she book passage on the next available ship. But Lucie had no intention of joining her husband. Finally, his patience exhausted, Dr. Aber had threatened to return to Berlin to collect Renatta and Evelyne, whatever the cost and risk to himself. His wife gave in.

Now, inside shed 76, Renatta and Evelyne looked up at their mother as she repeated to them how exciting it would be traveling alone.

"Then why don't you come, too?" Renatta persisted.

Lucie Aber shook her head. "Maybe later, darling." Then, looking around to see no one was watching, she opened her purse and produced a child's gold watch. "Take this, quickly, put it in your pocket."

"No, Momma," Renatta replied, frightened. "It's not allowed. I know it's not." The child, terrified of the men in uniforms she saw all around, adamantly refused to accept the going-away present.

An elderly couple joined the group. They had agreed to act as guardians to the children. Lucie Aber hugged her daughters and then turned away.

"I'll look after Evelyne," the seven-year-old called to her mother. "I promise."

Taking her sister by the hand, Renatta slowly walked toward the ship. Only once did the two small children look back. Their mother was not to be seen.

By midmorning Saturday, Purser Ferdinand Mueller had achieved the impossible. By bribery, pleading, and manipulation, he had carried out the captain's order to ensure that the ship's larder was properly provisioned. Since dawn he had supervised the loading of pounds of caviar, sides of salmon, smoked and fresh, hundreds of cases of choice German wines and beers, and medical supplies, and he had even managed to scrounge an adequate supply of "fine quality" toilet paper.

Periodically he left the loading bays to watch over the embarking passengers, making sure his stewards settled them comfortably in their cabins. Now, with the last of the supplies safely stowed, he began to knock on those cabin doors, introducing himself, offering to be of service.

When he arrived at the Weilers' cabin and knocked, Recha Weiler opened the door. Behind her, Mueller could see her husband, seated with a leather-bound book on his knees, an embroidered skullcap on his head. Recha explained that they were saying prayers; it was not, she asked anxiously, forbidden?

An embarrassed Mueller said there were no such restrictions on board, and went on to explain that during the voyage the first-class social hall would be converted into a synagogue. The look of utter disbelief on Recha Weiler's face further discomfited the purser; it brought home to him the true meaning, he later told a steward, of what people like the Weilers must have suffered.

Recha asked him for which faith the synagogue would be used: Orthodox, Conservative, or Reform.

Mueller was startled by the question. He had never before considered that Judaism was anything other than a single belief.

Several times during the afternoon, Aaron Pozner tried to ask one of the crew whether the ship would leave on time, but did not dare. Instead, he stood on A deck apart from everyone else, and watched his fellow travelers boarding. One particular group caught his attention: a man in a topcoat, holding a woman's arm. Behind them came two chattering youngsters. Even from that distance, Pozner felt the man's apprehension.

Down on the quay, Max Loewe's anxiety gave way once again to fear. The swastika flag was flying at the stern. He suddenly realized the *St. Louis* was a *German* ship; once aboard, he would still be on *German* territory. Perhaps he had not given the Gestapo the slip after all; perhaps there were Gestapo on the ship who would yet turn him in.

Elise Loewe had had to choose between staying with the aged mother she loved who refused to leave Germany, and going with her husband. She knew that if she had stayed, her husband would have remained as well; eventually he would have been caught, and that might well have meant his death. She had chosen her husband. She felt sure she would never see her mother again.

In shed 76, Elise had shielded her husband as best she could from the officials; fortunately they had seemed much more intent on her pretty, seventeen-year-old, dark-haired daughter Ruth. They successfully passed the emigration formalities, only to receive a cruel blow: the precious container holding everything in the world the family owned had been mistakenly shipped to Shanghai.

The formerly prosperous Loewes were leaving Germany with little more than the clothes they wore. Max Loewe knew there was now nothing left for the Nazis to take but himself and his family. He was barely able to control his anguish as he walked up the gangway.

High above the quay, forward on the promenade deck, First Officer Klaus Ostermeyer and Purser Mueller watched the scenes below. Mueller had tried to explain his problem of a choice of Orthodox, Conservative, or Reform services to Ostermeyer, but the first officer replied merely: "If that's the *only* problem we'll have, then we will escape lightly." Both men were conscious of the stiff, motionless figure of Captain Schroeder standing once again on the nearby bridge wing. Mueller wondered what he was thinking.

The captain was wondering what the people boarding the ship thought. Most moved a trifle too fast or too slow, staring around, turning their heads, looking for a friendly face in the crowd. Though he could not see their faces too clearly, he imagined that not a few were suppressing tears. Gustav Schroeder was a romantic man; he wanted to believe that if they had a common thought, it was probably one of sadness that they, Germans, were being thrown out of their country; he hoped any bitterness would be assuaged to a considerable degree by the behavior of his crew.

Then, by the first-class boarding gate, Schroeder saw a photographer taking pictures of the passengers, as many tried to shield their faces from the camera. Sensing trouble, he hurried to the gate to find the man reloading his camera.

"Who are you?" Schroeder barked.

The man said he was from the Ministry of Propaganda, and began to explain that his films were to be rushed to Berlin at the "express request of Minister Goebbels."

"Get off my ship!"

The man paused, uncertain, and then, possibly believing that nobody had the authority to countermand an order from Goebbels, prepared to resume photographing. A furious Schroeder shoved him toward the gangway. "Get off—or I'll personally throw you overboard. And you can report that to the minister!"

The man slunk off the ship.

As the captain walked briskly toward the bridge, a sixth sense drew him back toward the nightclub on B deck, the *Tanzplatz*. From inside came the sound of a piano and singing. Recognizing the words, he hurried the last few steps to throw open the club's door. Inside, grouped around the baby grand, Otto Schiendick and the Gestapo "firemen" were chorusing their way through a medley of Nazi songs. Their voices died away as the captain entered.

Gustav Schroeder walked over and slammed shut the piano lid. Schiendick, a note of defiance in his voice, asked what exactly was the captain objecting to?

Apart from breaking a company rule forbidding crew to make use of passenger areas, they had deliberately flouted his order to cause no embarrassment to the passengers.

"Embarrassment, Captain?" said Schiendick. "Where is the

embarrassment? There is no law that forbids us to sing party songs."

The steward produced a piece of paper. It was authority from Hapag for the crew to use the *Tanzplatz* "when, and if it is reasonable."

Schroeder handed it back to the steward.

"Get out! All of you! If I find you in here again you will need more than a piece of paper to save your skins!"

The sullen group filed out.

Down on the quay, in the late afternoon, the man from the Propaganda Ministry continued to photograph passengers as they trudged towards the *St. Louis*. He chose his subjects carefully, selecting only those who would later, with the help of a Nazi caption writer, be presented as "documentary" pictorial proof that the refugees were "subhuman savages," "furtive-looking fugitives," not "worthy" of German citizenship.

The men, women, and children were in fact frightened people whose faces bore the mark of years of stress. The quayside scene was all the more painful for many of them as the Hapag band, present to give the ship its traditional musical farewell, played tunes from a bygone era.

Yet for Babette Spanier, that music suited perfectly her arrival in shed 76. All afternoon she had prepared her husband and children for this moment. She had told Fritz they would leave Germany in a fitting manner so that nobody could say a scion of the Seidemann family did not depart Germany in style.

First she had dressed the twins in their best party frocks. Then she had made Dr. Spanier wear a dinner suit beneath his topcoat. Finally she herself had put on a close-fitting evening gown and fur wrap.

A taxi had carried them to the Hapag pier. Inside shed 76, the officials and the other refugees were amazed by the appearance of the four people dressed as if they were going to a ball; the contrast with the shabby dress of many of the other passengers was total. Babette Spanier had inserted a monocle in her eye.

The family were waved through by the cheap-suited party men. Outside, at the foot of the black-and-white cliff of the *St. Louis,* stewards were ready. Willing hands grasped the Spaniers' luggage; cheerful voices gave their first assurance of friendly service.

In a grand cavalcade the party swept toward the first-class gangway, toward the ministry photographer.

"Excuse me," said Babette Spanier to her husband, "but it looks as if someone is going to take our picture."

She turned to the photographer and asked him how they should pose. He looked away: the Spanier family did not fit the image he required.

At that moment the band, perhaps catching the mood, launched into "Vienna, City of my Dreams."

"Fritz," Babette said with a smile. "Remember the music? The night you proposed."

She began to hum the tune. Her voice shook. And both then realized how frightened she was, that her insistence on a splendid entrance was really no more than a brave try at hiding her fears. Fritz was proud to see that she was still humming as she stepped on board, bestowing a gracious smile on the steward who stepped forward to guide them to their cabins.

During the afternoon, Purser Ferdinand Mueller dealt with passenger inquiries swiftly and sympathetically, though not always entirely to their satisfaction. He had to turn down a request from a couple who wanted to change cabins, making clear that the ship was fully booked and there were no spare cabins available. Recha Weiler came to ask whether kosher food might be served. Mueller regretted that it would not, at least not immediately, but asked if it would suffice to offer a plentiful supply of egg and fish dishes. A group of young passengers came, wanting to know where the swimming pool was. Politely postponing the discussion on kosher cooking, the purser told the group that the pool would be erected in the opening above the cargo hold, aft on A deck, after leaving port; it would be filled with water once the ship neared the warmer Gulf Stream.

By six o'clock Saturday evening, the purser was pleased that many of the passengers were already behaving like the travelers he was used to serving.

Babette Spanier thought the crew acted as if they had been

told to put on a show. Since boarding she had watched them, wondering what they *really* thought. She asked her husband, who said it did not matter.

"All that matters is that we sail on time and get away from Germany," Dr. Spanier said.

Even if the ship was a thousand miles away it could still be recalled by radio. Babette wondered whether her husband had considered that, but decided not to ask him.

Gustav Schroeder dined alone in his day cabin. As the steward, Leo Jockl, served him, the captain noticed he was obviously fumbling. What was the matter?

No more than "the general tension of the voyage," he told the captain.

The trip must be regarded as the same as any other. "These people are passengers, no different from others we have carried."

The steward nodded and hurried from the cabin before the captain could pry out the truth that he had been asked to inform on him.

Schroeder watched him go with some misgivings. The fact that Jockl was a half Jew made the voyage nerve-racking for him. The captain decided he must watch his steward more carefully. He then made another entry in the diary he was keeping of the trip.

"There is a somewhat nervous disposition among the passengers. Despite this, everyone seems convinced they will never see Germany again. Touching departure scenes have taken place. Many seem light of heart, having left their homes. Others take it heavily. But beautiful weather, pure sea air, good food, and attentive service will soon provide the usual worry-free atmosphere of long sea voyages. Painful impressions on land disappear quickly at sea and soon seem merely like dreams."

He walked to the bridge to prepare for the moment he always enjoyed, the moment of departure.

By half past seven on Saturday evening, the crowd at the railing had grown quiet. From high above came a piercing blast. Below, on the quay, the band struggled to compete. Bellowed commands echoed between ship and shore. Then the gangways were hauled clear and ropes slipped. Still the crowd remained quiet, waiting.

Even the band was now silent, its leader standing stiffly to attention, baton poised. Aaron Pozner felt the deck tremble under his feet, and a sigh stirred among the people wedged around him.

"The ship's moving!" somebody cried. "The space between us and the land is growing."

It widened steadily and surely before their eyes—too wide for anybody to jump from the ship, or onto it.

Babette Spanier looked at her watch. "Right on time. Eight o'clock.

"The Germans are never late, especially when it comes to Jews," her husband replied.

Shortly after 8:30 P.M., the radio room aboard the *St. Louis* received a priority message from Claus-Gottfried Holthusen. It made Gustave Schroeder angry: he had been deliberately deceived by Holthusen at his earlier meeting, for now the Hapag director had cabled in the message the captain decoded:

IMPERATIVE YOU MAKE ALL SPEED HAVANA IN VIEW TWO OTHER SHIPS THE ENGLISH ORDUNA AND FRENCH FLANDRE BOUND THERE WITH SIMILAR PASSENGERS BUT HAVE CONFIRMATION THAT WHAT- EVER HAPPENS YOUR PASSENGERS WILL LAND. NO CAUSE FOR ALARM.

The cable had come too late to discuss the matter directly with Holthusen, since the *St. Louis* was not fitted with a ship-to-shore telephone. Schroeder believed that Holthusen had timed his message to arrive at the moment when the *St. Louis* was steadily gaining speed.

The cable had given no positions for the *Orduna* or the *Flandre,* but a check in a reference book revealed that both ships were smaller than the *St. Louis,* and faster. Once the *St. Louis* was clear of its next port of call, at Cherbourg, she must maintain her maximum speed of sixteen knots all the way to Cuba. Ostermeyer said he would explain to the passengers that they were hurrying because the ship had a tight summer cruise schedule to follow.

It was a relief to have a reassuring and quick-thinking senior officer, the captain thought. Ostermeyer had ordered the radio room to locate the *Orduna* and *Flandre* as soon as he read the cable; the *St. Louis* must get to Cuba with its cargo before they did. But no matter how they interpreted the cable's message, its contents seemed to warn of trouble, with its "imperative," "all speed" and "whatever happens." If the fate of his passengers would not be endangered, the captain thought, he would abandon the voyage here and now. He was more than ever determined to resign at the journey's end.

"I'm being used," insisted Gustav Schroeder, "and, by God, I don't like it!"

By nine o'clock that Saturday night, news of the ship's departure was being telephoned and telegraphed to various parts of the world.

Claus-Gottfried Holthusen spoke to Morris Troper, European director of the Joint Distribution Committee in Paris.

"All will be well," the Hapag director told him. "They are at sea, which is the main thing."

Troper sensed that they both knew it was not the case, but he kept his reservations to himself. Afterward, he sent a telegram to the American Jewish Joint Distribution Committee in New York stating that the *St. Louis* would arrive in Havana "around May 27" with almost 1000 on board.

In Berlin, the departure was a signal for action in the Ministry of Propaganda. Goebbels was telephoned at home. He authorized the Nazi national news agency to carry a long, virulent diatribe on the voyage. Within the hour, newspapers and radio stations through Germany were preparing stories accusing the *St. Louis* passengers of fleeing with stolen hoards of money, and much else. Aryan Germans were reminded to protect themselves against the "machinations of those still among us."

A ministry official cabled Robert Hoffman at the Hapag office in Havana. Hoffman was instructed to ensure that the fourteen agents provocateurs in Havana created the maximum hostility among the people toward the ship's passengers, and also those on the British and French ships. Further orders were cabled to the German embassies in Washington, London, Paris, and Rome, briefing the ambassadors to exploit the propaganda value of the *St. Louis* voyage. Those on board were to be branded as criminals; the question was to be planted everywhere: Who would want to take such people? It was crude, but such methods had been effective before.

Commander von Bonin, who had briefed Otto Schiendick

about his rendezvous with Hoffman in Havana, learned of the departure over dinner in a call from a duty officer at Abwehr headquarters. There was no need to disturb Admiral Canaris with the news.

Around that time, an Associated Press correspondent in Berlin filed a story to New York on the sailing. He did not give it much play, guessing it might end up as a back page item for the Sunday editions.

In London, Sir Herbert Emerson, like Gustav Schroeder, was furious with Claus-Gottfried Holthusen. The director of the International Committee on Political Refugees felt that Holthusen had purposely snubbed him by ignoring his earlier, carefully considered cable warning that the *St. Louis* should not sail. Emerson believed the refugees on board could jeopardize his negotiations for the wholesale resettlement of Jews outside Germany. Hitler had threatened to withdraw his offer of allowing the orderly emigration of 50,000 a year because of a "lack of response" from other nations.

There had been no lack of response, but how were the schemes to be financed? Official Jewish opinion was divided, and also questioned the suitability of the areas offered.

The refugee director had begun to lose patience, confiding to an aide that there "is always some other scheme in the background for which [the Jews] are prepared to sacrifice schemes which are already in being." Emerson knew the crucially important British white paper on Palestine, due to be published in just four days' time on May 17, was almost certain to exacerbate the situation. The *St. Louis* was at the very least an irritating distraction. The voyage had come at the worst possible time.

Seated by her husband's bed in cabin B-108 that Saturday night, Recha Weiler kept telling him that the nightmare was finally over, they were out of the darkness into the light.

Professor Weiler nodded, but he was too tired to speak. "Recha," he murmured. "It is enough sometimes just to travel."

Babette and Fritz Spanier settled the twins to sleep and went out to inspect the ship. They walked from one public room to another, most plush-carpeted with crystal chandeliers, gilt-framed mirrors, and polished woodwork.

The ship's purser also strolled from deck to deck, pausing to speak with a steward, barman, or cabin boy. Babette wondered if he was briefing them on some anticipated action; the voyage could still be stopped.

But her spirits revived as they inspected the elegant ship. It seemed to represent "the good life ahead," as her husband had promised. "It was glossy and smart, just like America," she later recalled. They would become closer on the voyage. "Fritz was more attentive than he had been for years. He had not even looked at another girl on board, and there were plenty of pretty ones around."

As he walked through the ship, Ferdinand Mueller had been disturbed by the signs of distress or fear on many faces. Even if he had not received clear orders from the captain that everything possible must be done to please the passengers, he was sure he would still have done so. So, when the Spaniers walked into the Schanke Bar on C deck, the purser invited them to join him for a cocktail, "to show we are all Germans."

It seemed a great pity, Dr. Spanier replied, that not until he and his wife were fleeing the country had a German said such a thing.

Two decks above, Max Loewe peered out and down. The lights onshore blinked, but around the ship, the sea was black.

He wished, he whispered to his wife, that the protecting darkness would never lift. She touched his arm. His children, Ruth and Fritz, although intent on looking toward shore, could not help but overhear what their father had said.

"Do you know what it's like to be a Jew?"

Otto Schiendick's question stunned Leo Jockl. The group of stewards grew silent around one of the tables in the dining salon. Jockl desperately wished he had gone to his quarters instead of remaining to gossip after the last diners had gone. Schiendick repeated the question. One of the stewards looked at him speculatively.

"How do *you* know what it is like to be a Jew, Schiendick, unless you are one?" he asked.

There was a wave of laughter. Schiendick pushed back his chair and left the group.

The *St. Louis* departing Hamburg, May 13, 1939. Photo: *Stern*.

Captain Gustav Schroeder. Photo: *Stern*.

A picture postcard sold to the refugees aboard the *St. Louis*.
Courtesy: Liesl Joseph-Loeb.

The social hall of the *St. Louis*. Photo: *Stern*.

Front-page headline of the May 1939 issue of *Der Stuermer*, the Nazi propaganda sheet: "Jews Emigrate." Photo: *Stern*.

The refugees board the *St. Louis* in Hamburg, May 13, 1939. Photo: *Stern*.

Lilly Joseph, photographed just before the
St. Louis sailed. Photo: *Stern*.

Ten-year-old Liesl Joseph. Courtesy:
Liesl Joseph-Loeb.

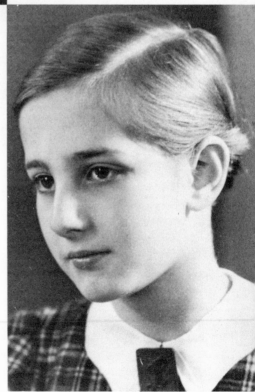

June 18, 1939. The day after her eleventh birthday, Liesl Joseph was presented with this bouquet of two dozen roses by Morris Troper on the ship. Courtesy: Lilly Joseph-Kamin.

Children who traveled alone on the *St. Louis:* seven-year-old Renatta Aber and her five-year-old sister Evelyne. Courtesy: Dr. Max Aber.

The Spanier twins on departure at Hamburg. Photo: Associated Press.

The passenger committee. Front: Josef Joseph, chairman. Behind, left to right: Dr. Max Weiss, Herbert Manasse, Dr. Arthur Hausdorff, Dr. Max Zellner. Courtesy: Lilly Joseph-Kamin.

Otto Schiendick.
Photo: Paul Bendowski.

SUNDAY, MAY 14, 1939

By Sunday, May 14, a bright and sunny morning, the ship had begun to settle down. Captain Schroeder was gratified to see that some of the passengers even smiled at the small party of deck officers he led on the inspectiion tour he regularly carried out on the first full day of a new trip. The inspection was primarily an exercise in public relations.

Within an hour the entourage had put in a brisk appearance in the social hall, peered into the deserted gymnasium on A deck, and strolled around the sports deck, where a few younger passengers tried their hand at shuffleboard. Then he led the officers inside, down to B deck, to the *Tanzplatz;* it was being prepared for an afternoon tea dance. They moved farther down, to C deck and the dining areas, where stewards flitted, laying tables for lunch. The arrangement of white linen, crystal glass, and silverware never failed to please Gustav Schroeder; it reminded him of his own humble upbringing, when he had eaten from enameled plates.

The captain led the way past the ship's laundry and into the crew quarters, with its pungent air of men who worked, relaxed, and slept in close proximity. His mellow mood gave way to rising anger as he saw a bulletin board festooned with the current issue of *Der Stuermer* and party notices bearing the signature of Otto Schiendick.

He ordered the steward to be summoned, and tersely told him to clear the board of all propaganda. Schiendick protested. As the ship's *Leiter*, he argued, it was his duty to keep the crew informed of party doctrines.

"Take that stuff down."

"But, Captain, I must respectfully—"

"Take it down—now! Like this!"

Gustav Schroeder ripped down the pages of *Der Stuermer,* and dropped them in a trash can.

Crimson-faced, the steward began to remove the offending material.

The Spaniers were among the first to enter the first-class restaurant. A steward showed them to a table and handed around menus.

Babette Spanier was content to watch other passengers arriving. An attractive, well-dressed woman caught her attention; she had a cosmopolitan air. Babette Spanier listened, with shocked disapproval, as the woman spoke to the table steward; for all her elegance, she used the broad, brutal Berlin dialect of the streets.

"Excuse me, but I think we'll have to be careful with whom we mix," Babette said to her husband.

Nearby on a podium, the musicians talked quietly among themselves. Soon the diners came in a concerted rush. Stewards advanced, bowing and smiling, escorting them to tables. The orchestra struck up briskly; its clarinetist sang a love song. Babette Spanier thought the performance "far too leery," and gave her attention to the menu.

In the tourist-class restaurant, Renatta Aber solemnly read aloud the contents of the entire menu to her five-year-old sister.

"Can I have it all?" asked Evelyne.

Aaron Pozner watched the two girls. Their innocent enthusiasm reminded him of his own two children. He pushed aside his plate, his appetite gone, and left the restaurant.

Otto Schiendick watched him go and told another steward: "There goes a typical Jew. Ordering all that food and then leaving it."

"I shouldn't let the captain hear you say that," came the reply. "Otherwise you'll be in more trouble."

Schiendick turned away, apparently furious that his latest clash with Captain Schroeder had made him the butt of crew gossip. For most of his colleagues, he was only tolerated because of his official party role on board. That knowledge smarted most of all, making him more determined than ever to seek his revenge.

In the kitchen area, which served both first and tourist classes, he cornered Leo Jockl and demanded to know what information he had gleaned.

Jockl replied blandly with a detailed recital of the captain's movements since he had awakened that morning, bathed, shaved, and breakfasted.

"That's not what I want to know."

"But there's nothing else to report," Jockl replied. "Unless you want me to make it up."

Schiendick glared, and for the first time the captain's steward did not avoid the stare.

Alice Feilchenfeld lunched quickly, having no interest in joining the excited chatter all around her. Afterward she went on deck, but the sight of children playing reminded her of the uncertainty over her own children's future. But, returning to her cabin, she was depressed even more by the empty berths and the folded-up baby's cot in the corner.

Three months earlier, Alice Feilchenfeld had sent her four children to Belgium for safekeeping. They were to join the ship at Cherbourg; in Havana her husband waited to complete the family reunion. But just before boarding in Hamburg, she had received word from Belgium that the Cuban visas for her children had not yet been received. Without them they would not be allowed to board. She wondered whether she should cable her husband to let him know the permits had not arrived, but decided that if he had not already sent them it was now too late.

Rather than sit alone in the empty cabin, Alice Feilchenfeld went for a walk on the promenade deck, where she noticed a man standing alone by the rail. She decided to speak to him and was pleasantly surprised to find that Max Loewe came from her home town, Breslau. She tried to begin a conversation, eager to have a man's advice, but he seemed hardly to comprehend, and fidgeted nervously. When she began to explain her dilemma about the children, he became even more agitated, as if she had "touched a raw nerve in his mind." Embarrassed, she excused herself.

One-year-old Raphael was the one Frau Feilchenfeld especially worried about; the three older children were tougher, particularly ten-year-old Wolfgang. In Germany, the boy had looked at the world around him and hardened himself to the suffering and taunts. By midafternoon, she was exhausted and fell asleep in her cabin, as she would recall, "actually trembling with anxiety."

After an excellent dinner, Dr. Spanier and his wife joined the throng heading for the ship's cinema; the main feature was to be a romantic story.

Few noticed Otto Schiendick slip into the back of the dimmed theater. He wanted to see the passengers' reaction to the newsreel. A murmur of consternation stirred through the audience as the face of Adolf Hitler filled the screen and his voice shrieked familiar invective about "worldwide Jewish influences clamoring for an interventionist war against Germany." The Fuehrer was followed by shots of German mobilization, and the strident commentary warned those in the darkened room that the day of reckoning for Jews was at hand.

Dr. Spanier had seen enough. He escorted his wife to their cabin and then stormed to the purser's office.

Mueller was mortified when he heard Fritz Spanier's complaint. In all the careful checks the purser had made to ensure nothing would give offense, he had inadvertently overlooked the newsreel. Dr. Spanier was not placated; nothing less than a personal explanation from the captain would satisfy him. Mueller began to plead there was no need to go to such lengths since the mistake would not occur again. But the doctor coldly insisted that either the purser would take him to the captain or he would seek him out himself.

The captain had years of experience in handling difficult problems involving passengers. Now, he dismissed Mueller; he would deal with the purser later. Alone with Dr. Spanier, the captain listened sympathetically and silently.

But the doctor's anger stemmed from no ordinary complaint. The captain decided to do the only thing he felt proper in the situation: he admitted frankly that there had been a lapse of good taste. It would not occur again.

"A lapse of good taste!" said Dr. Spanier. "Is that what you call insulting people? Do you know what it is really like to be persecuted and then have to endure this?"

The captain conceded that he had no such personal experience. "What further do you wish me to do? You have my assurance it will not happen again. I have apologized. What else can I do?"

There was no more to be done. With a stiff *"Gute Nacht,"* Dr. Spanier left the cabin. Nothing, after all, would be so very different on this ship from life in Nazi Germany. He felt that the captain had behaved correctly, but coldly, in his apology.

Gustav Schroeder felt dejected after the encounter. He had tried to avoid just such an incident, and yet it had happened—and early in the voyage. Dr. Spanier did not, however, seem the sort to make further trouble. The captain respected the force of the doctor's words. His eloquence and sense of moral decency made him a formidable figure. He marked Fritz Spanier as a man of substance.

Fritz and Babette Spanier's exit from the cinema had been witnessed by Otto Schiendick. Others had also left the theater in disgust, and the steward was pleased that the newsreel had achieved the effect he had hoped for. He had followed Dr. Spanier to the purser's office and watched the two men head for the bridge. When Mueller returned alone, Schiendick had tried to question him, but the usually placid purser erupted in fury.

Otto Schiendick retired to his quarters, determined to add Mueller's name to the captain's as men to be revenged upon.

MONDAY, MAY 15, 1939

The sun sparkled on the wheelhouse windows. They had not, Gustav Schroeder observed to the helmsman, been properly cleaned. It was one of several caustic observations he made early that Monday morning.

The captain had slept badly. He had questioned Jockl about the passengers' mood, and when the steward had not replied quickly enough, he had sharply demanded to know what was the matter.

Jockl then told him of Schiendick's demand that he become an informer. Gustav Schroeder listened in stunned silence. His hopes of a peaceful, ordinary voyage faded.

His first thought had been to send for Schiendick, confront him, and then dump the steward ashore at Cherbourg. But he realized that was not possible. Six months ago an order had been issued by Hapag to all its masters that party *Leiters* on company ships could not be removed without the written authority of the marine superintendent.

If the captain faced Schiendick now, the steward would probably gain the upper hand. He decided for the moment to take no action. His mood was not eased by another cable from Holthusen ordering Schroeder to curtail his Cherbourg stop. The 15,507 *Orduna*, with 154 emigrants on board, was only fourteen hours astern of the *St. Louis*—and gaining steadily. The *Flandre*, smaller and faster than either the *St. Louis* or the *Orduna*, had 104 refugees, but her exact position was unknown. Suppose they arrived first, and unloaded their human cargo. Would there still be room for the *St. Louis*'s passengers? The message had ended:

REPEAT YOU MAKE ALL POSSIBLE SPEED VIEW FLUID SITUATION HAVANA.

84

Gustav Schroeder dispatched a reply to Holthusen demanding to know what he meant by "fluid situation Havana."

Shortly afterward the Cherbourg pilot came on board and eased the *St. Louis* toward the harbor. Passengers on deck could clearly see traffic on the waterfront streets, and more than one expressed relief that there were no Nazi symbols in sight.

At 9:30 A.M. the ship was positioned and anchored; minutes afterward the electrically powered starboard accommodation ladder was lowered, and from the shore a number of launches headed toward the liner.

Gustav Schroeder summoned First Officer Ostermeyer and showed him the latest cable from Holthusen.

"I want to be out of here in half the usual time," he added. "I don't care how it's done, but I want it done."

Otto and Rosemarie Bergmann watched as the first of the launches rose and fell against the accommodation ladder.

The young couple were happy to have a break from their charges, the two most elderly women on the ship—Rosemarie's mother, aged sixty-nine, and Otto's aunt, Shalote Hecht, eighty. Aunt Shalote had already proven herself particularly trying, and Rosemarie's ailing mother had complained incessantly about having to leave Germany despite the fact that the Nazis had confiscated her home, requiring her to pay rent for living in the house that had been hers for over half a century.

Rosemarie Bergmann, too, gave her husband cause for concern. Superstititous, she had been disturbed by the departure date—the thirteenth—the more so since the journey had begun on the Jewish Sabbath.

They watched the crates of fresh fruits and vegetables being loaded, and she noticed something else that bothered her. No water was being taken on. Otto Bergmann wondered whether the story his wife had heard, at breakfast, could possibly be true—that the ship would not take on water because of a fear that the French could have poisoned it. He discounted it; if someone wanted to kill them all, it would have been possible for them to poison the stores being loaded.

Yet Rosemarie Bergmann thought it strange that no water was taken on. She decided to note it in her diary of the voyage.

All through the long morning, Alice Feilchenfeld watched the
supply boats coming and going. The only break for her had been
when the mail was brought on board, the last the St. Louis would
receive before Havana. But there had been no letter from her
husband in Cuba, and none from her children.

The lunch gong sounded. She refused to leave the rail. Still no
one boarded the ship.

Early in the afternoon, a tender filled with people approached.
It carried thirty-eight passengers, mostly children and Spanish
refugees from the Civil War.

Alice Feilchenfeld saw no sign of her family. In that moment,
she made her decision: she would leave the ship and go to Belgium
to be with her children, even though it meant she might never see
her husband again. With tears streaming down her cheeks, she
looked for an officer to whom she could convey her decision.

"Momma!"

She turned, and Judith and Heinz, followed by Wolfgang
carrying baby Raphael in his arms, ran down the deck toward her.
They had been the last off the launch; their arrival made a total of
937 passengers on board.

Shortly afterward, the St. Louis glided forward into the
English Channel toward the Bay of Biscay.

In Havana, some 4000 sea miles away, the news that the St.
Louis was on her way did not please the Cuban president;
Frederico Bru was determined to stop the ship's passengers from
landing.

Throughout the whole of this humid Monday, Manuel Benitez, director of immigration, reassured the refugees and the local
Hapag agent, Luis Clasing, that the passengers would land; that
President Bru's recently published decree 937, which forbade
them entry, was no more than a piece of paper, "just like Hitler
gave Chamberlain at Munich."

Clasing had not been amused by the comparison, nor was he
able to hide his anxiety that Bru's decree would bar the St. Louis
passengers and end the profitable partnership between Manuel
Benitez and Hapag. Benitez had barely concealed the fact that he
had amassed a fortune by capitalizing on the plight of refugees.
He could not accept that he was callously profiteering from their

desperation, as had been suggested by at least one of his cabinet colleagues, the commanding Secretary of State, Dr. Juan Remos. Only that day Benitez had heatedly told Remos that in granting refugees sanctuary, however temporary and restrictive it was, he saved their lives. Remos retorted he could not share Benitez's view of himself as an idealistic humanist—or that the money Benitez made was of secondary consideration.

Nevertheless, Remos had promised his support for allowing in the *St. Louis* passengers. Benitez had been surprised; he knew that Remos usually backed Bru's line at cabinet meetings. The Secretary of State had dryly remarked: "Sometimes conscience is more important than anything. You should try and remember that."

Other cabinet members had proved evasive when Manuel Benitez had tried to enlist their support to have decree 937 repealed. They recognized that the law was more than a device to keep out refugees; it was the instrument Bru wanted to force a head-on clash with Manuel Benitez and, more important, his benefactor, Fulgencio Batista, chief of staff of the Cuban army, and effectively the most powerful single voice on the island.

By late afternoon, having forgone his siesta, Manuel Benitez was tiring of all the unaccustomed activity. Nowadays, the most onerous side of his partnership with Hapag was writer's cramp. In the past months he had signed his name to some 4000 landing permits at $150 a signature, bringing him about $600,000 for an outlay of some seventy-five cents for a new fountain pen.

There had also been periodic and handsome kickbacks from Hapag, and this Monday he received another one when Clasing arrived with $5000 in small bills. The agent explained that Hapag didn't want the "problem" of taking the *St. Louis* passengers back to Europe, and the company was happy to make Benitez this "gift of friendship" to ensure that the "problem" would not arise.

Benitez had graciously accepted the money, seated Clasing in a corner of his large office, and begun a rereading of decree 937, to see if there was a loophole, to see if a way could be found which would avoid a confrontation with the president, and yet allow the immigration director to realize his daydream of becoming one of the wealthiest men in the Caribbean.

In the fall of 1938, Benitez had opened a strictly unofficial, private, and illegal "Bureau of Immigration" in the Hotel Plaza, next door to Hapag's offices. He waited for the promulgation of the long-expected decree 55, published in early 1939, drawing a clear distinction between tourists and immigrants.

Decree 55 made it mandatory for an immigrant to have a visa, jointly approved by Benitez, Remos, and the secretary of labor. Further, each immigrant had to post a bond of $500 as a "guarantee of sustenance." Few such legal visas were issued because Benitez, Remos, and the labor secretary disliked and mistrusted each other.

Tourists, on the other hand, were still welcome in Cuba, and could enter unhindered by any such visa restrictions.

Manuel Benitez, with the foresight that made him peculiarly suited to Cuban politics, had prepared his "Immigration Bureau" for just this eventuality. He discreetly let it be known that his "Bureau" would issue not visas, but landing permits, to *anyone* who paid $150.

The permits were individually typed in Spanish on Department of Immigration note paper which Benitez had purloined. They all carried his flourishing signature. Benitez carefully made sure the permits had the right legal jargon to give them further authenticity; there was a firmly couched warning that the permit holder could not work in Cuba, and that he was only authorized to stay "for such time as may be necessary to obtain a visa for the U.S.A. or any other country."

There had been an immediate rush for the permits. Some of the refugees already settled in Havana, caught up in the spirit of happy corruption, bought them in job lots at $150 apiece, and resold them in Europe at up to $500 each. The profits were reinvested in more permits, and a number of refugees grew prosperous exploiting their kinfolk still in Germany.

Hapag had been quick to see advantages in the scheme, and offered immigrants a bumper package deal—a permit *and* guaranteed passage on a Hapag ship. The passengers on the *St. Louis* were just such a package, each of them described on his landing permit—had they known it, it would doubtless have surprised them—as "a tourist, traveling for pleasure."

Manuel Benitez now knew that the "tourist" loophole had been closed. He believed the decree 937 was an act of revenge on Bru's part because Benitez had refused him a share of the profits.

REPUBLICA DE CUBA

SECRETARIA DE HACIENDA

DPTO. DE INMIGRACION

La Habana, Febrero 28 de 1939.

Sr. Agente General de la
Cia. de Vapores
A quien pueda interesar.
Ciudad.

Señor:-

De conformidad con lo que disponen el Apartado
(A) del Artículo Cuarto del Decreto #55, del 13 de -
enero del año en curso y el Párrafo Tercero del Decreto #2507, del 17 de Noviembre de 1938, esta Dirección
General ha tenido a bien, permitir la entrada y estan-
cia en Cuba, por el tiempo que autorizan las leyes de
la República, en calidad de turista y al objeto de ges-
tionar su visado y entrada en los EE. UU., u otro país
cualquiera, de la señora GERTRUD SCHEUER, que por su na-
cionalidad de origen no usa otro apellido, natural y -
ciudadana de Alemania, de veinte y cuatro años de edad,
soltera, del comercio y residiendo en la actualidad, en,
la Ciudad de Kowln-Muehlein, Alemania, calle de Ruchheimer
número seis; siempre que no sufra enfermedad ni defecto
físico alguno, que porte su pasaporte y que no venga a
dedicarse a trabajos de ninguna clase durante el tiempo
que se encuentre en el Territorio Nacional.-

Lo que digo a usted, por si estima oportuno cur-
sar el cable a su Agencia en el puerto de embarque, a fin
de que le sea expedido el boleto de pasaje al menciona-
do pasajero.

Atentamente de usted.,

Manuel Benítez González.
DIRECTOR GENERAL DE INMIGRACION.

The immigration director lay aside his paper, rose from his couch, and looked quizzically at Clasing. How much would Hapag pay to get decree 937 rescinded?

Clasing asked, equally carefully, how much Benitez had in mind.

"Say $250,000," replied Benitez blandly. "You understand it is not for me, but for Bru."

"Impossible! Hapag would never agree to such a figure."

Benitez sighed; with $250,000 from Hapag, he could have made the magnanimous gesture to Bru of "splitting" the profits with the president, while at the same time not actually having to touch any of the money he had already made from selling illegal permits.

Clasing spoke again, and his criticism of Manuel Benitez was barely concealed. "I have given promises to my company on your word and there seems to have been a gross miscalculation about Bru's opposition."

Benitez bridled. The remark hurt his Latin pride. But even if Hapag would not make such a "gesture," it did not matter. Clasing was panicking unnecessarily; he did not understand the Cuban mentality. Benitez argued that Bru could still be outmaneuvered.

To prove his intention, he telephoned the presidential palace for an "urgent and immediate" appointment with Bru. It was granted. Clasing left, promising to return later that evening to hear the outcome of the meeting.

Shortly afterward the immigration director set out to walk to the palace, content for the moment to be carried along in the undertow of Havana life. On the way he was offered prostitutes, dirty movies, and postcards from pimps who solicited him automatically but with no real hope.

Manuel Benitez enjoyed such experiences. He had grown up with some of the touts, and the sight of them, he often said, was a constant reminder that all men were born equal, and that success, wealth, and position were only a matter of planning and seizing opportunities. Such an attitude had earned him the kind of respect and homage that in America a Mafia clan bestows on its "godfather." And, like all good "dons," he cultivated his popularity.

Along his route this evening Benitez stopped at a news vendor to inquire after the man's family, paused for a chat with a shoeshine boy, slipped a few coins to an old crone minding a coffee stall, and patted a number of children on the head.

Those he touched or talked to were flattered by his attention, and the image of Manuel Benitez as a sharp but likable wheeler-dealer, an image that he enjoyed, was enhanced by such contacts.

At exactly 6 P.M. he arrived at the palace. From a distance the building gave the impression of solidity and elegance; the walls were thick to resist the summer heat. Closer up, one could see they had suffered the ravages of tropical hurricanes and time. It appeared a quietly crumbling monument to Spanish colonialism.

Frederico Laredo Bru had returned from his siesta to his office late in the afternoon. Now, in the evening sunlight, he stood by one of the tall windows overlooking the landscaped palace gardens, lean and impeccably dressed in a white tropical suit and black bow tie.

He reviewed the reasons that led to decree 937. In part he had published it because the secretary of labor had questioned the wisdom of letting in more refugees—in relation to its size and population, Cuba had more than almost any other country—arguing that though they were legally barred from working, many did in fact get jobs Cubans would otherwise have had. The labor secretary believed public opinion was against further immigration.

Then, the secretary of the treasury had urged a curb on immigrants because of the island's economic stagnation. Finally, Dr. Juan J. Remos, the secretary of state, had eloquently urged the ban on refugees to end Benitez's "disgraceful" flouting of Cuba's immigration laws. That, Bru knew, had been the key factor in his decision, more so because Benitez had refused to share the profits from his private "bureau" with him.

But the mounting public clamor against the refugees had also influenced Bru. What the president did not know was that the outcry had been deliberately whipped up by the fourteen propaganda agents Goebbels had sent to Cuba a full month before, and who had then been carefully briefed by the Abwehr spymaster on the island, Robert Hoffman.

From a Nazi standpoint, the results had been spectacular. An alliance was forged between the newly legalized Cuban Nazi party and the older and stronger National Fascist party to engage in a virulent propaganda war against the refugees. Every move was guided by the Nazi propaganda experts, who, in turn, through Hoffman's office in the Hapag building, received their instructions from Berlin.

The Nazis had persuaded a local press baron to launch a campaign in his three newspapers to drive all Jews out of Cuba. On May 4, one of those papers, *El Diario de la Marino*, had announced in bold banner headlines that, far from the government driving them out, more would soon be on their way aboard the *St. Louis*. The Cuban secretary of labor planned to "interfere with the ship." Imprecise though those words were, there was no doubting what was intended when Bru had been asked in Congress to "prohibit repeated immigration of Hebrews who are inundating the republic and making a joke of its laws."

Decree 937 had been passed ten days ago, on May 5. Now, all signs suggested it was a popular move. Yet Bru remained worried because Batista had not yet expressed a view, and the president knew the army chief's attitude was a crucial one.

Ever since Batista had assumed command of the army in the revolt of 1933—the same year Hitler and Roosevelt assumed office—Batista had manipulated political power from behind the scenes. Since 1933, there had been no fewer than nine presidents of Cuba. One had probably the shortest stay in office ever. The first thing he did when installed in the presidential palace was to take a bath in the presidential tub. While he was drying himself he received notice that his term was over.

In 1936, Batista eased the then president from office, and put in his own nominee: Frederico Bru. But by May 1939 Bru had deliberately set himself on a collision course with Batista. He had ousted many of Batista's nominees from office. By stopping Benitez's "bureau," the president would widen the rift, for Batista had also put the immigration director in his post. But Bru was more than a puppet on Batista's string; he was now politically strong enough to show who really ruled Cuba—himself, and not the ex-army sergeant.

Bru seated himself behind his desk to await Benitez, an austere and worried man. He knew that the issue of the *St. Louis* had brought matters to a head.

He cut short the minister's cordial greeting by saying bluntly that he was already late for a dinner engagement.

"What exactly do you wish to see me about?"

Benitez tried to remain unruffled as he explained that he had come to discuss the "wider implications" of decree 937.

Bru rose, and in his cold, flat voice declared there was nothing to discuss. "The law stays as it stands."

"But Señor Presidente—!"

Bru walked swiftly from behind his desk toward his office door. He held it open.

"I am not going to discuss the matter further with you, or with anybody."

He wished Manuel Benitez a curt good evening.

At around the time Benitez left Bru, American naval attaché Ross E. Rowell and his opposite number, Henry Barber, the military attaché, kept the cocktail-hour date they had arranged in Havana's American Club to discuss how the arrival of the ship would affect them.

The two intelligence agents liked each other. Rowell was impressed by Barber's long experience of Cuban affairs, and Barber thought Rowell's enthusiasm for his new job "very commendable."

The military attaché's field of acquaintances was far wider than Rowell's: he knew many members of Havana's large diplomatic community by their first names, he had carefully nourished friendships among the more influential classes of Cuban society, he knew he could walk into police headquarters and be greeted more like a colleague than an intelligence agent for a foreign power. Barber was also a cautious man. He carefully considered all aspects of a situation before pronouncing, let alone acting. For that reason, the less experienced naval attaché was keen to have his views on the *St. Louis.*

Major Barber believed the passengers would "somehow" be allowed to land. Given that, Rowell inquired, how best to screen them? Clearly he alone could not scrutinize each one as they came ashore. Barber thought little purpose would be served by Rowell's being on hand when the ship arrived.

"If there are infiltrators among them," he told the naval attaché, "there will be plenty of time to watch them once they are
on land."

Rowell disagreed. He felt the moment of arrival would be
crucial: "That is when they will be at their most vulnerable."

The two men then debated whether there would in fact be
German agents on board. Barber thought it unlikely—"surely
there are enough here already"—and then went on to describe a
wider view, held by many of his informants, that the voyage was
inspired by pure politics.

"Some believe Germany is sending these immigrants here with
the express intention of creating the impression abroad that Cuba
does not want to accept the very people the world criticizes
Germany for wanting to get rid of," he told the naval attaché.
"And remember, to Germany, Cuba is part of the United States."

Rowell persisted in his view that the *St. Louis* was a perfect
vehicle for transporting agents under the guise of refugees.
"When all these people arrive," he said, "there will be
pandemonium. Surely among a thousand people, the chances are
there will be at least one agent."

Barber had to admit that on a balance of probabilities, Rowell
was right. In the end, the military attaché agreed to be on hand
with Rowell when the ship arrived: they would split the surveillance duties, then pool the result.

It was a novel arrangement. The main branches of American
intelligence were notorious for the way they jealously guarded
their secrets, competed with each other, went their own ways, and
seldom came together. Even at this meeting, Rowell had not told
Barber of his suspicions about Robert Hoffman, or of his continuing
surveillance of that most unlikely of all Abwehr agents on the
island, the dwarf Otto Ott. Nor had the two men discussed the
possibility of checking on *St. Louis* crew memebers, as opposed to
the refugees, when they came ashore.

Now, as they parted, Barber told Rowell: "The whole matter
stinks. I intend to tell Washington in my next report what is really
happening here. These forlorn and desperate fugitives are being
unscrupulously fleeced by Cuban officials."

As Barber went to send his report to the War Department in Washington, Rowell paid one of his regular calls on the one main Jewish organization the "fugitives" already in Havana had to turn to: the Jewish Relief Committee. This small organization, run by two dedicated workers, Milton Goldsmith and Laura Margolis, had become by May 1939 almost alone responsible for the well-being of nearly 5000 refugees. Both officials feared that the *St. Louis* passengers would strain their meager resources to breaking point.

Goldsmith was middle-aged, and during his long career in relief work, he had become used to disappointment. Younger than Goldsmith, Laura Margolis had, like him, retained many of the old-fashioned Jewish virtues. She had been taught to feel an obligation to help those worse off than herself, and she continued to do so in the years she had worked with refugees.

Laura Margolis had made repeated requests to New York that someone should be sent to Havana to see the conditions they were laboring under. Goldsmith had asked for more money from the Joint in New York, the agency that financed the committee. Neither request had brought results. As a consequence, the committee was not able to enlarge its overworked and now demoralized staff.

Each day an increasing number of refugees had called at the committee headquarters at Aguiar 556. Some had even followed Goldsmith to his room at the Hotel President. They wanted more money to live on, or information on how to get out of Cuba to the United States more quickly, or how to get relations and friends into Cuba. Goldsmith found himself painfully inadequate on all three counts.

The harrassed committee was besieged by other worries. The Joint in New York had also refused to give Goldsmith the authority he felt he needed to act independently. There were the anti-Semitic newspaper reports: Goldsmith felt he must raise funds in order to "persuade" editors to modify their attitudes. There were the continuous queries from refugees in Havana awaiting relatives on the *St. Louis:* would they be allowed to land? Goldsmith replied reassuringly that they would, but privately he was far from confident. And finally there was the Advisory Board, composed of eminent Jews living permanently in Cuba, always ready to offer Goldsmith the benefit of their knowledge.

Havana had a nucleus of such wealthy Jews who had established themselves in the nineteen-twenties. They had integrated well into the community, building a synagogue, opening kosher shops, and starting religious schools. But the existence and experience of those earlier immigrants was far removed from that of the refugees who later crowded into Cuba. The established Jews knew the language and had made the island their home, but the new Jews did not speak Spanish, and did not intend to stay. It was the prosperous Jews who advised Goldsmith and Laura Margolis on how to run their Relief Committee, and often those settlers found it difficult to identify with the poverty-stricken refugees.

Now, as Ross Rowell passed through an outer office crowded with people and knocked on his glass door, Goldsmith wondered whether the naval attaché had come to add to his troubles; his ususal reason for calling was to question him about Nazi agents among the refugees.

To Rowell's "Anything to report?" Goldsmith replied that he had discovered that a person who had recently applied for relief had previously lived for nine years in Mexico. He had been expelled from there for selling secrets to the Germans, and therefore Goldsmith had refused his request for money. Goldsmith told Rowell he believed the man was still a Nazi informer.

Well satisfied with his visit, Rowell thanked Goldsmith and departed to write another report to Washington. As Goldsmith watched him go, and saw at the same time the long queue of refugees outside his office, he must have feared that if the St. Louis was allowed to disembark its passengers, his Relief Committee might collapse altogether.

On this Monday night Luis Clasing and his assistant, Robert Hoffman, came to Benitez's office to learn the result of his meeting with the president.

The immigration director told his visitors that Bru was "just playing politics." In the manner of a born opportunist, Manuel Benitez reduced the whole complicated issue of the St. Louis to a single question. Would Bru allow the ship to enter Cuban territorial waters, let alone Havana Harbor, if he intended to bar the passengers from landing?

It was a tenuous argument and, unhappily for Benitez, Clasing virtually demolished it when he replied that the ship was not yet in the harbor, and even if it were, there was a great difference between the *St. Louis*'s "being there, and actually disembarking refugees."

Benitez brushed aside the comment, believing the German "incapable of appreciating the finer points of argument. He behaved like a permanent tourist," he was to say later. But now the immigration director kept such thoughts to himself, anxious still to appear friendly toward the Hapag men, sensing that at the right moment another generous "gift" would be forthcoming.

It would not be on this night. Before coming to the meeting Clasing had told Hoffman that "tactically" it would be wrong, as the Abwehr agent had recommended, to offer further bribes "at this stage"; Clasing had added that Benitez "must now show results for his money."

Hoffman wanted the *St. Louis* to have a smooth passage in and out of Havana just as badly as did the Hapag agent; if there were difficulties over the passengers, Hoffman feared that Otto Schiendick might not get ashore to collect the secrets he was holding for him. But how to ensure that the ship landed? Hoffman thought it only a matter of bribing Benitez; Clasing was convinced that to pay more would inevitably lead to further demands later, and would guarantee nothing.

Disagreements between them had become common since Hoffman had been foisted on Clasing a year earlier when the Abwehr spy ring in Cuba was being developed. Clasing, a professional shipping man, had resented such intrusion, the more so as it had impinged on company affairs on numerous occasions. When he had angrily protested, Hoffman had merely shrugged.

The question of when and whether to offer Manuel Benitez yet another handout had touched a raw nerve in Clasing, further exacerbated when Hoffman had insisted that he come to the meeting. Clasing had objected, and been told curtly by his assistant that Hoffman would not be there in behalf of Hapag.

"Why don't you keep your spying outside my business?" Clasing demanded sourly.

"Why don't you complain to Hamburg and see what happens?" Hoffman retorted.

In Benitez's presence now, both men maintained a seemingly united front, arguing volubly that the *St. Louis* passengers must land "no matter what happens." Manuel Benitez played his trump card. He reached into a desk drawer and produced a handful of notices.

"These are being posted publicly throughout Havana today," he told them.

The notices stated that though his "bureau" would no longer be issuing landing permits, those Benitez had issued prior to May 6, when decree 937 became law, would be honored.

"The permits for those on the *St. Louis* were signed in this office before May 6, my friends. The legislation is not retroactive. Therefore those permits are entirely legal. The passengers will be allowed to disembark."

"And if they are not?" asked Hoffman.

"If they are not, I give you my personal assurance I will carry them off the ship, one at a time, myself, if need be."

Dr. Max Aber dressed for dinner with extra care on Monday night. Though the fun-loving doctor looked forward with considerable anticipation to an evening with Benitez's secretary, the vivacious Gloria Spira, it would present only a pleasant interlude in his hours of worry about the safety of his two small daughters, Renatta and Evelyne, now traveling toward him on the *St. Louis*.

After he had gotten the landing permits at Benitez's "bureau"—seizing the same opportunity to make the acquaintance of Gloria—and sent them off to his wife, he had heard rumors on his frequent visits to the city's gay and gaudy center that had made him uneasy: there was talk that the permits were "not quite kosher."

Aber had called again on his original Cuban contact, José Estedes, to express his concern, and had been taken by Estedes to see the powerful ally of President Bru, Secretary of State Juan Remos. The two Cubans had conversed rapidly in Spanish. Aber, not understanding what was being said, watched Remos carefully; he seemed to display enormous sympathy and friendliness. His kindness and concern was already well known to other refugees.

"Do you have enough money to maintain your family?" Estedes asked Dr. Aber in English.

Dr. Aber, who was trying to live on the money provided by Milton Goldsmith's Relief Committee, replied that he had virtually none.

Estedes turned back to Remos and said in Spanish: "Yes. He has plenty."

Remos scribbled a message in red ink and ordered a secretary to telegraph it to the Cuban consulate in Hamburg. It was authorization for bona fide visas to be issued for the Aber children.

Later, Max Aber cabled the prefix number of the telegram to his wife with the request that she collect the visas. Lucie Aber had replied that the original permits issued by Benitez's "bureau" seemed "perfectly adequate." He had not heard from her since.

Earlier that day, he had received a telephone call from a relative in New York. She had just learned from Aber's sister in Germany that Renatta and Evelyne were on the *St. Louis*. It was enough reason for their father to celebrate tonight, but he still did not know whether his wife had collected the visas from the Cuban consul in Hamburg.

Now, as he dined with one of the most beautiful women in Havana, he asked what could be done for his children if they brought with them only landing permits, and if President Bru enforced decree 937. Gloria Spira laughed—and revealed how Manuel Benitez intended to interpret the decree.

Much later, Max Aber walked back home convinced all would now be well.

TUESDAY, MAY 16, 1939

At first the wind had barely rippled the sea. But within an hour it brought waves rolling against the starboard freeboard of the *St. Louis*.

In the early hours of Tuesday, May 16, as the motion became more pronounced, First Officer Ostermeyer ordered thirty degrees' wheel to starboard, bringing the ship head-on into the wind and seaway. Five minutes later he reversed the order, completing a zigzag to port, satisfying himself that the maneuver reduced the roll and yet allowed the *St. Louis* to maintain the maximum speed possible through the Bay of Biscay.

The change, of course, jolted Aaron Pozner awake. For some minutes he lay still in his bunk in cabin D-375, soaked in a cold sweat, so real was his dream that the screams of his family still rang in his ears.

But the rhythmic motion of the ship slowly relaxed him, reminding him that every rise and fall of the *St. Louis* brought him closer to Cuba and the chance to earn enough for his family to join him.

Recha Weiler hardly noticed the ship's motion, for by this early Tuesday morning her world had shrunk to her husband's bed.

At some point during the night, Moritz Weiler had begun to sweat profusely, and Recha had given him two of the tablets the ship's doctor, Walter Glauner, had prescribed. She remembered, and had been grateful, that the doctor had been solicitous, insisting that no matter what the hour he would come to the cabin if she felt it necessary. Recha thanked him, but deep down inside her she knew her husband needed more than the ship's doctor and his pills; his frail body required the will to live.

Throughout the night she had sat by his bed, caressing his hand and murmuring gentle encouragement. Now, as dawn lightened the cabin, the tablets took effect; Moritz Weiler fell asleep.

Purser Mueller viewed the heavy swell with unhappiness. Seasickness was the surest way to dampen the growing gaiety among passengers. Since departing Cherbourg, he had been pleased to see smiles on more and more faces. One had even cracked a joke about Hitler. It had brought laughs from the passengers, and also from Mueller, but not from Otto Schiendick. Schiendick had told the passenger the comment was "not funny. All of you owe your lives to the generosity of the Fuehrer for allowing you to travel on this ship."

The passengers had been surprised to be addressed by a steward in this way, but one or two laughed.

Schiendick stalked off, making a further note about the purser in his "book of offenses," which he so often flourished in front of fellow stewards.

Down in the crew mess hall, he once again harangued those present on the dangers of mixing with passengers, and especially "polluting our purity by having sexual relationships with non-Aryans." He warned that any crew man suspected of such an offense would face severe penalties under the Law for the Protection of German Blood and Honor.

The threat was greeted with barely suppressed grins from some stewards, for by this Tuesday morning the crew quarters were rife with stories that some of the women passengers "were the hottest ever to come on the ship."

Similar stories reached the ears of Babette Spanier, who "could not understand why our nice-looking girls should want to fool around with crew members."

Fritz Spanier ventured that "even Hitler cannot control the mating instincts of the human race," and went on to point out that he had heard that some of the young refugee men on board had "not been doing badly with the German crew stewardesses."

"That's different," said Babette Spanier.

The conversation was overheard by the Spanier's breakfast

steward. When he relayed it to his colleagues, they thought it confirmed their impression that Frau Spanier was one of the most likable, but "unusual," passengers on the ship. She had an enormous appetite which she maintained despite the ship's rolling, so severe that the wooden sides had been raised around the dining tabletops. Her husband sat patiently while she rapidly ate her way through most courses at every meal. No one could understand how Babette Spanier remained thin.

The eating habits of Otto Bergmann's Aunt Shalote also came in for their fair share of comment by the crew. The night before, at dinner, she had caused raised eyebrows by hectoring her steward, demanding that he serve her first, and then sampling all the food as it arrived before deciding what she would eat. When Otto had tried to remonstrate with the eighty-year-old, Aunt Shalote had turned on him: "Young man, *you* don't know how to handle servants."

When the old lady appeared for breakfast this Tuesday, Otto, wanting to be spared further embarrassment, excused himself, saying he was leaving to go to the gift shop to buy a birthday present for his mother-in-law. Aunt Shalote sniffed: "Why all the fuss? Rosemarie's mother is *only* seventy."

Renatta and Evelyne Aber felt the trip was getting even more exciting than their mother had promised. They had a cabin to themselves, and now, with the storm, the entire ship seemed theirs as passengers slumped on deck chairs or in their bunks.

After breakfast, Evelyne traipsed behind Renatta on a new adventure: soaping every door handle they passed. They peeped back down a corridor and watched a steward stop at a cabin door, carefully balancing a tray against the ship's motion; he grew angrier the more he tried to turn the handle. Finally his hand completely slid off the doorknob, and he lost his balance, and the tray skidded out of his grasp.

Laughing gleefully, the sisters sought a new diversion. On the promenade deck, they found some string; they dangled it over the rail and let it trail across the passengers dozing in chairs below on A deck.

The high spot of the morning came when they made friends with the Bardeleben and Fischer children. Though they could not know it, their fathers, waiting for them in Havana, had also become friends.

Ten-year-old Marianne Bardeleben and Ruth and Hans Fischer were standing conspiratorially outside the ladies' restroom on B deck when Renatta and Evelyne joined them. Marianne explained that Hans would stand guard while the four girls slipped into the rest room. Inside, each child went into a cubicle, locked its door from the inside, and then crawled out under the door, left the room, and waited expectantly outside.

A woman, clutching at a dressing gown, hurried into the washroom. The children giggled delightedly as they could hear her rushing from one locked door to another. Eventually she was ill in a washbasin.

The gang decided to repeat the prank in another washroom, but a suspicious stewardess followed and caught them red-handed. She threatened to lock them up if they continued. Not very frightened, the children returned to their cabins, whispering to each other that they would meet again.

WEDNESDAY, MAY 17, 1939

After breakfast on Wednesday, May 17, Gustav Schroeder remained alone in his cabin. As he peered through the scuttles at the squally weather outside, he speculated on other and more unpleasant possibilities that could soon face his passengers and himself.

He had received no reply to a second and even terser message to Claus-Gottfried Holthusen, demanding to know the situation in Havana and exactly why the *St. Louis* was engaged in a race with the two other ships carrying refugees. All Gustav Schroeder knew for certain was that the *Orduna* and *Flandre* were steadily cutting down his lead, and he had been forced to chart a new course, taking the *St. Louis* north of the Azores, thus gaining five hours. But even that lead would be canceled out if the other ships followed a similar route.

The new course had sent the *St. Louis* plunging through the bellicose Atlantic rollers, setting the breakfast crockery tumbling and bringing from the purser a plea for a reduction in speed during the morning meal.

The captain had brusquely refused, and was irritated with himself for venting his temper and frustration on the person who least deserved it.

By midmorning, the wind and swell held the ship in their sport, sending the few people who had braved it to the sports deck hurrying to their cabins and bringing on a further wave of seasickness throughout the *St. Louis*.

At noon First Officer Ostermeyer arrived with the daily summary of radio news broadcast to all German ships by the *Deutsches Nachrichtenburo,* Goebbels' official news agency.

Schroeder was horrified to read that the *St. Louis* was the

104

main item, that its journey was being exploited as part of the gathering Wagnerian murk of Hitler's New Order, and that, in the summary, his passengers were dismissed as *Untermenschen,* subhuman. He ripped up the news sheet. Turning to Ostermeyer, he snapped: "I'll get these people ashore in Havana even if the whole Propaganda Ministry tries to stop me!"

Unknown to the captain, that Wednesday, in Berlin, the ministry had another, bigger, event on which to comment; it would adversely effect not only the reception his passengers would receive in Cuba, but also the plight of thousands of other refugees.

On May 17, the British government published its long-awaited white paper on Palestine. As Sir Herbert Emerson, director of the International Committee on Political Refugees in London had feared, it further complicated his problems, for the paper set new and stringent limits on the number of Jews to be admitted to Palestine. Worse for Emerson, Britain and Germany found themselves in unusual agreement with each other, for Hitler welcomed its proposals, and Goebbels exploited the apparent British attitude to the full.

Embarrassed by the German attitude, and by world opinion —apart from Germany almost uniformly critical of the white paper—Britain would quickly offer for Emerson's consideration 40,000 square miles of land in British Guiana for the use of refugees. Most of it was within five degrees of the equator and 250 miles from the sea, but planning soon began for an initial settlement of 5000 people. Not to be outdone, America matched the British offer with the Philippine province of Mindanao. The Dominican Republic, just southeast of Cuba, then announced it would make room for 50,000 to 100,000 refugees, while suggesting a trial settlement of just over 200 families.

In Cuba itself on this Wednesday, the newspapers concerned themselves with the white paper and mass refugee-settlement areas, and more with the anti-Semitic attacks, which they had begun to narrow down to the *St. Louis* specifically. Robert Hoffman arranged for the editor of the Havana *Avance* to write about the ship's arrival:

Against this invasion we must react with the same energy as have other peoples of the globe. Otherwise we will be absorbed, and the day will come when the blood of our martyrs and heroes shall have served solely to enable the Jews to enjoy a country conquered by our ancestors.

But on the *St. Louis,* no one yet knew of the white paper, nor of the increasing attacks on the passengers in the Cuban press.

Recha Weiler was so completely absorbed in the matter of administering her husband's medicaments that she did not notice the weather had brightened that Wednesday afternoon.

The ship's doctor, Walter Glauner, had made two visits to her husband's bedside that day, and on the second he had prescribed new tablets, and medicine to be taken hourly.

Now, at 5 P.M., Dr. Glauner returned, this time to give Moritz Weiler an injection. Recha winced as the needle was jabbed into the skin, and later told other passengers she wondered what was the point of it all, for she now believed that no tablet, no sip of medicine, no injection, could alleviate the true cause of her husband's suffering: the pain of having to leave his birthplace.

After the doctor left, she sat by her husband's bed, mopping away his perspiration and struggling to control her own fears. She wanted to say that being together was all she wanted, and that being together was possible only as long as he stayed alive. But when she looked at him, she could find no words. Moritz Weiler had grown more haggard, his eyes more sunken, his bone structure more pronounced, his face more white. It made his words all the harder for her to bear when he whispered: *"Liebe,* do not be distressed."

The distress Aaron Pozner first felt at the question he had been asked had given way to relief this Wednesday evening. There was, he finally decided, no ulterior motive behind the query; it was no more than curiosity that had prompted Leo Jockl to ask him quietly what it was like to be a Jew in Germany.

Aaron had encountered the steward that afternoon near the first-class restaurant. Seeing the room empty, Aaron had slipped inside to inspect the elegant tableware. The steward had emerged from a pantry and had eagerly conducted Pozner around the gracious salon, stopping with special pride at the captain's table.

Then Leo had invited Aaron for a coffee in the pantry. At first Pozner had refused, suspicious and reluctant to accept that a German could be so friendly. His memory was still fresh of a day in Dachau when a guard had offered a prisoner a cigarette; when he accepted it, it was smashed into his face by a savage blow from the guard's riot stick.

Nevertheless, Leo Jockl's obvious friendliness persuaded Aaron to join the steward for coffee, and he soon found himself unaccountably relaxing. The steward was, Pozner later wrote, "very sincere with his questions." Jockl had listened carefully to Pozner's bald description of Dachau, and how afterward he had fled Germany without his family. Though he had not wished to sound bitter, Pozner had added: "That is what it is like to be a Jew in Germany."

"But have you never lost your faith?"

It was the first time anybody had asked Aaron Pozner such a question, and it left him momentarily speechless. He later realized it would have been easy to have said he was a Jew through an accident of birth, but he knew it would have been less than the truth; that for him being a Jew was far more than merely observing the ritual of his faith, that it reached deep into every aspect of his life.

He had decided to say none of these things. Instead he rose to his feet and simply replied: "No, I have not lost my faith, but only a Jew would understand why." Then Aaron Pozner hurried to his cabin, ashamed of himself for the obvious hurt he had seen in Leo Jockl's face. He promised himself that should the opportunity arise, he would redress his rudeness, even thought it seemed baffling to Aaron Pozner why any German should be interested in a religion proscribed by the Nazis.

THURSDAY, MAY 18, 1939

That moment in the afternoon of Thursday, May 18, when Otto Bergmann followed the engine-room officer past the steel fire door leading into the crew quarters, he wanted to turn and run, to leave behind the raucous singing that swept toward him. He wished he had never asked to visit the engine room.

Bergmann, an engineer, had thought it would be an interesting way to pass the time, and had been pleased when the first officer, Klaus Ostermeyer, agreed to arrange the visit. He was also happy with the prospect of a few hours' respite from the constant all-female company of his wife, his aunt Shalote, and his mother-in-law. After lunch, he had gone to D deck to keep the appointment Ostermeyer had made for him with the engine-room officer. The man had greeted him coolly, and instead of grasping Otto's proffered handshake, he had motioned Otto to follow him down the metal steps, past the sign saying "No entry—crew only," past the fire door, and now into the crew quarters.

Though Bergmann could not see the men who were singing and banging their fists on the table, the sound sickened him much more than the smells of sweat, cigarette smoke, grease, stale cooking, and the sheer stench of close living. Loud and clear, Otto heard with horror the words of the *"Horst Wessel,"* the Nazi rallying song.

He looked back at the fire door, but someone had closed it behind him. Ahead the officer was leading the way toward the engine-room entrance. Bergmann followed him.

"Stop! Passengers are not allowed here!"

He turned to the group of men seated in an opening to his right. Their singing died down as one of them got up, and, staggering slightly, walked up to him. It was obvious the man had

108

been drinking, and although Bergmann did not know it, it was Schiendick. From the end of the room the officer called: "He has been given official permission to visit the engine room."

Schiendick stared balefully at Bergmann, and then returned to his comrades. As Bergmann hurried to catch up to the officer, he heard the men whispering: *"Juden raus, Juden raus!"*

With a terrible sense of shock, he realized that "down here, where no passengers had been, it was a totally different world. Up above, the officers, stewards, musicians, bartenders, and bellboys had made us feel welcome. But below, it was different. Perhaps it was more real."

He saw more evidence of Nazism on the crew notice board. In spite of Schroeder's specific order, Schiendick had once again plastered it with Nazi slogans and propaganda.

Bergmann finally reached the engine room. He did not enjoy his tour of the boilers, generators, pumps, switch gear, dials, and alarms that made up the mechanical heart of the *St. Louis*, however shining and spotlessly clean it all looked. Here once more crew members gave him "dirty looks."

As he retraced his steps through the crew quarters, the words of a Nazi song followed him again: *"Wenn das Judenblut vom Messer spritzt, dann geht's nochmal so gut."* ("When Jewish blood flows from the knife, things will go much better.")

FRIDAY, MAY 19, 1939

After breakfast on Friday, May 19, Fritz Spanier was invited to visit the captain on the bridge, and his astonishment was equaled only by his curiosity at the purpose of the invitation.

Following that earlier, and brittle, encounter over the screening of the Nazi newsreel, Dr. Spanier had not seen the captain, apart from one glimpse of him standing on the bridge wing.

As he reached the bridge, he found Schroeder once more on the wing, this time with two other first-class passengers, Josef Joseph and his pretty daughter, Liesl, aged ten.

Like many on the ship, Dr. Spanier had yet to form meaningful relationships with any of the other passengers, but he immediately liked Josef Joseph, and saw in Liesl a possible playmate for his own twin daughters. Yet he was still puzzled at why he had been asked, and frankly said so to the captain. Gustav Schroeder disarmed Dr. Spanier by openly admitting that he hoped the gesture of a tour of the bridge would, in part, go some way toward repairing the damage caused by the newsreel incident.

Josef Joseph followed this exchange literally, and he, too, asked if there was any special reason for his presence. Gustav Schroeder laughingly remarked that his only purpose in inviting the Josephs was simply because on every voyage he had a number of passengers along to see over the bridge.

But there was another reason why Josef Joseph and Fritz Spanier had been invited. It gave the captain a chance to assess them, to confirm for himself the opinion of the first officer, Ostermeyer, that the men were two of the strongest personalities on the ship.

110

For, by this Friday, almost halfway to Cuba, still with no news from Hapag, still being pursued by the two other refugee ships, with the daily Nazi news summaries still attacking his passengers, Gustav Schroeder had begun to plan. Uppermost in his mind was the need to have, should events dictate it, allies among the passengers, men who could firmly quell any trouble. Fritz Spanier was an automatic selection; Josef Joseph had been recommended by Ostermeyer.

Schroeder had been fascinated to learn that Joseph was once a friend of Goebbels, initially attracted, as many were, by the man's intellectual brilliance; their friendship had ceased when Goebbels joined the Nazis, and still later, Joseph found his livelihood as a lawyer proscribed by numerous Nazi edicts, trumpeted abroad by Goebbels' machinations.

In spite of his experience, Joseph, like Spanier, simply refused to be cowed by past events, and that, too, had impressed Schroeder.

Now, as he led his visitors around the bridge workings, the captain further believed that Joseph would be an ideal man in a crisis; he displayed a lawyer's shrewdness in his questions, yet remained warmly human.

By the end of the visit the captain was satisfied.

Around eight o'clock on Friday evening, the port side of the *St. Louis* was crowded with passengers peering through a steady drizzle at the Azores. They were close enough to the coast to make out the windmills through the mist.

"We're nearly halfway to Cuba," Elise Loewe told her husband.

SATURDAY, MAY 20, 1939

On Saturday morning, passengers made their way to the first-class social hall, now converted into an Orthodox synagogue. Reform worshipers were in the *Tanzplatz,* those of the Conservative faith prayed in the gymnastic hall.

The Spaniers had decided to worship with the Orthodox, and were surprised to see the number required before a service could be held—ten men—had been exceeded ten times over. Perhaps they had been drawn by the novelty of worship aboard a ship.

The prophetical reading from Hosea seemed to Babette Spanier particularly appropriate, dealing as it did with infidelity and fornication. She looked at her husband, seated apart with the other men in the congregation, and thought he intentionally avoided her glance. Once more her worries about their marriage returned.

A few of the crew stood above, in the gallery of the social hall, looking down on the scene. Behind them, Otto Schiendick pushed his way to the front. He looked below contemptuously, and told the crew members that their education would be better served reading *Mein Kampf.*

TUESDAY, MAY 23, 1939

In the three days that followed, Recha Weiler had quietly intoned, in the privacy of their cabin, every prayer she knew for intercession for her husband. She had interrupted her keening only to feed him some broth or the medicine and tablets Dr. Glauner increasingly prescribed. She had hardly slept, apart from fitfully dozing in her bedside armchair, nor had she eaten properly.

By Tuesday morning, May 23, she was close to nervous and physical exhaustion. When her husband started to moan, a low and choking sound, she leaned forward and gently wiped his face, and then resumed her chanting, her voice rising and falling, corresponding with the labored breathing.

Once he looked at her and said something. But even when she bent closer his words were too slurred to understand. Recha kissed him gently on the cheek and sat back, looking searchingly into his face. As she watched, his breathing seemed to ease and the pain to go from his eyes.

For a long time she stared at his face, and then, suddenly, Recha began to sob, oblivious to the urgent knocking on the door, or Dr. Glauner standing by the bed, checking and confirming that her husband was dead.

When Gustav Schroeder learned of the death, his first thought was to offer what comfort he could to Recha Weiler. Together with purser Mueller, he hurried to cabin B-108, where he found Dr. Glauner trying, and failing, to calm the widow, slumped across the bed on which her husband lay.

The captain motioned Dr. Glauner to join himself and the purser in the corridor outside, and there he quietly explained to

113

them that he believed Recha Weiler's weeping was linked with
the "ritual of death" of her faith, and therefore no attempt should
be made to curtail her grief. They must give her time "to rend her
garments and that sort of thing" before reentering the cabin.

In the meantime, he told Mueller, the purser should bring a
supply of candles. Mueller, surprised, asked what sort.

"It doesn't matter. Just candles," replied the captain.

He was aware that both men were looking at him oddly, and,
guessing their thoughts, Gustav Schroeder told them that years
before he had read a book on the funeral arrangements of various
religions.

Then, followed by the ship's doctor, he went back into the
cabin. Recha Weiler's face was tear-stained, her neatly coiled
hair was now disheveled, and she had rent her blouse and un-
derslip to expose the skin.

Gustav Schroeder gently explained they had come to offer any
help they could, but would leave if she felt they were intruding;
or if she preferred to have present any friends on the ship, he
would have them called.

"I know nobody," she whispered. "But I will need a rabbi if
there is one among the passengers."

"I will see to it," replied Gustav Schroeder. "Can we be of any
other help?"

She looked at the captain, weighing in her mind a decision.
Then she nodded, and said she needed help to lay out her husband.

Together, the three of them moved to the bed. There, sighing
deeply, Recha gently removed a feather she had placed on her
husband's lips. Looking at her watch, she saw it had remained
there well past the ritual eight minutes following his death, a
period when, for religious reasons, nobody could touch the body.

Now, she closed her husband's eyes and mouth, and extended
his arms beside his body, as Mueller returned with the candles
which he had removed from the first-class restaurant.

Recha looked at the captain, thankful and surprised that he
had anticipated another of her needs. She took one of the candles
from the purser and Gustav Schroeder lit it; again Recha glanced
gratefully at him.

She placed the lighted candle on a bedside cupboard, murmuring to the three men, standing awkwardly, not knowing what next to do or expect, that for her the candle symbolized the flickering of the human soul.

She then asked them to place the body on the floor, explaining that that, too, was an essential part of the ritual. Under her guidance, Gustav Schroeder and Dr. Glauner positioned the body with its feet facing the cabin door, as directed in the Torah.

Recha placed the lighted candle close to her husband's head and draped his body with a sheet. She knelt for a moment in prayer, and then arose. In silence, she took the remaining candles and placed them at various points around the cabin, lighting them as she went along, intoning prayers for the dead.

Gustav Schroeder whispered for the doctor and purser to leave and to try to find a rabbi from the passenger list. Then he waited, anxious not to disrupt the prayers, hating the fact that even with death, bureaucracy still had to pursue Recha Weiler, knowing that no matter how sympathetic he felt, there was no way of avoiding pain for the elderly woman.

"Frau Weiler," he began. "When do you wish the funeral to be?"

She appeared not to have heard the captain's words, as, standing with her back to him, she continued to pray aloud.

Embarrassed, believing he should not have asked the question at that time, Gustav Schroeder started to edge toward the door.

"Wait. I wish my husband to be buried in Havana."

Recha Weiler turned and faced the captain, and he saw abject misery and pleading on her face. In that moment, he would "willingly have given up my command to have helped her."

Instead, he explained that the ship was still four days from Cuba, that there were no adequate facilities on board for keeping the body, that even when they reached Havana he would still need permission to take the corpse ashore.

What he did not say, but which was also in his mind, was the very real problem of handling the other passengers and crew if it became known they were carrying a dead man. Gustav Schroeder believed that the knowledge would create "a low mood," heightened by a traditional belief shared by many seamen that a corpse on a ship was the harbinger of bad luck.

"Please . . . my husband would have wished it."

The agony behind the words moved Gustav Schroeder to promise to try to meet her wish. He hurried to the radio room and sent a priority radio message to the Hapag office in Havana requesting permission to bring the body ashore. The reply came within the morning:

PERMISSION DENIED FOR HEALTH REASONS

The captain returned to Recha Weiler. With her was a tall, well-built, bearded man who introduced himself as Rabbi Gustav Weil, a tourist-class passenger. The rabbi was able to calm the widow. She accepted the decision that her husband must be buried at sea.

Purser Mueller invited Rabbi Weil to his office to discuss the funeral.

Mueller asked whether he should arrange for the ship's carpenter to make up a coffin, "complete with brass handles." The suggestion was gratefully received but delicately refused, by the elderly rabbi, as was the purser's offer to turn the ship's small hospital into a chapel of rest. Rabbi Weil told him, "It is death, not rest, which we are concerned with."

The purser then offered the ship's orchestra to play "somberly" at the service, and was told there should be no music. Next he raised the question of flowers; Rabbi Weil explained that under Judaic law, they would not be required.

Mueller protested that "the body can't just be thrown over the side. It wouldn't be Christian."

Rabbi Weil patiently explained to the purser that a Jewish funeral was an unostentatious rite, a "democracy in death," where no one need be ashamed of the simplicity of the coffin or shroud. Weiler's body, he suggested, should be sewn into a weighted sailcloth, and slid over the side from a plank as soon as possible.

Mueller discussed the timing. "If it is held during the day, it will create a bad effect on everyone. The majority of the passengers are now in good humor. The sight of a body going over the side would be bound to depress them."

The rabbi agreed. Many of the passengers, he observed, had themselves "been recently near to death, the funeral could bring back unpleasant memories. We should try to avoid that."

They agreed to hold the burial service at eleven o'clock that night.

Soon after Gustav Schroeder returned to the bridge from his meeting with the widow, a coded cable brought very bad news indeed from Hamburg.

A day of intense telephoning between Hamburg, London, and Paris had preceded that cable. It had begun with Claus-Gottfried Holthusen calling Morris Troper in the French capital to say that Hapag's *Orinoco* would leave Hamburg for Havana on May 27 with over 200 refugees. Holthusen had added: "So, Herr Troper, you can see there is nothing to worry about over the *St. Louis.*"

Troper was glad to receive some reassuring news; he had been worried ever since reading that morning's Paris newspapers with their reports that Cuban President Bru's opposition to *all* refugees had hardened.

Holthusen had been placatory, reaffirming that Hapag was in close contact with developments in Cuba and that the company had "highly placed" connections on the island. He had urged Troper to dismiss the press reports. What the shipping director did not say was that as soon as he was off the line he planned to send Gustav Schroeder a cable based on information Hapag had received from Luis Clasing in Havana which clearly confirmed the French newspaper stories.

After Holthusen's call, Morris Troper contacted Sir Herbert Emerson in London to tell him the *Orinoco* was sailing. The director of the International Committee on Political Refugees replied that the *Orinoco*'s voyage was "just another bit of moneymaking by Hapag," and in his view it would only worsen the "devilish" situation already created by the *St. Louis*. Emerson did not reveal that Britain's ambassador in Havana, H. A. Grant Watson, had earlier that week filed a "most confidential" report indicating that he believed President Bru would stand firm on not admitting the refugees. The news had caused a flurry in both the Foreign Office and the Home Office, and Emerson faced a question being asked by more than one Whitehall mandarin: If Cuba would not accept any more refugees, where on earth could they go?

It was against this background that Claus-Gottfried Holthusen sent Schroeder the cable. It read:

MAJORITY YOUR PASSENGERS IN CONTRAVENTION NEW CUBAN LAW 937 AND MAY NOT BE GIVEN PERMISSION DISEMBARK. ORINOCO SAILING DOUBTFUL. YOU WILL MAINTAIN SPEED AND COURSE AS SITUATION NOT COMPLETELY CLEAR BUT CERTAINLY CRITICAL IF NOT RESOLVED BEFORE YOUR ARRIVAL.

The captain immediately sent for Dr. Fritz Spanier.

Dr. Spanier faced Gustav Schroeder across the captain's desk, uncomfortably aware of the strength of Schroeder's argument, yet unable to lend practical support for reasons he knew must sound painfully inadequate.

"No, Captain, I cannot do it," Dr. Spanier said. "I am simply not the right person for such a committee, let alone chair it."

Gustav Schroeder hoped his silence would express his disappointment more than words.

"Captain, please understand me. I am not good at such things. My experience of committees is that they spend all their time talking with little result. If I can help, I will gladly do so, but I will better serve you, and the passengers, outside it."

"But you will help?"

"You have my word."

"Very well. But I must ask you to treat this talk in the strictest confidence."

Dr. Spanier nodded, still stunned by the cable the captain had shown him. Schroeder had also told him of his own fears of "serious trouble" when they reached Havana "unless things improve." He had then explained that he proposed to set up a small passenger committee, made up of lawyers and others, to confer with him in dealing with the passengers should it become necessary.

Fritz Spanier proposed his own choice for the chairmanship of that committee, Josef Joseph.

The captain sent for the lawyer, who immediately accepted the post and went off to select people to serve with him.

At four o'clock that Tuesday afternoon Gustav Schroeder welcomed the members of the passenger committee assembled in his day cabin. As Josef Joseph introduced them, each man stepped forward and shook the captain's hand.

As he gripped each hand, Schroeder looked into the man's face and was reassured by what he saw. On Dr. Max Weiss's face he saw quiet resolution. Max Zellner and Arthur Hausdorff had the cool, appraising faces of experienced lawyers. The fifth member of the group, Herbert Manasse, though younger than the others, still seemed a man versed in the vicissitudes of life.

Behind them Leo Jockl attended a table set with coffee and cakes. As the steward served, the captain began to explain the reason why they had been assembled. Herbert Manasse interrupted. "Are we here to prepare for returning to Germany?"

The directness of the question and the manner in which it was asked decided Schroeder to confide completely in the group.

"At this stage, the answer is no. We will sail to Havana. But I cannot say what will happen when we reach there."

The committee members then listened without interruption as the captain read Holthusen's message. He said it presaged trouble, explained the significance of the reference to the *Orinoco*—"it means resistance to refugees must have hardened"—and revealed the race for life between the *St. Louis* and the other two refugee ships. Using a chart, Gustav Schroeder showed the group that the latest position of the *Orduna* placed her only seven hours astern with the *Flandre* twelve hours behind.

The silence in the room, Josef Joseph was to remember was "deadly. The voyage had assumed a menace nobody had suspected." He asked a number of questions: Was decree 937 permanent? What pressures could Hapag bring directly on the Cuban government? What attempts were being made to enlist support from recognized welfare agencies in Cuba and elsewhere? How could landing permits clearly issued by the Cuban authorities be revoked?

Gustav Schroeder quietly replied that he had no answer to any of the questions.

Dr. Weiss took up the probing. What would the captain do, if on reaching Havana, they could not disembark?

"We will wait."

"For what?"

"For instructions from Hamburg."

Each man pondered those words. Then Arthur Hausdorff spoke the fear they all felt: "Captain, what if Hamburg insists that you cannot wait and that you must return to Germany?"

Once more, silence. Schroeder was uncomfortably aware they wanted a reassuring answer from him. He knew he could not lie to them; to do so now, at the start of their relationship, might destroy any confidence they had in his credibility. Instead, he said, "I give you my word that I will do everything possible to avoid going back to Germany. I am only too well aware of what they would do to you."

"Captain, we thank you for your honesty," said Josef Joseph.

The lawyer had one request: Could they cable the Jewish Relief Committee in Havana for further information on the situation? Gustav Schroeder agreed, adding that Hapag would pay for the cost of the radiogram. After some discussion the committee took its first collective action. Their cable read:

WE HAVE JUST HEARD PASSENGERS WITH LANDING PERMITS ON ORINOCO MAY NOT BE ALLOWED TO SAIL. PLEASE TELL US IF WE CAN EXPECT SIMILAR DIFFICULTIES. ST. LOUIS PASSENGER COMMITTEE.

As soon as Otto Schiendick heard of Moritz Weiler's death, he called on the purser. In his capacity as the party watchdog on board, he demanded details of the funeral arrangements. Mueller gave them.

Schiendick said he was satisfied on all but one point. Party regulations stipulated that for burial at sea, the bier must be draped with a swastika flag; he could see "no reason for an exception to be made in this case."

Recha Weiler—indeed, all on board—would regard it as sacrilege if such a thing occurred. Mueller flatly refused.

That afternoon Schiendick called another crew meeting in their mess hall. About fifty attended. He reminded them of the Nazi edict banning Aryans "from attending in any way" Jewish funerals, except in a "professional capacity."

Aaron Pozner heard the news of Weiler's death from Leo Jockl early in the evening when the steward called to apologize for not keeping their afternoon appointment. "The ship's routine has been disrupted by this unhappy event," he said.

"It is I, not you, who should apologize," replied Pozner, referring to their previous meeting.

Rosemarie Bergmann was told of the professor's death by her husband. Later, while bathing her mother, now bedridden and unable to look after herself, she and her mother agreed it was probably something to do "with our leaving Hamburg on the thirteenth."

Elise Loewe learned the news on a visit to Dr. Glauner after dinner. That morning her husband had complained that he had been unable, again, to sleep the night before. She knew his depression was made worse by lack of sleep, and Elise Loewe was determined to get something to remedy the situation. She had seen Dr. Glauner earlier in the day, and told him she needed "something strong" to help her sleep. Elise Loewe had decided it was better to conceal the fact that it was really for her husband, since his behavior was already being commented upon by some of the passengers. Dr. Glaunder had asked her to return in the evening for the potion.

Now, as he told Frau Loewe of Weiler's death—"he simply lost the will to live"—the doctor handed her a glass partly filled with a milky liquid, and asked her to drink it. Still feeling unable to explain that the sleeping draught was for her husband, Elise Loewe drank it. By the time she got back to her cabin, it had already begun to take effect.

Recha Weiler had spent the day fasting and praying. From time to time Rabbi Gustav Weil had joined her, and they sat beside the body, reading from the Bible or murmuring a prayer. Frau Weiler had covered the mirror over the washstand with a hand towel, drawn the curtains over the porthole, and replenished the candles. Several times during the day she had lifted the sheet to peer at her husband's face; in death it had a peace which had not been there for many years.

At ten o'clock—she later was to remember the time exactly, as she also recalled all the events of that day—Rabbi Weil returned to the cabin. The moment had come for Recha to complete the final preparations for burial. She produced her husband's tallith, the long prayer shawl she had given him on their wedding day, which had served as a canopy during the marriage ceremony.

The shawl was fringed at the corners. Recha pulled the tassels from the cloth, a ritual rending of the garment, and placed it over her husband's body. Then she rose, uttering fresh prayers, and nodded to the rabbi.

He opened the cabin door and motioned inside Purser Mueller and two sailors carrying a folded stretcher and sailcloth. The seamen laid the stretcher on a bed, and rolled out the sailcloth. It looked like a long envelope, open at the top, with iron bars sewn into the sides.

Recha Weiler picked up the candle at the head of the corpse and placed it on a table. At a nod from the rabbi, the sailors carefully lifted the body up from the floor, and slid it inside the sailcloth lying on the stretcher. Screened by Mueller and his companions, the other sailor sewed up the shroud. The purser produced a large Hapag flag, loaned by Captain Schroeder, and draped it over the body. Preceded by the stretcher party, Recha Weiler and Rabbi Weil walked slowly from the cabin.

An elevator carried them to aft on A deck, where, waiting by the swimming pool, were Captain Schroeder, Ostermeyer, and a handful of passengers, some of whom had also symbolically torn their upper garments.

As the cortege emerged on deck, the ship came to a stop. Captain Schroeder had ordered the speed to be reduced gradually, hoping to minimize curiosity among the passengers, and consequently the *St. Louis* had steadily lost way for nearly an hour, a fact mentioned to Schroeder by Ostermeyer, who also thought the time could be ill afforded with the two other refugee ships now in close pursuit. Schroeder had overruled the objections of his first officer. Now he led the way to the ship's railing.

A gate in the deck rail had been opened and a plank placed in position, protruding over the side. The shroud was put on the board, the sailors standing on either side of it, their hands resting lightly on the flag. Mueller stood behind the body, his hands on the end of the plank.

The mourners grouped closer; the ship's officers, bareheaded, stood to one side.

The committal service was brief, conducted in Hebrew, and

ended with the mourners intoning, "May he come to his place in peace." Rabbi Weil looked to the seamen: they tautened the flag over the shroud, Mueller tilted the plank, and the body slid over the side.

From far below came a dull splash, signal for the mourners on deck to utter, "Remember God, that we are of dust." They stepped to the rail, sprinkling into the sea handfuls of sand which they had taken from the children's sandbox a few feet away. In a series of crisp movements, the sailors folded up the flag and stood to attention beside the plank. During the service Captain Schroeder and his first officer had remained rigid; now they turned toward the sea, donned their caps, and saluted.

Schiendick, watching from a position in the shadows of a lifeboat, noticed that the salutes were not Nazi-style, and was seen to enter the fact later in his party notebook.

The formal proceedings on deck ended when Schroeder handed to Recha Weiler what was to become for her a treasured memento of the occasion: a map marked with the place where her husband had been buried.

Below in his cabin, Max Loewe had heard the splash of the body as it entered the waters.

His children, Ruth and Fritz, looked down from their upper bunks at their parents. Their father, unable to waken Elise Loewe from her drugged sleep, seemed to cringe, to retreat again within himself. Even twelve-year-old Fritz had come to recognize this as abnormal, and his father's behavior distressed the boy deeply. It was not until he was older that he could put his feelings into words. "Father was becoming increasingly mentally disturbed. He was paranoiac."

Max Loewe's mind filled with confused thoughts: perhaps the ship had stopped so *they* could come and get him; perhaps he should hide on the ship as he had had to hide in Germany? His children felt helpless in the face of their father's confused suffering.

In the first-class cabin she shared with her mother, the silence before the *St. Louis*'s engines started made ten-year-old Marianne Bardeleben think of the father she had not seen for months.

The girl had much in common with her friends, the Aber children. Like them, her father was a doctor who had fled to Havana. Like them, Marianne had a non-Jewish mother, and had spent time in a home before boarding the ship. During those days, she had become accustomed to "noise, sirens, marching feet, and shouting crowds." For her, the silence of this night on the *St. Louis* was "ominous and threatening." She waited, almost too frightened to breathe. Only when the engines started up again was Marianne able to shut her eyes to the darkness.

Rosemarie Bergmann had realized that the ship had stopped to bury Moritz Weiler; she carefully noted it in her diary. Her husband wrote in the diary he was also keeping: "At least the old professor has not died or been buried in the hell of the Third Reich."

On B deck, shortly after 11 P.M., Fritz and Babette Spanier took their customary prebed stroll, relieved that the ship was back at full speed. It was a cool night, and the deck was now deserted, lit only by a few lights.

Babette Spanier felt like talking. She reflected that their fellow passengers had turned in early possibly because of the funeral, but more likely in order to rest up for the gala costume ball to be held two nights later. She had not yet decided what to wear; she had heard that a number of passengers were going as sheiks or harem girls, but she felt that would be in poor taste in view of the Arab opposition to Jews settling in Palestine.

Dr. Spanier paid little attention to his wife's chatter until suddenly she whispered: "Fritz, did you hear that?"

A giggle, quickly suppressed, came from farther down the deck, straining their eyes in the darkness, the Spaniers could see a close, unheeding couple. They found similar pairs in niches and tucked away under the companionways.

"The whole deck was full of these goings-on," Babette Spanier was to recall. "They were like rabbits in a cornfield."

Suddenly, from the deck above, toward the stern of the ship, came muffled shouting and the pounding of feet. As the runners came closer, Dr. Spanier could make out the words. He turned to his wife and said: "My God!"

The excitement barely ruffled the quiet on the bridge when

one of the Gestapo "firemen" reported by telephone: "Man over-board!"

"Did you see him?" asked the voice of the watch officer.

"Yes, he jumped, port side, A deck."

"Thank you," acknowledged the voice with a detached calmness.

The watch officer ordered helmsman Heinz Kritsch to stand by to go hard about, and then contacted Captain Schroeder, who bolted to the bridge to take charge of the rescue operation.

Schroeder was pleased to see Kritsch at the helm. Apart from the steersman's professional abilities, so necessary in an emergency, the captain had a genuine liking for the young Rhinelander. They shared a common off-duty pleasure, ornithology.

Where the watch officer had been relaxed and easygoing, Schroeder moved briskly. The engine room was warned that there was about to be a major course change, extra lookouts were posted, a motorboat was prepared for launching, and, as the ship came around, the bridge searchlight began to sweep the water.

First Officer Ostermeyer established in a series of telephone calls that the jumper was not a passenger but a crew member, Leonid Berg, a kitchen hand.

"Do you know him, Kritsch?"

"Yes, Captain. He's a Russian émigré."

A telephone call to purser Mueller provided further details: Berg was thirty years old, on his second voyage, and had jumped from the same spot where Moritz Weiler's body had been dropped into the sea. Mueller believed it "significant" that Berg had experienced frequent attacks of depression during the voyage, a fact which Kritsch confirmed.

Though the night was clear, Schroeder thought the chances of finding Berg were slender: there was every likelihood the kitchen hand had been sucked under by the ship's wake. If he was alive, he could be anywhere in several square miles of sea; meantime, the search would cut still further the *St. Louis*'s lead over the *Orduna* and the *Flandre*. At 11:55 P.M., the ship hove to. Two illuminated buoys were dropped and the motor launch lowered; it began systematically to quarter the area.

WEDNESDAY, MAY 24, 1939

At 1 A.M. Wednesday, Captain Schroeder officially ended the search by ordering three short blasts on the siren to recall the launch. Shortly afterward, the *St. Louis* resumed course.

By breakfast time, rumors about Berg's death were circulating freely. A favorite story cast the kitchen hand as a victim of a Nazi fight. "With a name like his, what chance did he have?" Shalote Hecht asked. Otto Bergmann wondered whether Berg had been dumped over the side for being "too friendly" with the passengers. Babette Spanier heard a more titillating tale: "Berg was a handsome man who had fallen in love with a passenger, and committed suicide when the other crew told him to give her up." Josef Joseph thought a love tragedy was unlikely. He favored the theory of a "simple suicide, clean and quick."

"Two deaths are unusual," Aaron Pozner wrote in the diary he kept of the voyage. "It has created new tensions. People are suspicious again. Today there was consternation when two stewards were seen carrying a large portrait of Hitler into the purser's office. People said some Nazi ceremony was being planned, but the portrait was being removed from the social hall for Shabuoth."

Gustav Schroeder had ordered the photo to be taken down after Rabbi Weil told him he felt it would be inappropriate for a sacred moment to be celebrated in the "presence of Hitler."

The rabbi had spent much of the morning preparing the hall for the service. It was now decorated with bowls of fruit and vases of flowers; two ornamental palm trees had been borrowed from the *Tanzplatz*. The service was well attended, and again members of the crew secreted themselves in the gallery, listening to the singing.

Otto Schiendick had not been drawn to the service, but later,

126

learning that the Fuehrer's portrait had been removed, he strongly protested to the purser about "this most serious offense." Once more the usually placid Mueller castigated the steward, telling him it was no concern of his, and that his "days on this ship are numbered."

Schiendick hunted down Jockl and found the captain's steward in a first-class pantry. Here was something he could revenge himself upon. Closing the door, Schiendick angrily demanded to know why Jockl had failed to make any reports on the captain. He was told there was nothing to report.

His voice quite devoid of its usual hectoring tone, Otto Schiendick revealed that he knew about the visit of Josef Joseph and the other passengers to the captain's cabin. Then he raised his voice.

"Why, Jockl, why were they there?" he demanded. "You were there. You haven't mentioned it. Why?"

As he recalled later, at that moment, Leo Jockl felt again the urge to hit the dumpy little man who seemed so bent on destroying the captain. Once more he controlled himself, and calmly repeated what Gustav Schroeder had told him to say: the passengers had formed a committee "in case of any trouble in Havana."

At the mention of trouble, Otto Schiendick became uneasy, lowered his voice, and asked what the captain meant.

Sensing that the balance had tilted in his favor, Leo Jockl partly drew upon his own imagination to tell Schiendick that while the trouble was some vague threat against the ship, it had been enough for the captain to contemplate banning all shore leave for the crew.

"Are you sure?" blurted out Schiendick.

"That's what the captain said, but it won't bother me. I hear Havana is not much of a place," replied Leo.

If Otto Schiendick was unable to go ashore, he knew his Abwehr mission would fail, assuring him of unpleasant complications back in Hamburg. In that case not even producing cast-iron proof against the captain or the purser was likely to return him to favor, or get him promoted by the Abwehr.

For the first time since joining the *St. Louis,* Schiendick felt that it was he who was threatened.

The *St. Louis* plowed through a gentle sea toward the Bahamas. After lunch that Wednesday, passengers could choose a tea dance, language classes, or lazing around the swimming pool.

Aaron Pozner spent the early part of the afternoon in his cabin learning Spanish from a phrase book given him by his wife. He found it difficult to concentrate. His mind constantly returned to Leo Jockl. The steward now spent a good deal of his free time with Pozner, during which a conviction had grown in Pozner's mind. That afternoon, when Jockl arrived, he decided to test his theory. He asked the steward if he was a Jew.

Pozner realized "as soon as I put the question that it was a mistake. Leo was not ready for it. The thought that I was suspicious frightened him. He only shook his head and left the cabin."

Afterward, Leo Jockl felt ashamed he had been unable to admit the truth.

Elise Loewe finally awoke late on Wednesday afternoon, dazed from the aftereffects of the sleeping drug Dr. Glauner had given her. She had slept for nearly twenty-four hours.

Her husband's condition had deteriorated. His speech showed he had difficulty in distinguishing between fantasy and reality; his emotional problems were now not just in relation to life. He appeared to have a "death complex," dwelling morbidly on the Weiler funeral and the Berg suicide. Elise Loewe was very frightened.

At exactly six o'clock Havana time on this Wednesday evening, Milton Goldsmith, the director of the Relief Committee in Cuba, ended his telephone conversation with New York.

He had already told the American Jewish Joint Distribution Committee, who financed his work, that without further funds it would be difficult to maintain the 5000 refugees he supported, let alone any newcomers on the *St. Louis* and other refugee ships. The Joint official had said no extra money was available.

Desperately seeking some concession, Goldsmith had raised again the matter of the shiploads of refugees approaching Havana, but to no avail. Afterward he was left with the impression that the gravity of his situation had completely failed to register with the New York-based committee.

He and his assistant, Laura Margolis, received some financial help from the local Jewish community, but a businessman reflected part of the local feeling when he told Goldsmith, "Over the years we have all sent our donations to the Joint. Let them use that money."

Another had said, "Of course we feel sorry for the refugees, but the whole world should be helping, not just us."

Laura Margolis had wept at those words. Then, on hearing the Joint's reply, she told Goldsmith there was only one solution. The weekly handout to each refugee must be cut from $7 to $4.50. That would eke out a further few weeks' allowance, and in that time they could prepare another appeal to the Joint.

Laura believed that "they won't be able to refuse again. Not with the *St. Louis.*"

Later that same evening, in Havana, Robert Hoffman completed another phase of the plan to carry off one of his biggest espionage coups. He photographically reduced some of the American defense secrets smuggled into Cuba. Then he carefully rolled the films inside the barrels of fountain pens or stitched them onto the spines of magazines. Large documents he had secured in a hollowed-out, carved walking stick.

These were classic Abwehr methods and Hoffman was a skilled hand at such work. Nevertheless he was worried by a number of things, among them the virulent anti-Semitism on the island. He clearly saw the inherent danger in the situation he had helped to create: a climate of hatred now existed which might not only threaten the safety of the *St. Louis* passengers, but pose problems he had not foreseen in effecting a smooth pickup by Otto Schiendick.

Further, one of his agents, the humpbacked dwarf Otto Ott, reported that the Cuban secret police had started to watch all known Nazi agents on the island. Ott said this surveillance had been started on the direct order of Batista, and Hoffman had no reason to doubt this information, for he had had to pay substantial sums of money in the past for the secret police to turn a blind eye to the Abwehr's activities in Cuba.

What was especially troubling Robert Hoffman was his suspicion that strong American pressure must have been exerted on Batista to make such a move.

There was also evidence of American intervention on other fronts, such as the arrival of a new agent of the U. S. Immigration Service; Abwehr files revealed that the man had a formidable record. Also, the American naval attaché, Rowell, was becoming increasingly inquisitive. Overall, the German spymaster felt a determined American effort was being mounted to try to recover the secret documents he had now reduced to a few spools of film, secreted in his fancy walking stick.

THURSDAY, MAY 25, 1939

Thursday, May 25, the second day of Shabuoth was also the day of the fancy costume ball, the traditional end-of-voyage party held two nights before landing.

In the morning, on the *St. Louis*, once again the tables and chairs in the social hall had been rearranged and the room made into a synagogue; once again, despite Schiendick's protestations, Hitler's portrait had been removed.

After the service, an announcement requested all passengers to report to the purser's office to collect their landing cards for disembarkation Saturday morning. By midafternoon Thursday, the majority of the cards had been given out, and some passengers had even packed most of their clothes, putting aside the costumes they intended to wear at the gala that evening.

Now, seated at a table in the restaurant, Aaron Pozner wondered whether to reconsider his decision that it would be "improper" for him to join the festivities. Everyone else seemed set for a final fling; many were already in fancy dress. Though the dinner menu was not that different from what passengers had come to expect on the voyage, tonight it was particularly tempting after the mainly cheese diet many had maintained during the two days of Shabuoth.

But for Pozner, the contrast with his painful memories of Nazi Germany, of having had to hide among foul-smelling animal skins, of having to grovel in garbage for scraps of food, made it all seem so unreal.

Inside the gaily colored cover of the tourist-class menu, the refugee from the concentration camp was offered salmon mayonnaise, followed by clear soup with dumplings, veal marengo with buttered noodles and roast potatoes, or fried

131

chicken with grilled tomatoes, cauliflower hollandaise, and chips. For dessert there was orange ice cream, swiss or *harzer* cheese, fresh fruit, and coffee or tea.

The music program during dinner featured waltzes by Fucik and Robledo, a potpourri from *The Merry Widow*, and ended with a festival march by Blankenburg.

For the man whose memories of Dachau were still fresh in his mind, who had had to leave his family behind, the contrast was finally too much. Unable to finish his meal or to stand the growing boisterousness of his fellow passengers, Pozner returned to his cabin.

After dinner, Leo Jockl joined other stewards in the social hall, putting the finishing touches on the room which had changed its character four times in two days. The palm trees and fruit remained from the morning synagogue service, but now they were hardly noticed among the streamers and balloons suspended from the ceiling and hanging over the gallery rails. The wicker-work chairs, and tables with freshly laundered linen and a spray of flowers on each, had been pushed to the side to make space for the dancers.

Overlooking the entire scene, back in its proper place, was the portrait of the Fuehrer.

The Spaniers and the Josephs delayed going to the ball until it was well under way. Though both couples preferred formal evening attire to fancy costumes, Babette Spanier caused something of a stir by her entrance. She swept down the wide, curved double staircase leading from the gallery to the dance floor with a flourish, raising her long dress as she descended to reveal a pair of high black riding boots. She had exchanged her monocle for a pair of large frame spectacles.

Lilli Joseph thought the overall impression "a little strange." Babette explained that the boots under her evening dress were "because it might turn cool."

Some of the costumes demonstrated considerable invention; Arab djellabahs fashioned out of bed sheets and hand towels; many of the young men came appropriately as pirates and were rewarded by a liberal scattering of briefly clad harem girls wait-ing to be plundered; two geisha girls were particularly popular.

The band leader raised a cheer with a selection of Glenn Miller melodies. Later, even greater applause came from the younger set as the band swung into rhumbas and tangos.

As the night wore on, the passengers, knowing that what remained of their "shipboard money" would be worthless once they disembarked, spent it on drink. Babette Spanier was disquieted to see the dancing becoming more abandoned. One young couple who had fashioned palm leaves into a Hawaiian-type hula skirt were "swinging their hips in a way that was quite revealing." What disturbed her most, however, was the pretty girl dressed in the uniform of a ship's sailor. *"Excuse me,"* she said to her husband, "but how did she get hold of *that?*" Dr. Spanier thought the answer obvious.

The party finished for all but a few hangers on at three in the morning. Those with energy left began what they thought would be their last full day on the *St. Louis* by going on deck, from where they could now see the beam from the Bahamas lighthouse.

II

*A Chance
To Die*

FRIDAY, MAY 26, 1939

After breakfasting alone in his cabin on Friday, Captain Schroeder went to the chart room. There, as he made his calculations, he was joined by Ostermeyer. The captain said they would arrive in Havana before the two other refugee ships. What really concerned him, he went on to say, was not knowing what would happen when the ship reached harbor. He had sent two further cables to Holthusen, demanding amplification of the director's last radiogram, and the silence, the captain told his first officer, "was deafening."

The conversation then turned to the passengers. Apart from his meetings with Fritz Spanier and the passenger committee, the captain had maintained his stance of remaining aloof from them all, leaving the routine running of the ship to Ostermeyer.

The first officer replied that after some depression caused by the two deaths, all now appeared to be well with the passengers, and that the crew continued to respond to their orders to behave in an exemplary manner. Nevertheless, Captain Schroeder said, Schiendick and the Gestapo "firemen" would be "beached" once they reached Hamburg.

His determination to do so had been furthered by Jockl's recounting that morning his latest encounter with Schiendick.

Gustav Schroeder and Ostermeyer wondered why the party *Leiter* had seemed concerned over the remark that shore leave might be canceled. The captain said he had a good mind, in Schiendick's case, to carry out the threat "if there is any more trouble from that man."

Friday the passengers lining the rails tried to identify landmarks as the ship sailed down the Florida coast, passing Miami early in the afternoon.

The sight of the city was a signal scores of them had been waiting for. They hurried to the purser's office and used up the last of their "shipboard money" on telegrams to friends and relatives waiting in Cuba and the United States for their arrival. More than one message contained only the words "Arrived safely."

Late in the afternoon, suitcases were brought up on deck and the deck chairs folded away.

There seemed to Aaron Pozner "a feeling of anticipation, of release from the Nazi horror. People laughed and prayed, and the crew smiled, pretending to understand."

That evening Josef Joseph invited members of the passenger committee to join him for cocktails in the first-class bar.

He raised his glass and thanked them, even though, as he pointed out, there had been nothing in the end for them to do, for since that first meeting with the captain, they had not seen him again, nor had he sent any word of fresh developments.

Only Dr. Max Weiss uttered a cautionary note: "That does not mean there will be no problems." But even he had to agree with Joseph's opinion that it was the "best possible omen" that the Relief Committee in Havana had not answered their telegram. The lawyer believed that in this case the cliché that no news is good news was true.

While the men replenished their glasses, and talked about life after the *St. Louis*, Gustav Schroeder received a wireless message from Luis Clasing in Havana. It was not in code, and the portent of the words was immediately clear. Clasing had telegraphed:

ANCHOR IN ROADSTEAD. DO NOT REPEAT NOT MAKE ANY ATTEMPT COME ALONGSIDE.

The cable Luis Clasing had sent to Captain Schroeder had brought him into direct conflict with his assistant, Robert Hoffman. Hoffman had turned to Clasing angrily, saying the situation would not have arisen if Clasing had offered Manuel Benitez the further bribe he had suggested.

Equally furious, Clasing had retorted that the immigration director wanted $250,000, an impossible sum for Hapag to provide. He had sarcastically suggested that Hoffman should approach his Abwehr paymasters for the money. Hoffman had snapped back that it was a "matter of negotiation," and that he proposed to do just that with Benitez. He stormed out of the Hapag building to see the immigration director.

Luis Clasing spent the next hour preparing a long cable to Claus-Gottfried Holthusen in Hamburg. Now, well into Friday night, he was still unable to find the right words to convey the series of swift-moving developments which had begun earlier in the day.

The first indication of trouble had been a telephone call from President Bru's office to Clasing informing him the *St. Louis* would not be allowed to tie up at the pier Hapag shared with the American Ward Line.

Clasing made repeated attempts to contact Manuel Benitez, but the immigration director was suddenly unavailable. Next had come a further blunt warning, this time in the evening editions of the local press, that there would be a "dangerous situation" if the refugees landed. That had been followed by a visit from Milton Goldsmith, demanding to know the exact sitaution.

The relationship between the two men was at best barely polite, kept alive by a common interest in landing as many refugees as possible. It became icy when Clasing refused to give any assurances the *St. Louis* would berth as scheduled.

"You mean you don't know if they will land or not?" pressed Goldsmith.

"I mean you should put that question to the president," retorted Clasing.

After Goldsmith had gone, the shipping agent had telephoned Bru's secretary and pleaded that it was "now impossible" to turn back the ship, the *St. Louis* "should at minimum be allowed to anchor in the roadstead, to allow it to revictual, pending a continued search for a solution."

The secretary had telephoned back granting the request on Bru's orders.

Clasing had then cabled Schroeder. Now, he incorporated the substance of that message in his radiogram to Holthusen, adding:

STILL HOPEFUL COMMON SENSE WILL PREVAIL AND ALLOW DISEM-
BARKATION. ASSURE YOU I AM DOING ALL POSSIBLE AND WILL
EXPLORE EVERY MEANS TO ACHIEVE DISEMBARKATION.

A few doors away, Robert Hoffman sipped coffee and shared the optimism engendered by Manuel Benitez.

The immigration director had received him warmly, and asked Hoffman to apologize to Clasing for his earlier unavailability, explaining that he had been "fully occupied with the *St. Louis* in other quarters."

Benitez did not specify what those areas were, but when Hoffman revealed Bru's order that the ship must anchor out in the harbor, the immigration director had felt it was further confirmation that "Bru was weakening."

Then, in a dazzling display of verbal juggling which had convinced many others and now convinced Robert Hoffman, Benitez went on:

"My friend, Bru has to keep up a pretense. Tonight he lets the ship into Cuban waters. Tomorrow he allows it into the harbor. The next day it will be at the pier. Then, off they will come, and our worries are over."

"You are *that* sure?"

"Of course. I am a Cuban. I understand the Cuban mind," soothed Manuel Benitez.

Now, as they drank coffee, Hoffman felt especially satisfied that the situation would be resolved after all, that he could keep his meeting with Schiendick. Later, when he wrote his monthly report to the Abwehr, Berlin, he noted he had not even had to offer a small bribe, a nice footnote to his account of Operation Sunshine.

He left Benitez, totally unsuspecting that he had been hoodwinked.

Friday night passed uneventfully aboard the ship. After dinner, served early so that the passengers could get to bed, most of them had laid out their going-ashore clothes and turned in.

Some slept fitfully. Max Loewe had another restless night. Aaron Pozner was a "little anxious" of entering a country where he knew no one, and the Aber children kept each other awake chattering about the sights their father would soon show them.

In his day cabin, Captain Schroeder fell asleep in his favorite leather armchair still holding in his hand the cable ordering him to anchor in the roadstead. He had read and reread it, deciding in the end that nothing would be accomplished by contacting Havana at this late stage. After his experience of Holthusen, the captain had little confidence in any Hapag official, especially a "minor one in an outpost like Cuba."

SATURDAY, MAY 27, 1939

At 2:30 A.M., the captain was awakened by the watch officer, who told him the *St. Louis* had made up for the time lost burying Weiler and searching for Berg, and had actually gained on the other two refugee ships. The *Orduna* was now six hours behind, and the *Flandre* nearly twenty-four. There had been no incoming cables except a few of welcome for passengers.

At 3 A.M., Schroeder ordered the ship's speed be reduced to take on the pilot. He looked forward to questioning the Cuban, and as soon as he boarded Schroeder asked him why they were to remain at anchor in the harbor, The pilot was noncommittal. His English was poor and his German nonexistent. The captain spoke little Spanish, but enough to recognize the man claimed he was "only carrying out orders." The reply rekindled Schroeder's fears, but he realized there was no point in pressing the matter.

Precisely at 4 A.M., Captain Schroeder ordered the ship's klaxon sounded to awaken the passengers.

Rosemarie Bergmann delayed dressing long enough to capture the moment in her diary: "I have never jumped out of bed so quickly. The sky is dark blue but I can make out a few white buildings stark against it. There are still stars in the sky. It's like a dream."

All over the ship that dream was coming true for its passengers, almost half of whom were women and children being met by husbands and fathers already in Havana.

Soon the decks were overflowing with people trying to recognize landmarks they had seen in postcards. A few car headlights pierced the darkness on the shoreline. Passengers on the port side could see the murky outline of the towering walls of El Morro, the ancient fort guarding the harbor's entrance. The

142

movement of the ship was barely perceptible as it glided through the water, now beginning to sparkle in the dawn.

At 4:30 A.M., the breakfast gong sounded. Despite the hour, there was soon a hubbub of excited conversation in the dining rooms. Some passengers, Babette Spanier noticed, sported the watches and rings they had purchased at the last moment from crew members; the "shipboard money" the passengers had paid for them could be exchanged by the seamen for Reichsmarks on their return to Germany.

With the sound of the anchor being dropped, the Spanier twins rushed to a window in the first-class dining room. Their parents joined them, and on the starboard side, in the half daylight, they could see that the shore was a long way off; away in the distance was Havana Cathedral.

Returning to their table, Babette Spanier asked Leo Jockl why they had not tied up alongside. The steward did not know, he had never been to Havana before, but he suggested that perhaps the harbor was not deep enough to take a ship as large as the *St. Louis*.

Within minutes, half a dozen theories swept the room. Dr. Spanier, who had see the ship's yellow quarantine flag being hoisted, said that until they had been passed by the port's medical authorities, they would have to remain at anchor.

Rosemarie Bergmann, recalling her doubts about the drinking water at Cherbourg, believed: "We are being kept out now so that no illness is brought on board." Shalote Hecht said she had heard "some story" about the ship's papers not being in order.

By the time that rumor reached A deck, it had changed: now it was the passengers' papers which were in doubt. When he heard this, Josef Joseph kept from his wife his feeling that it "had an uncomfortable ring of truth about it," remembering what the captain had told the passenger committee about decree 937.

The ship's doctor, Walter Glauner, stood at the top of the accommodation ladder, waiting to greet a Cuban in a white tropical suit from the first boat to come alongside. Glauner escorted the Havana Port Authority doctor toward the bridge.

Aft on A deck, the ship's orchestra broke the early morning quiet of the harbor as it struck up *"Freut euch des Lebens."* Remembering the words of the tune, "Be Happy You're Alive,"

Aaron Pozner "felt good" almost for the first time since leaving Hamburg.

In his day cabin, Captain Schroeder gave to the Cuban doctor the thirty-two manifest sheets listing every passenger and containing his sworn statement that none of them was "an idiot, or insane, or suffering from loathsome or contagious disease, or convicted of a felony or some other infamous crime involving moral turpitude."

Despite the captain's signed statement, the doctor insisted that he personally view the passengers. Barely able to conceal his anger over his words being challenged, Schroeder curtly ordered the first officer, Ostermeyer, to assemble the passengers in the social hall for inspection. He then abruptly left the two doctors, and returned to the bridge.

Assisted by purser Mueller and his staff, the ship's nurse formed a long snake of people that wound its way around the hall. As the doctors entered, she took up position with them on the bandstand, and the queue began rapidly to file past.

Renatta and Evelyne Aber wriggled themselves near the front of the line, eager to be first. As Renatta looked up to the officials seated behind a table, she "became frightened, as I was in Hamburg, of men in uniform."

Elise Loewe had intentionally chosen a position near the end of the queue for her family. She hoped that by the time they passed the inspection committee it would not be so vigilant, would not see that "Max was not acting normally." The Loewes were passed by the Cuban doctor without comment, as were all the passengers. Satisfied, he authorized Dr. Glauner to arrange for the quarantine flag to be lowered, and left the ship. When Schroeder learned that the man had gone, he told Ostermeyer he thought "the entire business was a charade."

Shortly after 6 A.M., Otto Schiendick joined a group of stewards standing by the accommodation ladder watching the approach of a launch flying the Hapag flag. When Luis Clasing reached the deck, Schiendick asked him if he was Robert Hoffman.

"No. And who are you?"

"I'm the *Ortsgruppenleiter* on this ship."

Suspecting that the steward was involved in Hoffman's Abwehr work, Clasing sourly told him that his assistant had no business on the ship, and if Schiendick wanted to see him he should go ashore; in the meantime he could make himself useful by bringing on board the ship's mail, stacked in the launch.

Then, without waiting for an answer, Luis Clasing went to the bridge.

The captain awaited him in the day cabin, seated behind his desk, on which lay all the telegrams received since leaving Hamburg. He remained seated as Clasing entered. Nor did he offer his visitor any traditional hospitality. He was tired from a night of little sleep, and his mood was not improved by Clasing's breezy reassurance that things "would be well."

Then why, demanded the captain, had Clasing sent a cable ordering the ship to anchor in the roadstead?

Clasing began to explain. The captain interrupted.

"So. This man Benitez tells you it will be all right, and you believe him?"

Clasing, borrowing a sentiment from the immigration director's fund of reassuring phrases, replied that he understood the Cuban mentality.

"Then, by God, you had better explain these!" roared Gustav Schroeder, thrusting the cables at the shipping agent.

Luis Clasing began to wish he had never boarded the ship to face this fierce little man.

"Well? What do they mean," snapped Schroeder.

"Captain, the situation is fluid, and there are many problems I have had to overcome—"

"I'm not concerned with your problems. I just want these passengers ashore. Do you understand?"

The telegrams, said Clasing, referred "to events in the past." Then, borrowing another sentiment of Manuel Benitez, he added: "The truth is, you are here, in Havana Harbor. You may regard the voyage as over. The passengers are not your problem any more."

Gustav Schroeder rose to his feet, pressing his palms down on the desktop, and looked coldly at the shipping agent. Then, in a measured voice, he said, "These people are my responsibility until they are off this ship. If you ever forget that, I will personally see to it that soon you will be working for somebody else. Now, get off my ship and go back to Havana and get *my* passengers ashore. And do it quickly!"

At about the time Clasing was receiving his ear-bashing from Schroeder, Hoffman, in charge of the Hapag office in Clasing's absence, received his first unsettling news of the day. Otto Ott, the midget spy, telephoned to inform Hoffman in his distinctive high-pitched, panting tone that during the night the Cuban secret police had raided his Swiss Home Restaurant. Nothing had been found, but clearly the restaurant, long a meeting place of the Abwehr, could not be used for the planned *Treff* between Schiendick and Hoffman.

While Hoffman considered a safe alternative, his phone had rung again. This time a contact in the Havana post office told him that hundreds of telegrams were being delivered to President Bru urging him to keep out the refugees, and to order the *St. Louis* to leave.

The information came like a bombshell to Hoffman. The telegrams had probably resulted from the work of the propaganda agents he himself had briefed. Now, despite Benitez's previous assurances, if Bru acted quickly on the advice of those telegrams, the *St. Louis* would depart Havana before Schiendick had collected the espionage secrets from Hoffman.

The Abwehr agent cursed himself for not going to the ship with Clasing. He realized he must go immediately, taking the secrets and running the gauntlet of the American agents he guessed would soon be at the harbor.

The U.S. military attaché, Major Henry Barber, was already there. He had stopped counting the number of suspected Abwehr agents and contacts on and around the pier. "The place was a bees' nest of them, with the Cuban police and the rest of us playing the keepers."

Naval attaché Ross E. Rowell viewed the Abwehr strength with alarm: "Most of them were there as a smokescreen behind which anything could happen." His confidence ebbed as he realized the enormity of the problem. The plans he had laid—persuading the Cubans to tighten their immigration and custom checks for the *St. Louis,* having police boats patrol the area around the ship—seemed woefully inadequate to cope with the situation developing this Saturday morning. There was simply no way of properly shadowing all the Abwehr men. Rowell decided that, until Hoffman appeared, he would concentrate on Ott.

The dwarf was difficult to tail. Ott darted around the pier, playing the part of a successful local restaurateur awaiting the arrival of new customers. He greeted a number of people effusively, and waved each one farewell with his fat cigar before busily talking to someone else.

Rowell was disappointed to see that neither Ott nor any of the other agents gave a sign of doing anything unusual. By 7 A.M., Rowell's spirits began to wane.

They would have revived had he seen Hoffman striding purposefully toward the pier head, carrying some magazines and official-looking papers, and forcing his way through the crowds with a carved walking stick.

Hoffman was allowed through the customs point, and waited at the landing stage for the Hapag launch, now returning with Clasing. As the launch pulled alongside, Hoffman told Clasing it was urgent that he go to the ship. Clasing, still smarting from Schroeder's tongue-lashing, told Hoffman he was "welcome, but I suggest you avoid the captain. He's not in a very receptive mood."

Just as the launch was leaving, Rowell, talking to Milton Goldsmith and Laura Margolis, caught sight of Hoffman departing. Rowell borrowed the binoculars the refugee workers had been using to watch the passengers now thronging the upper decks of the *St. Louis*. Angry that he had not spotted Hoffman earlier, he now hoped he could see what the Abwehr agent did, even if he could not overhear what was being said.

"I am Robert Hoffman, assistant manager of the Hapag office," Hoffman told the Cuban police officer confronting him at the bottom of the *St. Louis* accommodation ladder.

"That does not matter. We have just received strict instructions from the highest authority to allow no one but Cuban officials aboard."

"Then I should like to have a certain crew member brought to me here."

"I am sorry. That is not allowed. There is to be no contact between anyone on the ship and anyone who comes out to it. Please leave."

"But I only want to give a friend these magazines," Hoffman pleaded.

For a moment, the policeman hesitated. Hoffman sensed he might be able to bribe his way up the ladder if the steward was present to receive the documents instantly. He shouted up Schiendick's name. At this, the policeman put his hand on his pistol, and ordered Hoffman back into the launch. Hoffman looked up: there was no reply to his call. He stepped into the boat, and it headed for the shore.

Rowell handed the binoculars back to Milton Goldsmith, relieved that Hoffman had not boarded the ship and had apparently only spoken to the policeman.

Like Rowell, Hoffman did not see nor hear Otto Schiendick approach the top of the ladder and ask Leo Jockl whether it was Clasing who was now returning to the shore in the Hapag launch.

"I don't think so," said Jockl to Schiendick. "He called out for you. I think his name was Hoffman."

On shore, watching the Hapag launch approaching shortly after seven o'clock, Rowell's attention was drawn by an excited murmur sweeping the crowd as people fell back to allow Manuel Benitez to walk to the pier head. Rowell presumed Benitez had come to "make good on his promises." Later, in a secret report to Washington, he would write that the swashbuckling minister had "arrived on the scene armed with two pistols."

At the pier head, a police captain and a detachment of patrolmen awaited Benitez. The captain saluted the minister and then shrugged apologetically, saying he had orders not to let him through.

"Do you know who I am?"

The captain did, and it was for that reason he was being barred, on specific instructions.

"Who issued them?"

They had come directly from President Bru's office.

"They cannot apply to me!"

The captain was even more apologetic, but stood firm; the president's instructions were that the minister must not be allowed to pass this point.

For a moment it seemed to Rowell that Benitez was about to

shoot his way through the police cordon. The minister's hands hovered over the pistol butts. Then, finally, he turned away, and headed toward his office, hands still on his pistols.

Milton Goldsmith had viewed the scene with disbelief, concluding that it was dismal proof that Bru was in total command. He, too, turned and pushed his way through the stunned crowd, pausing only to tell Laura Margolis he intended to telephone the Joint in New York.

By nine o'clock that morning of arrival, the Cuban police already aboard the *St. Louis* had been joined by immigration and customs officials.

Passengers and crew had watched the small uniformed group make their way up the ladder and then go directly into the first-class restaurant. There they ordered a breakfast of rolls, sausages, and beer. Otto Bergmann noticed that the officials seemed especially to like the German lager. "That will put them in a good mood," he told his wife.

On deck, passengers waited, watching the rowboats which now surrounded the ship offering a variety of fresh tropical fruits. A few tossed money down, and received a bunch of bananas or coconuts, which were passed up the ladder by the now more obliging policeman.

As the Aber children moved close to the companionway, Evelyne caught a glimpse of a black man; she had never seen one before. Clutching her sister's hand, she ran to the safety of their cabin.

Gradually a sprinkling of relatives and friends began to arrive in the rowboats. When they got too close to the *St. Louis,* the police ordered them back. Their shouted words could barely be understood on the upper decks, some seventy-five feet above the water line. In one of the boats were Dr. Aber, Dr. Bardeleben, and Hans Fischer. They circled the ship, shouting up their names.

Mrs. Bardeleben was the first to see them; she and her daughter Marianne had been standing at the rail ever since they passed the medical examination.

Ten-year-old Marianne was particularly excited. The night before, for the first time in her life, she had been taken to the hairdresser. This morning her mother had given her a further surprise: two Cuban hair clips sent by her father to Germany had been kept secret from her and brought out only as a special treat for this moment. Marianne excitedly peered down at the row-boats, hoping to find her father so he could see her new hair style. Her mother kept saying, "There he is. *There!*" but the distance was too great for the child to pick out her father; there were so many upturned faces, and so many boats. "There, Marianne, *there!*" urged her mother. Marianne was broken-hearted, for she still failed to see her father.

Dr. Aber called up to Mrs. Bardeleben, asking for his daughters. "After what seemed like hours," she returned with them, lifting first Evelyne, then Renatta, above the ship's rail so they could catch a glimpse of the father they had not seen for a year. They hardly recognized him.

Almost crying with delight, Dr. Aber then asked whether his children had visas. It took some time before he made himself understood, his companions thought the question irrelevant. Finally Mrs. Bardeleben returned again, waving two green passports. "Yes, they have Cuban visas inside," she shouted. Dr. Aber wept with relief.

Rosemarie Bergmann "hugged with her eyes" those in the boats. "At last we are among friends," she told her husband.

Mrs. Spanier heard someone call, "Don't worry, everything will be all right."

"Of course it will," she said to her husband. "What do they mean?"

Fritz Spanier did not reply.

About ten o'clock, the immigration officials finished their beers and began processing passports, Benitez's landing permits, and the landing cards that had been given out on board. The passports, each stamped in Germany with a red "J," were given a cursory glance, as were the permits. The Cuban officials stamped the landing cards with an "R." Passengers were then given a form telling them where their luggage would be found on the Ward pier.

By ten-thirty, about fifty passengers had been cleared, collected their hand luggage, and were standing at the top of the accommodation ladder awaiting transport from the ship.

Anticipation rose as they saw the launch return which had brought the customs and immigration personnel aboard. An official ran up the ladder, ignored the passengers, and walked into the ship.

Minutes later, he, and all the officials, left the *St. Louis*. Only the Cuban police remained.

Soon after ten o'clock, Milton Goldsmith telephoned Joseph C. Hyman, the executive director of the Joint Distribution Committee, in New York. Goldsmith explained to Hyman, some 1500 miles away, that "our worst fears have come true. The passengers have not been allowed to disembark."

Hyman liked and respected Goldsmith as an energetic worker for whom years of setbacks had not eroded the enthusiasm essential for the often thankless task of manning a welfare outpost.

Now, as he listened to his voice, he recognized that Milton Goldsmith badly needed help.

Hyman promised that two experienced relief workers, Lawrence Berenson and Cecilia Razovsky, would fly down. Berenson, a lawyer, would "negotiate a settlement." Razovsky was to "help take care of the passengers when they land." The pair would arrive on Tuesday.

Goldsmith quietly pointed out that that was still three days hence: "The position here has been allowed to drift too long already. President Bru is afraid to let the passengers off because of anti-Semitic campaigns. Hapag have told me that if the passengers don't land, they are sure Germany won't have them back."

Hyman agreed there must be "no question" of the refugees returning to Germany. He requested that Goldsmith cooperate fully with Berenson in his "difficult task," and promised the fullest support of the Joint.

Laura Margolis was pleased to learn that at long last they were to receive the help they had repeatedly requested, though the role Cecilia Razovsky was to play did not seem altogether clear. Laura told Goldsmith the woman had "a reputation for forthrightness which might not suit the situation."

Nevertheless, Berenson would come with one great advantage. He was a personal friend of Fulgencio Batista, and Batista had recently been warmly welcomed in America by President Roosevelt. With connections like those, if Berenson could not "do a deal," no one could.

A deal, in any form, was furthest from President Bru's mind as he stood at his office window and looked out across the bay at the anchored *St. Louis*. Behind him, on his desk, were the bundles of telegrams which had been delivered earlier that morning, each one almost identically worded in its warning of "serious consequences" if the refugees were granted permission to land.

The telegrams had not influenced Bru; he dismissed them for what they were, an organized attempt to manipulate the situation. What did concern him were the indications of a possible alliance aimed at circumventing decree 937.

The first had come, predictably, when Manuel Benitez, after his failure to bulldoze his way on to the ship, demanded another meeting with the president. Bru had refused even to speak to the minister on the telephone.

The next move had caught the president unawares. It came when Dr. Juan Remos, the secretary of state, had telephoned to express his opinion that while legally the refugees should not be allowed to enter Cuba, there "may well be a moral case to let them in." Bru had listened respectfully to the arguments Remos advanced in the quiet, controlled voice which in the past had lent steadfast support to Bru both within and without the cabinet, and had advocated closing Benitez's illegal immigration "bureau."

Remos reminded Bru that Batista had yet to pronounce on decree 937, and there was "also the question of the American attitude to consider."

Bru had replied that he believed Cuban public opinion was largely in favor of banning the refugees, whatever Batista might say, and that he did not share the secretary of state's fear of pressure from the United States. America, he told Remos, was increasingly sensitive to the immigration issue. Opposition had quickened in the past months across the United States in spite of a lobby demanding extra admissions for European refugees.

The telephone call left the president uneasy. Without the total support of Remos, his cabinet might be split, and that could be a critical factor with elections pending. Bru sensed that any alliance which came about because of Remos and Benitez's common aim would likely have the support of Batista, and together, if that happened, the three would make a coalition powerful enough to end Bru's hope of a further term in office.

And yet, with a politician's instinct, Bru still believed he was right to maintain his stand, and that in the end he would be proved right at the ballot box. Nevertheless, he decided that the ship anchored out in the bay must not become an election issue, must not split his cabinet, must not even be allowed to remain as an offending presence for a moment longer than necessary.

By the end of this Saturday morning, Manuel Benitez was concerned, to varying degrees, on three counts.

First, President Bru had effectively barred him from both ship and palace. Benitez was upset by such banishment, but he had been long enough in the rough-and-tumble of Cuban politics to know it would not be an impossibility, given the right moment, to reinstate himself in the presidential favor.

Second, Dr. Juan Remos had told him that the interests of the Cuban nation must come above any support he might tender for the refugees.

Benitez had pleaded that his only concern "was helping the refugees as a matter of conscience."

Remos said he was astonished that Benitez had the gall to offer "such a high-flying excuse for larceny on a grand scale."

Benitez had learned in his political life to ride with such insults, but the immigration director had made a third, and more unpalatable, discovery. His benefactor, Batista, had gone to ground. It had dawned on Manuel Benitez that it was a deliberate move on the part of the army chief, one designed to avoid Batista's becoming involved with the *St. Louis,* or with the way Benitez had handled matters. That *did* worry the immigration director.

Ironically, Batista's move was a parallel one to that which Benitez had himself adopted toward Luis Clasing earlier on Saturday. Benitez had become "unavailable" to the shipping agent, and he planned to remain so until he had found a way out of the crisis. By lunchtime Saturday, like Bru, Benitez began to feel that the only solution was for the *St. Louis* to weigh anchor and take her troublesome passengers elsewhere. Then, when tempers had cooled, he would resume his old relationship with Hapag.

But Benitez, an expert on the Cuban mentality, had greatly misunderstood the European mind, in particular that of Gustav Schroeder.

At lunchtime this Saturday, Captain Schroeder spoke frankly to the ship's officers assembled in his day cabin.

"Gentlemen," he said, "I fear trouble."

The first serious sign of trouble, he said, had come when the Cuban officials had abruptly departed, leaving only the police behind. The captain had sent for the senior policeman, and the man had been unable, or unwilling, to explain why the customs and immigration officials had left. Under Schroeder's pressing questions, the policeman had pleaded the language barrier; the only sense the captain had gleaned from him was a repeated, "In Cuba, things go slower than in Europe."

Next had been the arrival of the *Orduna;* she had also been ordered to anchor out in the harbor, and now a police detail guarded her gangway.

The captain revealed that Luis Clasing had made no further contact since returning to Havana. Gustav Schroeder wondered whether his earlier blistering attack on the shipping agent, far from galvanizing Clasing, had merely had the opposite effect, sending him bolting for cover. Now, to the assembled officers, he returned to that thought, producing and reading Clasing's telegram, which ordered the ship to anchor in the roadstead.

"I don't think we can expect much from him," Schroeder said, "or, it seems, from Hamburg," referring to Holthusen's cables.

He went on to reveal the existence of the passenger committee, which brought surprised murmurs and questions. One officer asked what authority the committee had; the captain replied that its sole function was liaison. Another wondered if it gave passengers "a status on the ship they did not have in Germany." Gustav Schroeder answered sharply, "We are not in Germany now." Nor, he reminded them, would he tolerate any sign of "the sort of thing some of these people have experienced back home."

Nevertheless, he went on, if the daily Nazi radio summaries were to be believed, a similar climate existed in Havana. He now personally discounted much of the broadcasts as typical propaganda, yet he admitted that if they contained even some truth, the situation could become unpleasant.

Therefore, he continued, he had decided to cancel all shore leave until further notice.

Another murmur rippled through the room, and purser Mueller, remembering the repeated inquiries he had had from Otto Schiendick about going ashore, expressed the view that the captain's decision would not only be unpopular but might lead to tension between crew and passengers.

"It's your job, all of you, to make sure that does not happen," retorted Gustav Schroeder.

In the meantime, he concluded, in spite of his fears, he was confident about one thing: "These passengers are eventually destined for America. If the situation here deteriorates, I am sure the United States will resolve matters by accepting them a little sooner."

The office of the American consul general in Havana, Coert du Bois, was on the first floor of the consulate at the foot of Obispo Street, near the docks, and from it he could clearly see the *St. Louis.*

Like Goldsmith's Relief Committee, du Bois's consulate was constantly besieged by refugees; on his decision depended which, and in what order, refugees left Cuba and were allowed into the United States. The consul general carried a further burden: the ailing American ambassador relied on him heavily for advice and daily information, information that was passed to the government in Washington and that would critically affect the future of the *St. Louis* passengers.

Early on the day of arrival of the *St. Louis*—which, unhappily, coincided with the removal of the American embassy to another building, and with the beginning of the Whitsun weekend—Coert du Bois cabled to Cordell Hull at the State Department in Washington an assessment of the *St. Louis* situation. It was to become typical of the attitude of the American government to the entire affair.

THERE APPEARS TO BE NO ACTION THAT THE EMBASSY OR CON-
SULATE GENERAL COULD PROPERLY TAKE AT PRESENT.

In the British legation, Ambassador H. A. Grant Watson discussed with his consul general the difficulties of the *St. Louis* in relation to the *Orduna*.

The important thing, stressed Watson, was to make absolutely clear the difference between the two ships: "The *St. Louis* is German, the *Orduna* is British." In addition, the refugees on the *Orduna* should be allowed to land, said the ambassador, because they, unlike those on the *St. Louis*, "started their journey before decree 937 came into force. Although the *Orduna* did not leave Liverpool until May 11, after publication of Bru's decree, many of the refugees were from Gdynia, and they left there before the 5th May. The *St. Louis* did not leave until May 13."

The consul general conveyed the legal niceties of the British argument to the Cuban government. An undersecretary of state promised it would be "duly considered, but in the meantime, 937 applies to the *Orduna*."

French diplomats received a similar answer when they raised the question of the *Flandre* passengers. Like the British, the French saw no way of pressing the matter further, and repaired to enjoy the Whitsun weekend.

The Sabbath service on the *St. Louis* had been poorly attended that Saturday morning; most passengers were too excited watching the activity surrounding the ship.

Although Alice Feilchenfeld and her four young children had not yet seen her husband, she had decided they should attend. The family were deeply religious, and had managed to eat kosher throughout the trip. Now was not the time to break with their beliefs. Alice Feilchenfeld had been pleased to see Recha Weiler present; she hoped the service would console her.

Elise Loewe had also persuaded her family to attend. She hoped the service would somehow give her husband strength: the prophetical reading dealt with the birth of Samson.

On deck, at one o'clock, the Spaniers and Josephs watched the *Orduna* weigh anchor and move slowly toward the quay.

"Excuse me," said Babette, "but weren't we here first?"

As always, Dr. Spanier had a comforting answer: "The *Orduna* is a much smaller ship, carrying many fewer passengers. I'm sure we'll be off after lunch."

Lunch came and went, and no one boarded or left the *St. Louis*. The Cuban police were by now freely mixing with the passengers, and to those who asked them when they would get off, their reply was always the same: *"Despues de Pentecostes."* It was reassuring, and seemed a genuine reason for the delay.

At three-thirty, a launch came alongside and a uniformed official boarded. Shortly afterward, Purser Mueller broadcast an announcement requesting Mrs. Meta Bonné, her children Beatrice and Jakob, and four Cuban passengers, to come to his office. About fifteen minutes later, the group were swiftly escorted to the launch, and their suitcases handed down by policemen.

They were the first passengers from the *St. Louis* to disembark.

Their departure caused immediate hope. Clearly it was possible to get off, but how? The reason the Cubans had been allowed to go was taken for granted, but the departure of the Bonnés was a mystery. Mrs. Bonné had kept to herself during the voyage; some knew five-year-old Beatrice had had her birthday the day before, as a party had been arranged in the ship's kindergarten for the child by a *St. Louis* stewardess. But there was no apparent reason why this one family had been singled out for special treatment.

Captain Schroeder sent for Mueller and demanded an explanation. The purser described how the immigration official had asked to see the Bonnés' passports, and looked at the visas inside. Mrs. Bonné had also produced her landing permits, each signed by Benitez, but, the purser reported, they were of no interest to the Cuban, who then said they could leave the ship.

Captain Schroeder shook his head, surprising the purser by saying the disembarkation of the passengers was a "bad sign," and asking Mueller to find out which other passengers had visas.

Dr. Max Aber had not seen the passengers come ashore. Along with many others, he was at Benitez's "bureau."

Much as Gloria Spira liked the refugee doctor, she could only tell him: "The situation is serious. President Bru won't let the people off. Minister Benitez has given me orders not to be disturbed. There is nothing I can do."

Max Aber walked back to the cafe where his friends, Dr. Bardeleben and Hans Fischer, were waiting to tell him of the disembarkation of the seven passengers.

From their sidewalk table, the men could see the *St. Louis*, its swastika hanging limply in the Cuban heat. All around them were relatives and friends of the passengers, bartering with the owners of rowboats for a trip out to the ship; twenty-five cents was the going rate; a few who had boats with outboard motors charged more.

From time to time, an agitated immigration officer passed the cafe. One stopped at Max Aber's table and told the doctor Gloria Spira had asked him to help get Renatta and Evelyne Aber off the ship. The official told Aber to meet him at noon the next day, Sunday.

During Saturday afternoon, refugees came off the *Orduna* and were greeted by people on the shore who had helped swell the crowd on the waterfront to some two thousand onlookers. But no more left the *St. Louis*.

As Max Aber returned to his room in the Havana suburb of Vedado around nine o'clock, he saw the *Orduna* slowly sailing past the *St. Louis* and out of the harbor; the German ship remained.

SUNDAY, MAY 28, 1939

The worry that the *St. Louis* might also sail while he was asleep kept Aber awake much of the night, but Sunday morning it was still anchored in the bay. Walking back to the harbor, a reverberating bang repeated again and again, made him quicken his step. He broke into a run. Guns were being fired. Dr. Aber relaxed only when he reached the waterfront: an arriving American warship had received a military salute.

Another ship also arrived that Sunday, May 28. The *Flandre* was now tied up where the *Orduna* had previously been berthed.

Max Aber went straight to the cafe where the immigration man had agreed to meet him. Just after one o'clock, Aber saw him, but the official brushed him off, saying he was "too busy with the French ship," and entered the customs area, where Aber could follow him no farther.

With growing concern, the doctor called on Luis Clasing, but the Hapag agent offered no help. Aber protested that "as a German and a holder of the Iron Cross I received while fighting for Germany in 1915, I deserve treatment for my daughters at least as good as those who've already gotten off."

Clasing told him that those who had disembarked from the *St. Louis* "were Cubans," and only forty-eight passengers had been allowed off the British *Orduna;* the others had been ordered to remain on board and the ship had gone in search of another port.

The doctor returned to the waterfront, depressed, and, after again visiting the *St. Louis* with his friends, saw the *Flandre* leave the harbor.

"Each day a ship comes in, disembarks passengers, and goes," said Dr. Bardeleben. "Why can't the same happen with ours?"

"Because they were English and French ships. Ours is German," replied Hans Fischer.

159

MONDAY, MAY 29, 1939

By nine o'clock in the morning of Monday, May 29, Max Aber had left his *pension* and was knocking on the door of the residence of José Estedes, the well-connected Cuban who had originally purchased the Benitez landing permits for his family, and then later introduced him to Secretary of State Remos, who had arranged the visas.

A maid answered the door. "Señor Estedes in Havana," she told the doctor.

"Where?" he asked.

The maid did not know.

Max Aber hurried to the town center, searching for the only man he now believed could help him. He walked the full length of the main business street, Obispo, without success. He tried the adjoining streets. By lunchtime, he had still not found José Estedes. Aber decided to try the better restaurants and hotels, and just after noon, he found Estedes at the Hotel Sevilla-Biltmore.

"Dr. Aber was in tears," Estedes later recalled. "He told me how his wife had left him for a German, and about his daughters on the *St. Louis* with no one to look after them. He seemed to me a fine, cultured man of capacity. He was in bad shape."

José Estedes took Max Aber to see Cuba's secretary of defense, the elderly, aristocratic friend of Batista, General Rafael Montalvo. Aber waited in an outer office while Estedes spoke to the general.

Montalvo listened as Estedes explained Aber's plight, then summoned two aides, an army captain, Gomez Gomez, and Captain Eiturey of the Cuban police. The general told them to go with Estedes and Aber and "get the girls off the ship."

The party traveled in the general's official car to Benitez's "bureau." Startled, Gloria Spira asked them to wait, but Aber was

160

staggered to see his three companions sweep past the secretary and into Benitez's private office.

Benitez was not impressed that they had come at the "suggestion" of General Montalvo.

"I will not permit anyone off the ship," he told the group. "If they put their money on the table—I want two million dollars, yes, that's what I said—they can come in. Otherwise there is no way they can come in."

At that point, Estedes was to recall, "Captain Gomez pulled out his revolver and said, 'You are under arrest.' It was unbelievable. Benitez went red in the face. He was speechless."

If the minister thought of using one of his own pistols, he gave no sign. Gomez kept his revolver trained squarely on the minister and, without taking his eyes off him, told Captain Eiturey to take Dr. Aber to the *St. Louis* and return with his daughters.

Max Aber followed the police captain to the crowded pier head. There the police motioned them through. They boarded a launch. "A little motor boat with a flag on," Dr. Aber noted, "steered by a huge Negro with only two teeth."

Standing at the top of the accommodation ladder of the *St. Louis*, waiting for them, was Captain Schroeder, surrounded by police, passengers, and crew.

At first, Max Aber thought the ship's captain "a Hitler man. He was in uniform. He clicked his heels together and said 'Good afternoon.' I was astonished. Then he talked to Captain Eiturey in broken Spanish. I couldn't understand. I just told him, 'I have come to pick up my daughters. They have visas.' Captain Schroeder said, 'Yes, you can take them.' He was very nice and friendly."

When Evelyne and Renatta were brought to their father, they were in bathing suits, and seemed to Aber "to be more interested in the fun they were having on the ship."

As they went away to change, passengers collected around the doctor, besieging him with questions: "When will *we* leave? Can *you* help us? What *is* going on in Havana?"

Max Aber hid his doubts:

"I tried to give them some consolation. I told them other refugees from Germany had been allowed in. They were crying. I didn't want to discourage them."

Renatta and Evelyne returned, dressed in lace dresses and light coats. When they got in the launch, Evelyne clung to her father, frightened of the big, black, toothless helmsman.

On the way to the shore, Dr. Aber remembered something "strange" his wife had written from Germany, telling him to "look carefully in Renatta's new coat." The doctor felt the lining. Sewn in the seams was jewelry. Though the little girl had refused to take the gold watch her mother had offered in Hamburg, she had been an unwitting accomplice in hoodwinking the Nazi customs officials.

Now, Cuban customs checks were waived as Captain Eiturey led the group through, and then escorted them across the street to Benitez's office.

"Gomez had kept his pistol pointed at Benitez the whole time Aber was away," Jose Estedes recalled, "and Benitez did not move or say a single word."

The party then drove back to Montalvo's office. Dr. Aber introduced his daughters to the general, and thanked him for "making me the happiest man alive."

The general telephoned Benitez:

"Thank you, Minister, for your cooperation and generous help."

There was a short pause before Montalvo put down the receiver.

"What did Benitez say?" asked Estedes.

"He said," replied General Montalvo, that "it was a pleasure to be of service."

President Bru had not allowed the weekend at his country estate to be disturbed by the refugee ship, but when he returned to the palace Monday afternoon, he learned that the saga of the *St. Louis* had been reported by *The New York Times,* and reporters were arriving in Havana from other newspapers to cover the story.

Bru did not welcome their presence. He still smarted from press jibes that he had often in the past demonstrated the courage of Batista's convictions. That sentiment, he mused, would soon be given the lie.

Even so, Bru was relieved to be told of Batista's "indisposition." Like Benitez, the president diagnosed it as one of convenience, and the danger of a head-on clash with Batista over the *St. Louis* seemed to Bru, at minimum, postponed. He was further heartened by the news that Benitez had been seen high-tailing it out of Havana that afternoon. The only decision remaining was whether Bru should order the ship to leave harbor before "Batista had a chance to surface." As he considered the question, Bru overheard his secretary taking a call from the Hapag office.

It was Robert Hoffman. The Abwehr agent had had a worrying weekend. Ever since his rebuff by the Cuban police on the *St. Louis*, Hoffman had considered how he could transfer the secret documents to Schiendick, what reason he could invent that would allow him onto the ship. A few moments before his call to Bru's secretary, Luis Clasing had provided the answer: he mentioned in passing to Hoffman that he had heard from Milton Goldsmith that a passenger committee had been formed on the *St. Louis;* Goldsmith had been given permission to board the ship to meet them.

Preoccupied with the problem of what to do with the 250 passengers in Havana who had booked passage on the *St. Louis* for its return voyage to Hamburg via Lisbon, and wishing not to face Captain Schroeder again, Clasing had agreed that Hoffman might try to visit the ship to meet the committee as his representative.

Hoffman's inquiry to Bru's secretary brought a favorable reply. With Batista and Benitez out of the way, Bru decided to be "generous." If Hoffman went to the ship at once, and did not stay aboard longer than the time the president had granted to Milton Goldsmith, he could visit the ship.

The German agent was jubilant. Taking his cane, magazines, and pens containing the secrets, he went immediately to the pier head. There he was stopped. Though the Cuban police officer, on checking Hoffman's credentials, agreed that permission had been granted for him to go to the *St. Louis*, he "regretted nothing could be taken to the ship."

Hoffman realized that if he objected too strongly, the police might become suspicious. He handed over the walking stick; the officer requested the magazines as well. Watched by press men, Hoffman did as he was asked, pleased at least that there seemed no

American agents present. With two pens which contained microfilm in the barrels protruding from his handkerchief pocket, the Abwehr agent walked to the Hapag launch.

From the bridge wing the captain watched Robert Hoffman climbing the accommodation ladder, and ordered that he should immediately report to his cabin.

There, after a perfunctory introduction, the captain demanded to know what news Hoffman brought from Luis Clasing about disembarking the passengers.

"None," replied Hoffman. "And I will be perfectly frank. Your passengers do not interest me."

"What!" stormed Schroeder. "My God, they had better —otherwise I'll have you thrown off this ship."

"I don't think so, Captain," replied Hoffman. "I don't think you have the authority to do that."

Hoffman then identified himself as the senior Abwehr agent in Cuba, and made it clear that, should the situation arise, he could rely "on the backing of Admiral Canaris himself."

Unable to assimilate what he had heard, the captain remained silent, feeling the atmosphere in his cabin had been "poisoned." Then Gustav Schroeder asked how the Abwehr was involved with his ship.

"There is no need for you to know that, Captain," said Hoffman. "All you need to know is what you will do now—"

"By God, you're not giving me orders!"

"They are not my orders. They come from Berlin. If you choose to disobey them, that is a matter for you. And so will be the consequences."

The oppressive silence returned to the cabin as Gustav Schroeder weighed what he had been told, bitterly regretting that he had let this self-assured, arrogant man on his ship, hating his power to summon help from Canaris, a figure the captain knew only by reputation as a member of the Nazi clique now ruling Germany.

Hoffman spoke again, asking if the crew had been granted shore leave.

Schroeder shook his head.

"Then you will do so."

The captain made no reply, merely nodding agreement, not trusting himself to speak.

"Thank you. The first group will go ashore this evening. I will settle arrangements with your purser."

"And then?"

Hoffman looked puzzled.

"What happens to my passengers?"

"Captain. I have already made it clear they are no concern of mine. But, if it will help you, the Americans are sending two people down here from New York tomorrow. No doubt they will find a solution."

With that, Hoffman walked out of the cabin.

For the first time since leaving Hamburg, Gustav Schroeder felt beaten.

Being deceived by Holthusen was one thing; being exploited by Goebbels was another; they were events outside his immediate influence.

But Hoffman was different: he *was* immediate; he had stood in the captain's cabin, and threatened him. Hoffman had introduced the presence of the Abwehr on board. And, Schroeder thought bitterly, "I had been unable to overcome those threats, or excise the Abwehr." He had a deep sense of failure, an attitude of mind which already had begun to affect his decision making and would later make him appear even more isolated to the passengers he wanted to help.

His first decision after Hoffman left was to abandon any thought of going ashore to investigate matters for himself, and to remain on board pending the outcome of any discussions the American negotiators would have with Cuban officials.

It was his second error of judgment since the start of the voyage, and it was a far more serious one than his first mistake, his decision to stay aloof from the passengers. For what the captain did not appreciate was that on this Monday afternoon, his "view from the bridge" of the worsening crisis was increasingly confined.

Robert Hoffman found Purser Mueller in his office, explained that the captain had granted shore leave, and suggested that a launch filled with crew should go ashore that evening.

"Would you also like to pick those to go?" inquired Mueller sarcastically.

"I'll leave that to you. But make sure the ship's *Orstgrup-penleiter* is among them. I want to talk to him about crew morale."

"You can do that now," retorted the purser.

In uncomfortable silence, the two men waited for Otto Schiendick. When the steward arrived, Hoffman pointedly asked the purser to leave.

Mueller was about to protest, saw the look on Hoffman's face, and slammed shut his office door.

Hoffman looked carefully at the man who had come over 4000 miles to keep this *Treff*—and was, as an Abwehr report later showed, singularly unimpressed.

Years would pass before the substance of their meeting, as with much else involving the two men, became available, pieced together from information provided by their former colleagues and from the files of German, American, and British intelligence. From these, it is clear that Hoffman summed up Schiendick as a servile, self-aggrandizing man. Schiendick had produced his notebook, filled with the trivia he had written down about Schroeder and Mueller, adding: "They are not party men and should be removed."

Hoffman indicated he was not interested in such tittle-tattle, and handed over the two fountain pens and their precious microfilm, no doubt saying that his only concern was the completion of Operation Sunshine. He briefed the steward on the pickup and on the situation ashore, telling him about the American and Cuban secret service men prowling the Havana waterfront.

However little Hoffman thought of Schiendick, like Gustav Schroeder, the spymaster found himself in a situation over which he had no control. There could be no question of aborting the mission, nor was there any way of replacing the steward as a courier. He, like Schroeder, was saddled with Schiendick.

At the same time another meeting was taking place on board between Milton Goldsmith and the passenger committee. The refugee director had been blunt from the outset, underlining that even with the imminent arrival of the Joint representatives from New York, the outlook was grim.

The committee members, their belief that the delay in disembarking was only caused by the holiday weekend now shattered, waited uneasily for the tired, middle-aged man to continue.

Goldsmith wished he had not been so outspoken. The men grouped around him explained that they had received no indication from the captain, or anyone else, that for the last three days their fate was in the balance. Milton Goldsmith guessed, accurately, that the captain himself was probably unaware of the true situation.

Into this already tense and depressed atmosphere walked Hoffman. Goldsmith introduced him as the assistant manager of Hapag in Havana, and expressed surprise when Hoffman "regretted" he had no positive news.

"When will these people get off?" pressed Goldsmith.

Hoffman shrugged. It was "all a matter of the proper authorities."

"Who, exactly, are they?" demanded Josef Joseph.

"Ultimately, the president of Cuba," replied Hoffman.

"Has he been approached by your office?" asked Goldsmith.

"Yes—and by others."

"And?"

"Herr Goldsmith, this is Cuba. You know as well as I that you cannot push. Cuba didn't ask these people to come."

"But Cuba, like Hapag, was quite happy to take their money."

Hoffman shrugged again.

"What will happen?" asked Josef Joseph.

Robert Hoffman said he did not know, nor, it seemed to the dejected passenger committee, did he much care.

With growing alarm they turned to Goldsmith, who outlined a plan to bring public pressure to bear.

Into a notebook, Dr. Max Weiss wrote the minutes of the proposal: "Goldsmith asks us to obtain three hundred names of friends or relatives of passengers in U.S. to give to the Joint, who will then cable influential Americans for help. Goldsmith says if we can't land in Havana he will work night and day to land us somewhere else. He says there is no question of us returning to Germany, and we must impress that upon the passengers."

The meeting ended as purser Mueller and a Cuban policeman arrived to say that Hoffman and Goldsmith's visiting time was over. While the committee members walked with Goldsmith to the accommodation ladder, Robert Hoffman again told Mueller to see to it that Otto Schiendick was among those crew members granted shore leave that night. By way of explanation, Hoffman added: "We did not complete our talk about crew morale."

After Schiendick's meeting with Hoffman, and while Hoffman was with the passenger committee, the steward arranged to see the ship's first officer, Klaus Ostermeyer, about the subject of crew morale. He was to find Ostermeyer surprisingly receptive to his scheme.

During his regular tours of the *St. Louis*, Ostermeyer had become aware of the increasing tenseness aboard ship. Since Captain Schroeder had delegated to him the responsibility for gauging the passenger's mood, Ostermeyer had mixed frequently with them, taking tea and coffee and buying drinks, and come to the conclusion that the monotony of three days' inactivity was causing tension.

There had been complaints from the tourist passengers that those in the first class were receiving "better treatment," when, under the circumstances, they argued, all should be treated equally. Ostermeyer ordered that the usual demarcation between the classes should be abolished, with passengers of both classes allowed to make equal use of all the ship's amenities.

But it was Schiendick who suggested to Ostermeyer that the ship itself and, more particularly, its crew were in danger. Reminding the first officer of his responsibility for the crew's morale, Schiendick told Ostermeyer he believed that a search of the ship should be made for "explosives or other dangerous devices." Such a search, he went on, was necessary "because of the situation we find ourselves in as a result of carrying these people." It would go some way toward alleviating the foreboding of crew members who "fear for their lives because of the way some passengers are acting."

Ostermeyer thought Schiendick was exaggerating; still, the

seeds of uncertainty had been sown, and he authorized a spot check of passenger cabins and public areas, unaware that Schiendick's reasons for suggesting the search were virtually the opposite to those he had given the first officer.

At four-thirty in the afternoon, Robert Hoffman left the *St. Louis,* having delayed his departure in the Hapag launch until Milton Goldsmith had made his way ashore in the boat that had brought him. The Abwehr agent was anxious to ensure that as few persons as possible saw him collect the cane and magazines containing the secrets for Schiendick which he had left with the Cuban police at the pier head.

As he walked with them to the Hapag office, he was again relieved to see that his arrival back on shore had not been witnessed by either Rowell or Barber, the American attachés.

At the office, Hoffman found Luis Clasing too busy. He did not ask how Hoffman's visit to the ship had gone.

During the afternoon, Clasing learned that Manuel Benitez had disappeared, and received two cables from Claus-Gottfried Holthusen, each impatiently insisting that he extricate the company from any blame in the situation. Holthusen had granted Clasing's request that the *St. Louis*'s departure be delayed a further two days. Trusting that the American negotiators would have succeeded by then, Clasing now cabled Hamburg:

HOPEFUL SITUATION RESOLVED BY WEDNESDAY. AM IN CONTACT HIGHEST CUBAN AUTHORITIES. SITUATION ON SHIP CALM. CAPTAIN AND CREW DOING ALL POSSIBLE TO ASSIST PASSENGERS.

Clasing then set out to make good his boast of top-level talks. A telephone call to Bru's office brought the response that the president did not discuss "such matters with commercial companies." Another call to the secretary of labor's office, drew the reply that if Clasing cared to read the newspapers, he would find that the secretary's views had already been stated: he was firmly opposed to further immigration.

Soon after five o'clock, he reached the secretary of state, Juan Remos. Clasing had held no great hope of getting past the outer secretariat and was astonished to be put through to the minister.

Remos listened sympathetically to Clasing's suggestion that

250 passengers be taken off the ship and put in a quarantine camp, so making room for the 250 passengers in Havana waiting for passage back to Europe on the *St. Louis.*

The minister said the idea would be considered, but it would be agonizing to have to select who would be allowed to leave the ship, and who would have to return to Germany. Clasing suggested that the passengers draw lots; Remos told him that that attitude hardly suggested that he cared in any way for his charges.

By late Monday afternoon, Max Loewe's paranoid schizophrenia, with its symptoms of being watched, followed, talked about, and plotted against, was acute. He told his wife there were "S.S. and Gestapo on board," specifically there to search him out and take him back to the concentration camp he had managed to avoid when he had been in hiding in Germany. Every moment longer he was detained on the *St. Louis,* Loewe believed, brought him closer to detection.

Desperately trying to conceal her own distress over his suffering, Elise Loewe tried hard to divert her husband's thoughts. That Monday morning she had organized a small family party in their cabin to mark the thirteenth birthday of their son, Fritz. It had not eased her husband's burden, and only reminded him they had lost everything of value when the trunk containing their belongings had been sent by the German authorities to Shanghai; the group had barely a change of clothes among their hand luggage, let alone a present to give Fritz for his birthday.

Max Loewe's fantasies were not far from the truth. The six Gestapo "firemen," who hated all the passengers on the ship, had managed to hide those feelings on the journey from Hamburg from all but a few, who simply thought them "different somehow from the rest of the crew." Since docking in Havana, the "firemen" had made their presence increasingly felt. They had patrolled the ship in pairs, unsmiling, chevying passengers at every opportunity. They were, according to Babette Spanier, especially threatening toward children. She had warned her twin daughters to keep well clear of the patrols.

Now, with Ostermeyer's authority to search the ship for bombs, the way was open for the "firemen" to do as Schiendick had planned, while posing as the official protectors of the passengers and crew. Two of them called on Recha Weiler and abruptly blew out the candles she was burning to mourn the death of her husband. The candles were, they sharply reminded the old lady, a "dangerous fire hazard." When she tried to explain the reason for them, one of the men interrupted: "Candles won't help him where he's gone."

But it was Aaron Pozner the men singled out for the toughest treatment.

He was standing at the stern of the *St. Louis,* not far from where the ship's swastika hung. During the three days they had been in port, Pozner had eaten little, spending as much time on deck as possible, moving from one shaded spot to another. Down below where the restaurants were, the ship was hot and airless, and many passengers had complained that the heavy food was totally unsuitable in the humid Havana heat. The sun had sent the temperature to nearly 100 degrees on the decks.

"You are to come with us."

The hand on his shoulder combined with the tone of the voice made Pozner swing around in fright.

"We must search your cabin. You have the key?"

The "firemen" placed themselves on either side of Pozner, and motioned him forward. To his repeated "Why my cabin?" they gave no answer, speaking only once when he walked toward a lift. He was told they "preferred to go down by the stairs, where we can look out for other suspicious persons."

Pozner unlocked the door to D-375, an inside cabin on the lowest passenger deck on the ship, and let the men in. They shut the door behind them, locked it, and ransacked the room, throwing everything on the floor, smashing against the washbasin a framed picture of his wife and children. As he bent down to pick it up one of them knocked Pozner to the floor. The other opened his suitcase, neatly packed ready for disembarkation, and scattered its few contents around the cabin, pausing only to rip to pieces a letter he had received from his wife at Cherbourg, and the Spanish phrase book. They missed the diary in his pocket.

Satisfied, the Gestapo men left. It was time Pozner had his head shaved again, the last man said as he went out. The former inmate of Dachau then knew why he had been beaten.

Even the crew were too frightened to object about the "firemen's" maltreatment of passengers; they too, they later admitted, feared revenge if they protested.

Not everyone on the *St. Louis* knew of the "search." With more than 1100 on board including crew, scattered throughout a large ship, many events took place of which the majority were totally unaware. What was not known was later invented and passed on, making it difficult to disentangle the truth from fiction. Passengers began to mingle less among themselves, preferring to keep to their established friends whom they knew they could trust.

On deck Rosemarie Bergmann looked excitedly down at a small boat bobbing amidships. Standing in the boat was a man holding a white dog.

"It's Oshey," shouted Rosemarie to her husband.

It was their fox terrier, which had traveled ahead of them on a freighter from Bremen. From now on, it would be brought out each day for them to see, but even Oshey was not allowed onto the ship.

At about five-thirty, Purser Mueller and a bevy of stewards and seamen took up position at the top of the accommodation ladder. Minutes later, fifteen passengers, most of whom had boarded at Cherbourg and were either Cuban or Spanish, stepped down the ladder into a waiting launch, which sped toward the shore. Their departure was so quick that few passengers noticed it. Aaron Pozner was one who did.

Trying to take his mind off what had happened to him, and afraid the Gestapo men might return, he had left his cabin to be among the security of other people. Now he watched the launch return empty after discharging its fifteen passengers. Stewards and seamen began loading cases into the launch. When his time came, Pozner wrote later in his diary, "I will carry my own case ashore."

Around 6 P.M. the launch returned to take a party of crewmen into Havana. Otto Schiendick was among them. As the launch sped across the bay he warned the seamen that they must not comment to any waiting newspaperman about the ship or its

passengers because it would "only be used to Germany's det-
riment." As the launch edged toward the Ward Line pier, his
colleagues noticed that Schiendick grew restive.

His anxiety further increased when they were each subjected
to a thorough search by Cuban officials, and questioned and photographed by the newspapermen keeping a vigil outside the immigration hall.

Seeking an interview, the reporters were balked by the crew's
insisting in German that they did not understand English. Those
same reporters would undoubtedly have been intrigued by Otto
Schiendick's first action after he left the pier. At a newsstand he
bought a number of English-language magazines, explaining to
the other crewmen that he wanted to "show his friends back
home the sort of lies foreigners write about Germany."

Next he led them to a gift shop, and there Schiendick surprised
his colleages by buying, and handing them, walking sticks. It was
the first time they could recall the steward's ever showing such
generosity, but they accepted it at face value, never suspecting
they had become pawns in Robert Hoffman's plan to complete the
last stage of Operation Sunshine.

As they filtered into the town, the crewmen split up into
smaller groups, and somewhere along the way Schiendick detached himself from one of those groups and made his way to the
Hapag office.

Inside, in Robert Hoffman's office, Schiendick exchanged his
recently purchased cane and magazines for the identical ones
Hoffman had carefully prepared to hold the remaining American
secrets.

Moments later Schiendick was back in the crowded Havana
streets, joined up with other members of the crew, and together
they returned to the Ward Line pier, their shore leave at an end.

Again the seamen were subjected to a thorough search, but the
Cubans hardly glanced at their walking sticks or the magazines
under Schiendick's arm.

Robert Hoffman watched from a safe distance and shortly
afterward cabled Berlin that his part in Operation Sunshine was
over.

Neither Rowell nor Barber had followed Otto Schiendick. To

them, he was just one of the crew who had gone ashore, and there was no reason for them to suspect that he was any different from the others.

As the crew returned, they saw that the number of police boats circling the ship had increased. Many swept the hull and super-structure with searchlights.

To Rosemarie Bergmann, it seemed the passengers were now imprisoned; Aaron Pozner, in his cabin, saw the lights pass his porthole and was reminded of those that scanned the Dachau compound.

Max Loewe's thoughts of being a wanted man remained with him: he often wandered off alone. Ruth and Fritz had gone in search of their father, but the ship had any number of hiding places. When he returned, he could not explain where he had been or why he had gone. Of all the people on the *St. Louis*, none was so tragic and pitiful a figure as this prematurely aged man.

TUESDAY, MAY 30, 1939

On Tuesday morning, the passenger committee filed into the captain's day cabin. Still shocked at Hoffman's revelation that the ship was somehow involved with the Abwehr and espionage, he had, nevertheless spent time preparing himself for this meeting, the first he had convened since forming the committee.

Mueller, the purser, had briefed him on the committee's earlier meeting with Milton Goldsmith. Of necessity the description was sketchy; the purser had gleaned sparse information by adroit questioning of the members after the meeting had ended. But the captain realized that Goldsmith's attitude had brought gloom.

Now, he found them not only anxious but also resentful. They believed he had been less than forthcoming in his earlier promise of regular consultations. Schroeder saw the justice of their complaint and conceded that, on reflection, he should have summoned them earlier; he had not done so because he had hoped he would have better news if he waited.

"And have you?" asked Josef Joseph somberly.

The captain, with no news from Luis Clasing, and having decided not to go ashore and seek his own answer to that question, could only reply: "Things don't look good, but we must never lose hope."

It was honest enough, but it gave rise to new uncertainties. They had expected more than talk of hope. Some even wondered whether this little man facing them really had the stature to resolve the crisis. They mistook his tiredness for lethargy, and his silence for indecision.

Like Milton Goldsmith, the captain was convinced that the committee would carry out specific tasks well, but would be unable to initiate their own ideas. Therefore, he reasoned, if they could be imbued with a sense of purpose, one he must give them, it would communicate itself to the other passengers.

Taking pains to convey a feeling of being "part of an equal partnership," Gustav Schroeder proposed that the committee itself cable influential figures to intercede. Goldsmith had suggested a similar idea, but this time the initiative would be in the committee's hands, and it would "be seen by all on board that you are striving to solve matters."

The committee accepted the idea, and decided the first message should go to the wife of President Bru, the man they knew controlled their immediate fate. To her they cabled:

OVER 900 PASSENGERS, 400 WOMEN AND CHILDREN, ASK YOU TO USE YOUR INFLUENCE AND HELP US OUT OF THIS TERRIBLE SITUATION. TRADITIONAL HUMANITARIANISM OF YOUR COUNTRY AND YOUR WOMAN'S FEELINGS GIVE US HOPE THAT YOU WILL NOT REFUSE OUR REQUEST.

Similar telegrams were sent to public figures in the United States, though the committee decided it would be premature at this stage to call for the help of President Franklin Roosevelt.

While they drafted their messages and dispatched them, taking care, at Schroeder's suggestion, to post carbons for other passengers to see on the ship's notice boards, a seaplane landed close to the ship.

It brought Lawrence Berenson and Cecilia Razovsky from New York. Ashore, they went directly to the Relief Committee office, where Milton Goldsmith and Laura Margolis carefully briefed them on all developments.

"It will take money more than anything else to buy them their freedom," Berenson said.

On board the *St. Louis* Max Loewe had watched the plane land with great excitement. But at three o'clock this Tuesday afternoon, the day after his son's thirteenth birthday, Max Loewe entered a lavatory on A Deck. He locked the door and slashed his wrists with a straight razor. He walked past the ship's doctor's office on his way to the deck, and at exactly the spot where Moritz Weiler's body had been put over the side, and where Leonid Berg had jumped to his death, Max Loewe leaped over the rail.

Captain Schroeder and the first officer, Ostermeyer, standing on the port bridge wing, heard Max Loewe's scream as he entered the water. The captain shouted for a long blast on the ship's siren—traditional signal for "man overboard"—and then followed Ostermeyer, who was already racing along the promenade deck.

Purser Mueller was on the boat deck, near lifeboat number 8, when the siren sounded. He peered down at the water and saw nothing. He looked toward the bridge, where the entire watch was crowded on the port wing, gesticulating and shouting toward the sea. He looked down again and saw Loewe thrashing in "a pool of his own blood." Mueller rushed to the nearby officer's quarters, where the night watch were still asleep, and bellowed: "Out! Out! Man overboard!"

In the stern of B deck, stewards and deckhands, including Otto Schiendick, were spending an off-duty period sunbathing. They jumped to their feet and ran to the rail. Below, a police boat went into a sharp turn as other launches also made for the *St. Louis*.

Some sixty feet below Otto Schiendick, a couple of cable lengths out from the hull, Max Loewe had somehow raised his arms over his head and was clawing at his exposed veins, "pulling at them like rubber bands."

Above, from A deck, came a woman's anguished voice, almost lost in the piercing cries from Max Loewe.

On B deck, the powerful figure of leading seaman Heinrich Meier elbowed Schiendick aside.

"Nein!" Otto Schiendick's shout halted Meier as he clambered on top of the rail. He turned for a moment to look at the steward and then dived into the water, dimly aware of the uproar sweeping the ship's upper decks.

Meier was one of the ship's best swimmers. Even so, the impact of the sea from the height he dived slapped hard against him. Underwater for seconds, he shot to the surface, and found his hands and body stained with Loewe's blood. Shouting filled his ears; Meier looked up, but could not make out the words. Then, from close by, he heard: "Murderers! They will never get me!"

The seaman reached Max Loewe and lunged at him, seeking a hold. Loewe spun away and plunged beneath the water. Meier dived after him, grabbed him by the hair, and pulled the desperate man to the surface. Max Loewe called out again: "Let me die!" as another sound came to Meier, blocking out the shouting. He turned and saw the police boat; hands reached down and pulled Loewe out of the water. Moments later Meier too flopped into the launch.

Loewe lay moaning in the boat's well, blood draining from his wrists. A policeman began to bandage his wounds, but with a sudden burst of strength, Loewe kicked the officer clear, tore at the tourniquet, and went toward the water, screaming again and again, "Let me die, let me die!"

Meier grabbed him and the pair rolled back into the boat. Two policemen straddled Loewe, rebandaged his wrists, and held him down as the boat turned to the shore.

At that moment the St. Louis's siren stopped.

On the boat deck, purser Mueller and the off-duty watch he had roused swung number 8 lifeboat back on its davits. On the promenade deck, Schroeder and Ostermeyer walked past weeping passengers back to the bridge.

Otto Schiendick made the only immediate comment on the tragedy. Turning to the other stewards, he said: "Meier was a fool to risk his life. He won't be thanked for it." Schiendick was wrong.

The ship's siren had caused consternation along the Havana waterfront, where several thousand people kept vigil over the St. Louis. Word spread like a brushfire that the siren signaled the ship's departure.

Robert Hoffman heard the blast and left immediately to investigate; President Bru's siesta was disturbed and he told his secretary to warn Hapag that such "demonstrations" would not help matters; Laura Margolis stopped the discussion she was having with Cecilia Razovsky about where the passengers would be accommodated on landing.

When Hoffman reached the Ward Line pier he found an ambulance backed close to the water. Standing nearby were attachés Rowell and Barber. Terrified that something had happened to Otto Schiendick and the secret documents, he pushed his way forward to look inside the ambulance. Max Loewe lay strapped on a stretcher, barely conscious. Seated beside him was Meier and two policemen. One of them warned everyone to stay clear, and pulled the door shut as photographers jostled for position. Its siren wailing, the ambulance drove from the pier to the Calixto García Hospital.

On admission, Max Loewe was sedated and put in a guarded room; Meier was given a pair of pajamas and coffee while his clothes dried.

The drama provided reporters with the break they needed. They pooled their resources to cover the hospital and comb the waterfront for eyewitness reaction. Two of them talked and bribed their way through the police cordon on the pier and chartered a boat to take them to the *St. Louis*. They nosed their way through the flotilla of craft around the ship and tied up at the accommodation ladder. With that confident manner peculiar to police and press, they went aboard, telling the Cubans guarding the ladder top that they had been sent to investigate the incident. They bluffed a gullible ship's officer to direct them to Elise Loewe, and then asked him to muster other eyewitnesses.

Elise Loewe, Fritz and Ruth, had gone to their cabins as soon as they heard the news. When the reporters arrived, they found two well-built passengers, George and Carl Lenneberg, standing in their way. Fearing just such an intrusion, they had stationed themselves outside the cabin. They eyed the reporters coldly. The newsmen tried another bluff, but the brothers would not move. Just as a scuffle was about to break out, the ship's officer arrived to say he had assembled some eyewitnesses on deck.

Realizing that they could not see Elise Loewe, the reporters admitted their identity, and silenced the angry murmurs by changing the subject to mention the arrival of Berenson and Razovsky. Many passengers did not know of this development, and directed a barrage of questions at the reporters, who did little to dispel their anxiety.

First Officer Ostermeyer ordered the newsmen off the ship, a gesture misunderstood by a few passengers, who from then on believed that the ship's officers had a policy of keeping the outside world uninformed of their plight.

But the reporters had seen enough to draw a graphic picture of the ship "that shames the world." Within hours of their returning to shore, that description was radioed to a dozen countries. It was almost opposite to the news reports Gustav Schroeder had become used to hearing; ever since the St. Louis had arrived on Saturday, Nazi news broadcast summaries to the effect that Cuba, "and soon the whole world," would show its attitude toward the refugees by rejecting his passengers.

Though the captain hoped this confident prediction would be proven wrong by the efforts of Berenson, his private diary spoke of "going back to Hamburg and having to live with my conscience." Like everyone else on the ship, the captain still found himself short on facts in a sea of conjecture. His notes to Clasing had brought only the vaguest of replies; his latest cable to Hamburg demanding to know what action he should take when the two-day extension expired had elicited no reply whatsoever. Conditions on board added to his worries. Instead of relying solely on Oster-meyer, he had begun to take soundings himself among officers and a few passengers.

Assistant purser Hans Reich, who had established a convivial arrangement with several of the prettiest girls on board, told the captain he had the impression they thought the delay was due solely to Cuban inefficiency; certainly, from Reich's point of view, they seemed happy enough to while away their days by the pool, and their evenings in his company.

Dr. Spanier took the more guarded view that the general feeling was "not uniform throughout the ship. It differs from person to person, and from moment to moment." The relationship between the two men had been maintained, even strengthened, despite Dr. Spanier's refusal to serve on the passenger committee. The captain genuinely liked the soft-spoken doctor, finding him not only a useful sounding board but a valuable independent, and outspoken, voice. Dr. Spanier for his part looked forward to any meeting with the captain because, as he said, "I thought he was in an impossible position and I wanted to be of use to him in any way I could—apart from serving on the committee."

From his soundings, and those of Ostermeyer, the captain judged the mood of his ship as "fragile."

Max Loewe's action had broken that fragility. Within an hour of the incident, Schroeder received reports of passenger reaction; many said Loewe jumped through a combination of fear of the future and harassment from the crew.

The last charge produced an explosion from Schroeder. He summoned all deck officers and blasted them in his saltiest language, warning of the severest reprimands if such conduct continued. He had the Gestapo "firemen" marched before him. Although word had not reached him of the way they had carried out their "search for explosives," the captain knew their reputation, and threatened to put them ashore if he heard the slightest criticism of their behavior. Then he sent for Schiendick and subjected him to the most violent tirade of all for not maintaining the "proper standards" as ship's *Ortsgruppenleiter.*

The steward, doubtless anxious only that the *St. Louis* returned to Germany quickly, mumbled to the captain that he would "be more observant in future."

Loewe's jump and the arrival of Berenson and Razovsky brought home to the passengers the real gravity of their position: those who had been quiet now became militant; the outspoken and confident became silent.

Leo Jockl, during a later afternoon visit to the bridge with the captain's tea tray, felt a ray of hope about the outcome of the voyage. He found Schroeder and Ostermeyer pouring over charts of the American coast.

Purser Mueller contacted the senior Cuban policeman on the gangway and pleaded with him to let Elise Loewe go ashore to see her husband. The officer eventually agreed to convey the request to the authorities, but returned with the answer that no passenger would be allowed to leave the ship under any circumstances.

Unaware of Max Loewe's act, or its repercussions, American ambassador Butler Wright waited at home for the Cuban secretary of state, Juan Remos. Wright had carefully prepared himself for the "informal meeting" during an all-morning conference with his consul general, Coert du Bois.

Du Bois had explained that telegrams were beginning to flood into his office on behalf of the *St. Louis* passengers. Because there were so many he had drafted a standard reply to be used for all of them, which the State Department in Washington had approved. It read:

ACKNOWLEDGING YOUR TELEGRAM RE EUROPEAN REFUGEES ON
BOARD STEAMER SAINT LOUIS PLEASE BE ASSURED CONSULATE
GENERAL DOING EVERYTHING IT PROPERLY CAN ALONG THE LINE OF
UNOFFICIAL GOOD OFFICES. HUMANITARIAN ASPECTS OF SITUATION
HAVE BEEN EMPHASIZED TO CUBAN GOVERNMENT. DEPARTMENT OF
STATE IS BEING KEPT CURRENTLY INFORMED.

Despite approval for his statement implying that pressure was being brought to bear on the Cuban government by America, du Bois was told that Undersecretary of State Sumner Welles was "distinctly against making representations" to the Cuban authorities about the refugees.

Ambassador Wright had wondered whether the view of Welles, notoriously ambitious and jealous of the power of Secretary of State Cordell Hull, coincided with that of President Roosevelt. Du Bois replied that the State Department had told him that various organizations were requesting eminent Americans to speak to the president, urging him to make direct representations to the Cuban government, but "no instructions along those lines had yet come from the White House."

The two men had then discussed whether, in the circumstances, the matter could properly be raised by the ambassador during his meeting with Remos. Much, they decided, depended on Remos himself.

Forty-three, a former university professor, Remos was known as a liberal intellectual. He had a considerable reputation as an author; at the age of fifteen he had written a history of the fall of the Bastille, and soon after he produced a standard work on the life of Donizetti. More important, Wright knew that Remos had the confidence of Bru. A few months earlier, Batista had announced the resignation of Remos; the president had refused to accept it, and Remos stayed on. The ambassador felt, therefore, that Remos was a man of considerable courage, to whom a carefully chosen word or two would not go amiss.

Secretary of State Remos arrived at the ambassador's residence precisely at four o'clock. After a suitable time exchanging pleasantries, Wright "improved the opportunity to inquire about the present status of the refugees on the *St. Louis.*"

Remos expressed "deep concern," and regretted that the situation had arisen through the "pernicious practice of a member of my government, compounded by Hapag's willingness to accept bookings without ensuring that passengers had a visa, in direct violation of my requests to them."

Wright asked for the secretary's own view on what should happen. "My personal opinion is that the aliens on the *St. Louis* should be admitted," Remos told Wright. "If they are not, the outcry in the press, and the statements which would be made about the way the Cuban government conducted itself, would be most derogatory."

Ambassador Wright hinted agreement. Then, calling on the skill thirty years in diplomacy had taught him, and while delicately affirming that he was acting "without instructions," the ambassador gently reminded the secretary of President Roosevelt's appeal to all nations to take into account "humanitarian considerations" when dealing with the refugees.

Juan Remos thanked the ambassador for his "informal good offices," making it clear that he appreciated that the observations were made "solely in a desire to prove of assistance to my country." As he left, he said the entire matter was to be discussed by the cabinet the next morning, and in the meantime the departure of the *St. Louis* would be delayed.

Ambassador Wright was pleased with the outcome of his talk. In a confidential report to Secretary of State Cordell Hull, he wrote: "I gained the impression that the awkwardness of the situation is becoming increasingly evident to Cuban government authorities."

Lawrence Berenson and Cecilia Razovsky had checked into adjoining suites in the Hotel Sevilla-Biltmore, one of the best in a city of expensive hotels. On the same floor were three of Hoffman's agents, who spent an anxious time believing the Joint representatives were from the F.B.I.

After checking in, Razovsky had gone back to see Laura Margolis, while Berenson began a marathon telephone session to his contacts. They were many. Berenson spoke fluent Spanish, was a prominent New York lawyer, and had been president of the Cuban Chamber of Commerce in the U. S. For all his flamboyant manner, he was a shrewd judge of when to act the corporation lawyer, and when the public relations man.

Berenson soon had little doubt that his original assessment was right. Money *would* be the key, probably the only, factor. The question was, To whom should it be offered, when would be the right moment, and above all, how much? He had come to Havana with no fixed sum in mind, simply authority from the Joint in New York "to negotiate." That, he knew, would mean having to go through the tedious procedure of regularly contacting and keeping informed the head office in New York. And the head office, Milton Goldsmith had told him, was "not always understanding."

Berenson's first contacts in Havana warned him that any approach to President Bru would be rebuffed at this stage. Nor was a search for Manuel Benitez to be seriously considered. He had left town, trumpeting that he wanted two million dollars to "guarantee" the passengers' freedom. It was a figure that Berenson believed showed at least a temporary aberration.

Berenson's feelers among other cabinet ministers left little doubt that they would follow Bru's dictates. He did not know Remos. That left Batista.

After several calls, Berenson realized Batista was avoiding him. Though they were friends, intermediaries hinted that the army chief saw no political gain to be made from the *St. Louis,* at least not for the moment. Batista, it seemed, was content "to sit this one out and watch Bru wriggle." Berenson was not depondent. He knew Cuban politicians well enough to know they would change their position with the first shift in public opinion. Max Loewe's action might provide the impetus for that change.

When reporters knocked at Berenson's door, he was friendly and forthcoming. He had come, he said, from New York to avoid just such tragedies. How desperate the position already was could be judged from Loewe's behavior. The issue now was, How many more would follow Loewe's example rather than be returned to Germany?

At 5:30 P.M., leading seaman Heinrich Meier returned to the *St. Louis* and a hero's welcome from crew and passengers alike. He brought the news that Max Loewe would "probably live."

The passengers had taken up a collection for Meier, and Captain Schroeder presented it to him. It totaled 150 Reichsmarks, a considerable sum considering the financial state of the refugees.

Schroeder, outwardly relaxed and smiling, hoped his public appearance would diffuse the tense atmosphere on board. Earlier he had listened in silence as the passenger committee had spoken of an "impending disaster unless good news came soon."

Now, as he returned to his cabin, Schroeder was met by Ostermeyer, who informed him that cabin 76 on A deck was locked from the inside and had not answered the purser's repeated knocking. The cabin was only a few feet from the spot where Max Loewe had slashed his wrists.

Captain Schroeder ordered the door be forced open and the ship's doctor despatched to the scene. A seaman jimmied open the door and Dr. Glauner and Purser Mueller entered 76. Its sole occupant, Dr. Fritz Herrmann, a middle-aged physician from Munich, lay undressed on the bed, unconscious. On a side table was a syringe and a row of empty ampules.

"Will he live?" asked Mueller.

"Who knows? And how many more will there be?" demanded Dr. Glauner, echoing Lawrence Berenson's earlier question to the reporters.

Captain Schroeder asked the committee later what could be done to ensure that no further suicide attempts were made. The reply was unanimous: news of this second suicide bid must be concealed from the passengers; the ship's hull must be lit by powerful floodlights at night; lifeboats must be prepared for instant launching in anticipation of further jumpers.

Schroeder agreed to the suggestions.

Fritz Herrmann survived and was kept in quarantine; few on the ship ever knew of his suicide attempt.

That Tuesday evening, lifeboats were lowered to the deck and sailors stationed by them; when darkness fell, lights were dangled over the side, illuminating the water.

By then, Aaron Pozner was not the only person to think the *St. Louis* now resembled a floating concentration camp.

That same Tuesday night, Lawrence Berenson and Cecilia Razovsky dined in the Sevilla-Biltmore. Over crayfish cocktails and steaks they assessed the situation.

For Cecilia Razovsky the critical factor was the attitude of the local relief committee and its advisory board.

"Worthy, and well-intentional," was her verdict on the board. "But out of touch, and with nothing to contribute—unless, of course, it's money."

It was a typically blunt judgment, the sort that had made Cecilia Razovsky a respected, if not universally liked, refugee worker. Berenson agreed with her assessment. The advisory board was to be shunted aside—a decision that later would lead to friction and the eventual resignation of its most prominent members.

But on this clammy Tuesday night, even if the couple dining in a quiet corner of the dining room had anticipated such an outcome, they would not have changed their minds. Both saw themselves as professionals, facing a professional problem which needed totally professional answers.

By the end of dinner, after less than a day in Havana, they came to a conclusion both crucial and far-reaching: Milton Goldsmith and Laura Margolis were undoubtedly dedicated, but in Cecilia Razovsky's eyes they "did not have the professional experience necessary to solve the crisis."

Berenson agreed. If they were too closely associated with the committee, "we lose the respect of the Cubans." But possibly his legal training caused him to hedge. "If we ignore the committee completely, we sever our connections with the other refugees on the island. The main thing is for us to be seen by all to be impartial."

Cecilia Razovsky had one further suggestion. Berenson should ignore what everybody had told him and make a determined attempt to contact President Bru. They left the dining room and went to Berenson's suite to telephone the palace.

Bru's secretary was courteous but evasive: the president's engagement diary was full "for the foreseeable future."

Berenson ignored the snub, and decided not to force the issue. Instead he thumbed again through his "contacts book." Eventually he produced a name: García Montes, the secretary of agriculture.

Berenson explained to Cecilia that he had a "close personal relationship" with the secretary, and also with his predecessor, Amadeo López Castro. He had met the two men when they had visited the United States to negotiate a sugar agreement.

As Cuba's acknowledged sugar expert, López Castro was a man of immense influence. Both he and Montes were confidants of Batista and, Berenson believed, might provide an entree to the army chief. Equally important, Montes, as secretary of agriculture in Bru's cabinet, would have direct access to the president.

With skillful handling, Lawrence Berenson believed, García Montes and López Castro would provide him with the hourly attitudes of the two men in Cuba who mattered, Bru and Batista, without "having to take sides or ostracize either of them."

He telephoned Montes. The secretary confirmed he was on "good terms" with Bru, and agreed that he and López Castro could be of assistance. All he asked for was time "to assess the situation." He promised to bring López Castro to his home to meet Berenson the following night.

It was, Lawrence Berenson told Cecilia Razovsky, "the first step on the road to a solution."

WEDNESDAY, MAY 31, 1939

By midmorning Wednesday, the bridge of the *St. Louis* registered a blistering 102 degrees, and the decks shimmered in the heat. Around the ship a flock of boats maintained watch, offering fruits and bringing relatives to wave and shout encouragement.

The response on board was subdued. Babette Spanier felt, "There was no more to talk about, because there was no real news. We had done all the waving, the calling of greetings, the chasing after rumors, the speculation about Berenson and Razovsky, and, after five days, we were still on board. We didn't know why—and that was the worst thing. Suicide attempts we could live with; none of us were strangers to death. That a few had got ashore, we could rationalize. But out there, on the decks, in the heat, near exhaustion, with no appetite, *just not knowing,* that was the terrible thing."

Yet for Babette Spanier there was one personal consolation. Her marriage seemed to have revived; her husband had never been more considerate or attentive, and that made everything else bearable.

Some passengers, though, were finding the situation on board intolerable, and began to blame everything on the passenger committee, feeling, as Otto Bergmann felt, that "they don't tell us anything and they don't do anything."

In some ways the committee *was* secretive. After discussions with Schroeder, they had decided not to spell out that decree 937 was the stumbling block to disembarkation. The captain felt the information might further depress passengers whose experiences in Germany had made them well aware of the futility of challenging laws. Nor had the committee explained in detail their initiative in telegraphing public figures. It might suggest a desperate situation. Nor were the implications behind the arrival of the Joint negotiators circulated in committee bulletins. The committee did not wish to postulate what Berenson and Cecilia Razovsky might or might not achieve.

Dr. Spanier's clinical experience made him believe much of the mental stress on board was closely associated with the deaths of Weiler and Berg, and Loewe's attempted suicide.

Passengers became obsessed with indefinable fears and fantasies. Those passengers—shy, timid people often without emotional reserves—especially worried Dr. Spanier. He felt that unless they received swift assurances they too might try to end their lives. Dr. Spanier did not mention his fears to the passenger committee, but he did convey them to the captain. Schroeder was horrified by the doctor's prognosis because, he explained, it matched his own.

That morning the captain had received a letter from a passenger saying that the man's aged mother, who was traveling with him, was on the verge of suicide, and "others will undoubtedly follow her lead." Schroeder sent the overworked Dr. Glauner to sedate the woman, a move Dr. Spanier thought "hardly satisfactory." He told the captain: "You may have to sedate the whole ship if we don't get off soon."

Some thousand miles to the north of Havana, in Atlantic City on America's Eastern seaboard, the saga of the *St. Louis* finally stirred the general public into action. That day, *The New York Times* had carried a sober account of Loewe's suicide attempt.

Atlantic City's liberal community became one of the first to show public concern over the *St. Louis* with a protest meeting and march. Other demonstrations followed in New York, Chicago, and Washington. Messages were sent to President Roosevelt, Cardinal Spellman of New York, Cardinal Mundelein of Chicago, Secretary of the Interior Harold L. Ickes, labor leader John L. Lewis, and Supreme Court Justice Ferdinand Pecora. They were urged to telegraph President Bru asking him to repeal decree 937, and many did so.

As the media sensed a bigger story developing, more reporters and radio crews were dispatched to Havana. In London, the press was slower; only the *Times* had mentioned the *St. Louis*. Its brief report was read by Sir Herbert Emerson, director of the International Committee on Political Refugees. He saw the item as "the public tip of a private scandal." Emerson had kept up to date on events in Havana through copies of Ambassador Watson's reports to the Foreign Office. Watson believed decree 937 was "of a temporary nature."

Emerson did not share the view. His sources among President Roosevelt's Refugee Advisory Committee told him Bru was unpredictable. The committee was "not optimistic" about the refugees' chance of entering America "before their quota numbers came up." Presumably the committee reflected the American president's personal stand on the matter.

In Paris, the newspapers handled the *St. Louis* story coolly. Although the anti-Semitism of some stories disturbed Morris Troper, he had other worries. The *Orinoco* had sailed from Hamburg with 200 refugees on May 27 as scheduled, but the Hapag liner seemed in no hurry to set course for Cuba, and was still hovering off the coast of France. Claus-Gottfried Holthusen had been blandly evasive about the ship's intentions, and Troper wondered whether he might soon have to assume responsibility for the *Orinoco*'s passengers.

In Germany, *Der Stuermer* urged that the 200 be sent to Dachau or Buchenwald if they set foot again in the Reich. The newspaper predicted the same fate for the *St. Louis* passengers if they returned. The Nazi-controlled press in Germany followed Goebbels' edict to use the *St. Louis* as a handle to attack all Jews remaining in the country. The campaign outside Germany had also satisfied the propaganda minister's instructions. In South Africa, South America, the Middle East, as well as Europe, the *St. Louis* was now a Nazi *cause célèbre,* used as proof that it was not just Germany who did not want the Jews.

Late on Wednesday morning, President Bru went to the cabinet room to join his ministers. The only absentee was his director of immigration, Manuel Benitez.

Bru gave a comprehensive résumé of the *St. Louis* affair. At the end, he blamed Hapag "for bringing these passengers here with documents obtained through bribery." The president reaffirmed his determination not to be influenced by "external forces," and asked for cabinet backing.

Secretary of Agriculture García Montes did not speak, deciding, for the moment, to keep to himself his telephone conversation with Lawrence Berenson.

Secretary of State Juan Remos raised the suggestion Luis Clasing had made to him: that 250 refugees on the *St. Louis* be allowed to land so that an equivalent number of travelers wishing to return to Europe could embark.

Bru rejected the idea: there were other ships available on which they could travel; if 250 refugees were allowed to land it would negate the very meaning of decree 937. The cabinet agreed with him.

Remos then stated the American government's "unofficial position as conveyed to me informally by their ambassador."

The president listened thoughtfully, then replied, "I appreciate the concern for 'humanitarian considerations.' I feel deeply the pitiable situation of the refugees. However, I believe this is an opportunity to end once and for all the abuses that have led to it. Sending the ship back to Germany is the lesser of two evils."

Juan Remos accepted the president's arguments. With a sense of relief, the president saw there would be no split in his cabinet. It voted unanimously to exclude the refugees.

Ever since arriving in Havana, Gustav Schroeder had eaten his meals alone in his day cabin, and lunch this Wednesday was no exception. Leo Jockl served the meal in silence, realizing that the captain did not want his thoughts disturbed. In fact, Schroeder was brooding on the meeting he was about to have with Juan Estevez Maymir, President Bru's special plenipotentiary. Schroeder had been told that Maymir would bring him news of the government's official position.

It would be the captain's first contact with the Cuban regime, and he recognized an important opportunity to make known his own views and perhaps change the situation.

Juan Maymir arrived just after lunch. He was much taller than the captain, and, even at sixty, he held himself as rigidly as the younger man. His face betrayed nothing of his real thinking. He conveyed the current Cuban position in a few sentences: the cabinet had just endorsed a decision to bar the refugees; a law had existed *before* the ship sailed, precluding such immigration; Hapag had chosen to flout it, therefore the company was now totally responsible for the refugees.

Schroeder argued that, blame apart, the refugees *were* in Havana Harbor.

Then, in the face of Maymir's silence, Schroeder showed him the passenger's letter containing the suicide threat. Maymir read and reread it before handing it back. The captain expounded on his fears of a "collective suicide pact." With slow deliberation, Maymir remarked that the Cuban government would not be blackmailed; a wave of suicides would be laid at the door of Hapag.

Schroeder sought another opening. World opinion might apportion blame differently; even if the shipping line had disregarded a Cuban law, in doing so it gave "these people an opportunity to begin a new life." If Cuba refused them sanctuary, "the world will say your president has acted inhumanely."

Maymir thought it was an "interesting view," and he promised to convey it to Bru, along with a personal letter the captain had written to the president, saying there was a "state of mutiny aboard" which he feared he could not control if he was forced to leave the harbor without disembarking his passengers.

The shadowboxing with Maymir was over; Schroeder felt he had never really gotten to grips with his opponent.

Shortly afterward, the S. S. *Iller* arrived from Bremen with twelve passengers. They too were barred from landing. The *Iller*'s captain signaled the *St. Louis*, asking how long he should wait in the harbor. Schroeder replied: "That is a matter for God and your conscience."

The *St. Louis*, anchored five days in the center of Havana harbor, was now a tourist attraction. Friends and relatives of the refugees, lining the waterfront, were joined by Cuban sightseers. They produced a carnival atmosphere. Fruit and nut vendors set up shop on the Prado Promenade. Boats of dubious seaworthiness augmented those already offering trips to the ship; the price rose to one dollar. Binoculars and telescopes were rented. Entertainment was provided by street musicians and performing monkeys. The ship had fostered a shore-based industry.

For those who were waiting for loved ones to disembark, the noise and frivolity was cruel. Goldsmith's Relief Committee continued to be besieged, and continued to counsel patience. On Wednesday afternoon, after hearing of the Cuban cabinet's decision, Luis Clasing decided he would give the crowd outside his office clamoring for news "something to think about." He posted a notice saying the *St. Louis* would sail "tomorrow, Thursday, June 1, for Hamburg."

The notice caused near-panic among those who read it. Clasing had the announcement removed, but the damage was done. Hysterical relatives tried to bribe policemen to get their families off the ship; the U.S. consulate was flooded with requests that America call a halt to all immigration from Germany so *St. Louis* passengers could enter without delay, taking priority over all others.

The most desperate turned to anyone who might offer hope or consolation. Some even sought the advice of a refugee fortune-teller, a middle-aged woman from Prague who had made quite a name for herself in Havana's refugee community. She was not optimistic. Mysteriously swinging a lead weight on a string above her left hand, she predicted that the passengers would not be allowed off the ship, and soon they would be returned to Europe.

The fortuneteller's predictions drove many of her clients to despair. A few openly vowed they would "commit murder" if they could not board the ship to see their relatives. One of them was actually to do just that. Twenty-seven-year-old Hildie Reading had found a way around the president's ban. Her mother and father, an aunt, an uncle, and a former boy friend were all on the ship. She had personally paid Benitez $750 for their landing permits. Hildie Reading, herself a refugee, had learned Spanish while in Cuba, and earned a comfortable living giving facial and body massages; there was a regular demand for the beautiful Jew's services.

During the siesta hour on Tuesday, she had made her way to the home of the Secretary of State Remos, an elegant mansion guarded by six soldiers. She had to see the secretary urgently, she said, and she meant him no harm. The soldiers had searched her and found no weapon. She invited them to accompany her to the door. Instead they had waved her by.

A maid let her in and told her the secretary's office was at the top of a spiral staircase, directly in front of her. The young woman had knocked on the door, and gone straight in: "Dr. Remos was sitting in a huge, heavy, green leather armchair. Before he could say anything, I apologized for disturbing him, told him not to be angry with his soldiers for letting me in, and said I would only take five minutes of his time, and then burst into tears."

Remos listened sympathetically to Hildie Reading's pleading for permission to visit her relatives on the *St. Louis,* and finally agreed that she could board the ship for three hours the following day.

On Wednesday afternoon, accompanied by two soldiers, she boarded the ship and located her parents. There was a tearful reunion, while scores of passengers crowded around.

"I climbed onto a box, and told them they had nothing to fear. It was just the Cuban mentality. I knew because I had lived there for months. I spoke to them for a long time, and then I said they must understand I wanted a little time with my parents."

Hildie Reading explained to the two soldiers that she would like to see her mother and father alone. They agreed. Inside her parents' cabin, she gave her father $1700. It was her entire savings, and in the end it would make the difference between whether they lived or died.

The reason for her visit accomplished, the young woman left the ship carrying dozens of unstamped letters from passengers, which she promised to post. As she climbed into the launch, she broke down. One of the soldiers put his arm around her. "He was very upset by what he had seen on the ship, and said it was only a temporary hitch—'Someone important who has to sign something is asleep in his hacienda'—and I believed him."

That "someone important," President Bru, had in fact allowed his Wednesday afternoon siesta to be disturbed when he agreed to take a telephone call from his secretary of agriculture and Lawrence Berenson's contact, García Montes. Afterward, Bru spent the afternoon alone in his office, placing Montes' call in context with, among other things, the morning cabinet decision, and the stack of newly arrived telegrams on his desk.

The telegrams particularly troubled him. They bore the names of influential people, moved to protest over the *St. Louis,* and, unlike the previous batch, most were from America. To one side was the cable the passenger committee had sent to Bru's wife the day before. It remained unanswered. Bru and his wife had been too upset by the message's reference to the children on the ship to reply; it reminded them that they had no children of their own.

President Bru, behind his narrow vision and stubbornness, was a sensitive man, capable of acts of generosity. So far he had resisted such feelings over the *St. Louis.* He had been able to sweep aside the protests from the British and French governments, but there remained a nagging unease about the attitude of the American ambassador. For all his outward independence, Bru was receptive to American thinking. At the cabinet meeting, Remos had made clear Ambassador Wright's feelings: the diplomat had appealed for compassion. That sentiment remained with Bru, and so far he had issued no instructions for the cabinet decision to bar the refugees to be carried out.

The letter from Schroeder added to Bru's concern. In conjunction with Juan Maymir's report on his visit to the ship, the letter had to be taken seriously. For the first time Bru accepted that the refugees were desperate enough to contemplate seriously mass suicide rather than return to Germany. The thought chilled him.

Further, there was the presence of Lawrence Berenson to complicate the issue; he was not the sort of man with whom Frederico Bru would choose to deal, but as the official representative of such a powerful American organization, he could hardly ignore him.

Yet Bru actively disliked and mistrusted Berenson. He even help him partly responsible for the *St. Louis* situation, because Berenson had been told months earlier that refugees arriving without visas would not be admitted to Cuba.

Over all other considerations in Bru's mind loomed the figure of Batista. The army chief had remained publicly outside the controversy, but the president knew there was no reason to believe he would continue to do so.

All Wednesday afternoon, Bru had wrestled with the issue. By five o'clock, he came to a decision of crucial importance to those on the *St. Louis.* He telephoned García Montes and told him he was willing to discuss the matter with him and López Castro the next morning at nine o'clock. The president made one condition: Lawrence Berenson was not to be present.

Around the time Frederico Bru made that telephone call, the passenger committee on the *St. Louis* assembled in the captain's day cabin. They found the captain standing between First Officer Ostermeyer and Purser Mueller.

All sensed immediately that Schroeder was showing open strain for the first time. His fingers clutched nervously at various objects on his desk. His face was drawn. His shoulders drooped. He appeared "an old man." But it was his voice, above all, that shocked those present. It had lost its confidence, its certainty, its very tone; it was tired and faded as he spoke.

First, he read a copy of the letter he had sent to President Bru, leaving his listeners in no doubt that Schroeder genuinely feared mass suicide. A melancholy silence settled over the cabin. Then, in his precise Hanoverian accent, the captain expressed his "great disappointment" that the Joint team from New York had not yet visited the ship. If they had, he added, they would have seen for themselves that the situation was rapidly worsening.

Mueller stared at the captain and struggled for something to say. Finally, he stammered that the "only expedient thing to do is to return home. We are seamen, not politicians."

Schroeder sighed. "Yes, perhaps. But we would reach Hamburg half empty." Then he repeated a phrase he had used before: "Worse, we might face mutiny on the high seas. That is a real possibility." Schroeder's eyes searched the faces of those around him, seeking reassurance. He found none. After a long pause, he spoke again.

"Very well then," he said. "Certain further steps have to be taken."

He planned to initiate "suicide patrols" at night. Fifteen male passengers should be selected to augment the Cuban police and crew already patrolling the ship after dark. Those selected were to be able-bodied and discreet.

"Why passengers?" asked Ostermeyer.

"Because they are better able to deal with their own people," said Schroeder.

A murmur of agreement came from the committee.

"But nothing must be done to destroy hope," Schroeder ended. "Hope must always remain."

Some of the committee felt afterward that those words were little more than an attempt by the captain to sustain his own rapidly ebbing confidence.

As he had done every evening since arriving in Havana, Aaron Pozner made his way to the social hall this Wednesday night, seated himself at a corner table, and listened to the gossip. For some days the hall had become a clearinghouse for rumor, speculation, and the few available facts.

A disquieting hush settled over the huge room as the passenger committee appeared. Its members dispersed and moved from one group to another, repeating a familiar litany: *Do not worry, stay calm, do nothing rash.*

Pozner admired Josef Joseph's extraordinary self-control. The lawyer gently chided a tearful young woman, smiled understandingly at a couple tightly holding hands, gave an old man a reassuring pat on the shoulder. Joseph gave no hint that in moving around the hall he was in reality choosing members for the suicide patrol. He recognized that the margin for error was high because he knew few on board well enough to make a sure judgment.

He chose a bank clerk; the man was small and wiry but gave an impression of toughness. He picked a tall, sparse, middle-aged man who looked energetic enough to restrain potential suicides. Joseph selected another, a stolid shopkeeper who, he judged, lacked the imagination to consider whether a person had a right to end his own life.

He turned down some of the younger men because he thought them immature: they might panic in an emergency. Others were rejected: they *looked* right for the suicide patrol, but Joseph suspected them of emotional instability.

The lawyer considered Aaron Pozner. Joseph found him a strange man: polite, apparently in control of his feelings, yet distant. He respected Pozner's right to isolation, but wondered if it masked an urge for self-destruction. He ruled him out.

Joseph turned to Werner Feig, a Berliner with strong opinions about most things on board. Feig was born to travel first class, and had boundless self-confidence. He was asked to join the patrol.

Fritz Gotthelf, another Berliner, was the last approached. The former sales manager was chosen because he was a man "convinced of the importance of life" and had become a cheering influence throughout the ship.

At eight o'clock, the men assembled in the purser's office, where they were briefed on their duties and assigned to their watches. The patrols began an hour later, and were changed every two hours throughout the night.

THURSDAY, JUNE 1, 1939

The next morning, Leo Jockl approached the captain's quarters. In one hand he balanced a breakfast tray. Its contents never varied: a pot of coffee, black bread, and sliced sausage. In the other, Jockl held a blue book which the watch officer had just given him. It was the night log, recording among other things that there had been no radio traffic during the night, nor had the suicide patrols encountered any difficulties.

Jockl entered the cabin, set down the tray, and drew the thick curtains. He watched as Schroeder dwelt over the log, plainly relieved that it had been a quiet night. Yet, Jockl saw, the captain's mood was still somber. He picked over his breakfast, and then walked listlessly to his bath. It was clear to Jockl that the captain's anxieties were as great as ever; worse, Gustav Schroeder showed no signs of overcoming them. The steward left the cabin with the feeling that the ship's master had finally succumbed to the pressure of events that were outside his control.

At nine-thirty, Lawrence Berenson elbowed his way through a throng of excited people stationed outside the Havana Relief Committee offices. Inside, a jubilant Milton Goldsmith showed him the Havana *Post*. Its front-page headline read:

HOPE IS SEEN FOR HOMELESS ON SAINT LOUIS

The first paragraph stated that the "European refugees will be permitted to land in Cuba."

Consul general Coert du Bois had also read the article. He telephoned Milton Goldsmith for verification of the story, but the call was immediately taken over by Berenson. The lawyer said it

199

was "close to the truth," adding that he had just spoken to Montes by telephone at the presidential palace. There, García Montes and López Castro had come out of their meeting with Bru, where, Berenson reported to du Bois, "They put out feelers on my behalf. Montes told me that 'everything is O.K. above.' I am much encouraged. Negotiations have now formally opened with the president for the passengers' release. The only remaining question is merely one of guarantees, and I will settle that when I see the president at noon today."

The diplomat made no immediate reply, mulling over Berenson's exultant outburst. All Coert du Bois's considerable experience told him that such an explosive situation could not be so easily defused. Yet the confident, experienced man at the other end of the telephone was now emphatically repeating: "It's all over but the shouting."

The consul general murmured, "I hope you are right."

"I'd stake my bottom dollar on it," said Berenson.

Even for a man who had the reputation of being a lucky gambler, it was a rash bet.

¿Qué hora es?

Liesl Joseph's question pleased the Cuban policeman on guard at the accommodation ladder. He told her it was just past *"diez hora."*

Like many children on the *St. Louis,* Liesl found the policemen good-humored and willing to enter into almost any sort of game. Children wore policemen's hats and paraded themselves around the ship. Policemen chased after them shouting in feigned indignation.

Liesl attempted another question.

¿A qué hora ir Havana?

The policeman replied in unison with Liesl: *"Mañana."* It was the most overworked word on the ship.

Just a few feet away from Liesl, beside the railing, Marianne Bardeleben, Hans Fischer, and Wolfgang Feilchenfeld amused themselves by throwing small coins over the side. Far below, a collection of young Cuban boys dived off their boats into the water, attempting to beat each other to the booty. After a few seconds, one of them surfaced, his face beaming, the coin held high in one hand.

The long stay in harbor had affected the *St. Louis* children in different ways. The Spanier twins, upset, clung to their parents. Liesl Joseph was unconcerned: "Father and his committee have everything under control." Hans Fischer and Wolfgang Feilchenfeld remained fascinated by the continuous activity in the harbor. Marianne Bardeleben soon found new friends to replace the Aber children, but the memory of Max Loewe's jump still haunted the child: "It was like being surrounded by a ghost you knew was there but couldn't see."

In general, the children accepted their situation much easier than the grownups. Otto and Rosemarie Bergmann were particularly worried about their "two old ladies." Otto wrote in his diary: "Aunt Shalote is standing up well to the strain, but she *is* eighty years old. Rosemarie's mother has again taken to her bed. Dr. Glauner fears for her life. She is suffering from pneumonia she contracted before leaving Germany, and keeps repeating she wants to return to her home."

Rosemarie Bergmann could not bring herself to tell her mother that returning to Germany was the last thing anyone else wanted.

That Thursday morning, her husband made another attempt to get his two elderly charges off the ship by pleading his case to assistant purser Hans Reich. Reich was not hopeful, explaining that similar appeals on behalf of the widowed Recha Weiler had been rejected by the Cuban authorities. Elise Loewe had not been allowed ashore even to visit her husband in the hospital.

"They are unbending," said Reich. "They won't make any exceptions, however mitigating the circumstances."

Bergmann, disconsolate, left the office knowing that the two oldest women on the ship were to be treated by the Cubans no differently from anyone else.

Hans Reich was upset by Otto Bergmann's visit. The assistant purser's outward bonhomie belied an inner concern for the passengers. On the way to Cuba he had shown himself willing at every opportunity to go out of his way to be helpful. Tall and handsome, he was also extremely popular with the women.

One of those women, twenty-four-year-old Gertrud Scheuer, thought Hans "exceptionally nice." She had been told by a steward that he had a Jewish grandmother; his curly hair seemed to confirm the suggestion.

Gertrud Scheuer entered Reich's office as Otto Bergmann was leaving. Hans told her how helpless he felt in the face of problems like the Bergmanns'. To cheer him up, Gertrud showed him a postcard she had received on arrival in Cuba. Its message read: "Welcome to American soil."

Their discussion was interrupted when, at ten-thirty, a seaplane landed in the harbor, once again causing great excitement. It was from New York, and brought mail for the *St. Louis*. The letters were hardly more welcome than the newspapers. Little groups of passengers crowded together, silently reading over each other's shoulders. Some thought the attention focused on them would lead inevitably to their being saved; others felt the reports simply confirmed the hopelessness of their situation.

Marianne Bardeleben's mother knew at least what credence to put in the Havana newspaper *Pueblo*. Tucked away on its back page was a reference to the *St. Louis*. In it, Max Aber—now languishing nearly penniless in Havana with his two daughters—was described as "a millionaire, resident of the United States."

Pueblo's front page was mostly devoted to an explosion in a cinema in Liverpool, England, thousands of miles away. Not for the first time, Mrs. Bardeleben wondered if anyone in Havana really cared about the ship on his doorstep.

Promptly at noon, an immaculately dressed Lawrence Berenson was ushered into Frederico Bru's office in the presidential palace. The lawyer strode across the room to where Bru stood behind his desk, shook the president's hand warmly, thanked him for the interview, and, virtually anticipating Bru's gesture, seated himself in a comfortable chair beside the desk.

His was a brash, hail-fellow-well-met performance of a man whose manner indicated that it was now only "a matter of tidying up the small print" before catching the first flight out to New

York, content in the knowledge that a difficult task had been successfully accomplished.

Bru's opening remarks crushed Berenson's complacency:

"I have asked you here in order to let you know that I have decided not to enter into any negotiations whatsoever about the *St. Louis* until it has left Cuban waters."

Stunned, failing to immediately comprehend the significance of Bru's words, Berenson automatically launched into his prepared speech:

"Mr. President. The situation on the ship is serious. Already there have been two suicide attempts here in the harbor. My guess is that there may be more. Human feelings make it imperative that . . ." Berenson's voice tailed off as he gradually realized what the man eyeing him from behind the desk had said, that it was far from being all over but the shouting.

In a cold, clipped voice which barely concealed his dislike for Berenson, Frederico Bru said:

"I do not need to be reminded of the situation by you. However, the prestige of my government is at stake. I have ordered that the ship, and all on board, must leave the port as soon as it gets up steam. After it is outside territorial limits I will be willing to listen to any plan which covers the passengers' maintenance in the Cuban Repulbic until such time as they can go elsewhere."

"Mr. President, does that mean—"

"It means exactly what I have said," snapped Bru.

"Mr. President, it is a very generous gesture—"

"Señor Berenson, do you have any other questions?" Bru asked.

Berenson's instinct to respond intuitively to any situation asserted itself. He asked the president whether the Isle of Pines, off the Cuban mainland, used for centuries as a prison, could be considered as a temporary haven for the passengers.

"Señor Berenson. I have already told you I will not discuss any such possibilities with you, or anybody else, until the ship has left. Nor, I further inform you, will I give you any assurance that its departure will not be permanent!"

"But, Mr. President, you just indicated—"

"Señor Berenson! I know what I have said. Now, if there is nothing else!"

Frederico Bru rose abruptly to his feet. The interview was over.

As he turned to leave, a crestfallen Lawrence Berenson tried for one last concession: Could he be granted permission to visit the ship before it left to allay the fears of its passengers?

"No," snapped Bru, his anger rising. "I absolutely forbid you to go aboard that ship."

Early that afternoon consul general Coert du Bois received a copy of Bru's decree ordering the *St. Louis* to sail from Cuban waters. It confirmed the diplomat's worst fears: the document was as legally watertight as it was possible to make it. Its lengthy preamble set out the background and justification for the decision to banish the refugees. The nub of the argument was contained in clause 4, a paragraph that effectively sealed the loophole Manuel Benitez had originally used to issue his illegal permits:

> The status of tourists claimed by the passengers is in every sense improper, tourists by definition being persons traveling for pleasure; it is not possible to attribute that characteristic to individuals compelled by superior force to emigrate to regions where the circumstances which caused their exodus do not exist.

The document ordered the ship to sail "this day," Thursday, June 1, and warned that the Cuban navy would "conduct" the *St. Louis* out of territorial waters if she refused to go.

As far as Coert du Bois was concerned, the decree signaled the end of an unhappy episode. He now believed there was nothing he, or anybody else in Havana who had been involved in the affair, could do. He began to draft a telegram to Washington to that effect.

He was interrupted by a telephone call from Lawrence Berenson. The diplomat was astonished by Berenson's mood. Berenson seemed as confident as ever.

"Forget the decree," insisted Berenson. "It's a piece of paper to save Bru's face. The important thing is what he told me."

Berenson then related his version of the meeting he had with the president, stressing Bru's "promise" to consider letting the refugees return, and stay on the Isle of Pines.

The diplomat pressed. Was it a definite promise? Berenson was confident it was, adding "even if they don't go to the Isle of Pines, I am sure they will be allowed back in."

Then, asked du Bois, what was the point of the *St. Louis* being drummed out of Cuban waters?

"I've already told you. It's the president saving face! Once they are out, I can work out a deal with him to let them back in and everybody will be happy."

Coert du Bois asked what sort of deal was involved.

"Money. It's just a matter of money. It always has been!"

Berenson concluded the conversation by saying he was leaving at once for the *finca* of López Castro, where, with García Montes, he would produce "financial guarantees" acceptable to Frederico Bru. Afterward Coert du Bois tore up the draft of his telegram to Washington, persuaded by Berenson's words that the lawyer might well succeed in his mission.

The man who had to act on Bru's decree, Captain Schroeder, was among the last to know of it, and even then, he heard about the order in a roundabout way. A small boat pushed to the ship, and a man shouted up a message for Herbert Manasse, the passenger committee's youngest member. The caller said the *St. Louis* had been ordered to leave within three hours.

Manasse immediately informed the captain of the news. He reacted with no apparent emotion, simply thanking Manasse for the information. But, in fact, the news came as a bombshell. He could not possibly prepare the ship to sail at such short notice.

"There was no one to whom I could turn for help," he wrote in his diary. "Everything was now up to me." At long last, he finally concluded, "the time had come for me to leave the ship."

He took off his tropical whites, changed into civilian clothes, and called in his first officer.

"Ostermeyer, it looks bad. I am going ashore. I will leave alone. In the meantime, please start up the engines."

The first officer did not press for an explanation: "The fact that the captain had changed out of his uniform was enough to convince me the matter was serious." For a moment, he wondered whether Schroeder was leaving the ship for good. The captain answered the unspoken question by saying he expected to return "in an hour or so," and then walked out on deck. He was relieved to see the message shouted to Manasse had apparently not yet registered with the passengers. They lined the rails, looking as they had for the last few days—drained of emotion, numbed.

Dressed in a single-breasted gray suit, white shirt, tie, and brown felt fedora, Schroeder passed unrecognized among the passengers. His dress made him appear one of them. He hoped his "disguise" would also enable him to remain anonymous ashore, for the last thing Schroeder wanted was to be hounded by the press.

Near the accommodation ladder he saw a knot of passengers, mostly women, one of whom he noticed was pregnant. A sailor saluted somewhat hesitantly; the captain looked a tired, insignificant little man as he left his ship precisely at one o'clock to step off his ship for the first time in nearly three weeks.

During Thursday morning, the shifty figure of Otto Schiendick had prowled the ship's decks and public rooms, watching passengers and crew. As the captain left, the steward told one of the Gestapo "firemen," "That man is a fool over the Jews."

In all his time on the *St. Louis,* the last few days in Havana Harbor were perhaps the most anxious Schiendick had ever spent. He had expected the ship by now would be on its way back to Hamburg, where he would receive a rapturous welcome from the Abwehr. Schiendick had hidden the American secrets in his berth, in a steel box the Abwehr provided. He believed the box contained sufficiently important material for his debriefing officer in Hamburg to forget about the considerable sum of money Schiendick had been given for expenses, and which he had not found it necessary to use.

But the steward knew that his authority as ship's party *Leiter* was increasingly being challenged. Typically, he looked again for a scapegoat. Early this Thursday afternoon he settled on the person so often the object of his revenge, Leo Jockl.

Schiendick watched the captain's steward using his rest period to amuse children around the swimming pool. A few of the smaller ones called Jockl "Uncle." Schiendick wondered if the word had a deeper meaning than its childish connotation. Jockl, with his non-Aryan nose, could well be, thought Otto Schiendick, a real uncle to some of the boys and girls grouped around him.

No doubt with a sense of satisfaction, Schiendick devised a plan to confirm his theory.

In her first-class cabin, Elise Loewe tried to conceal from her children the anxiety she felt about her husband. Fritz sat on his father's berth, telling his sister and mother he was now the man of the family; he was, after all, thirteen years and two days old.

At about the same time, on shore, in the Calixto García Hospital, Max Loewe was receiving a visit from someone he had never met before. Hildie Reading, the only woman to board the *St. Louis*, had once more talked her way past administrative restrictions, and into his room.

Only hours before she arrived, Max Loewe had got out of his bed, and with the same resolve which had led him to slash his wrists, he had crossed to a wall mirror, and smashed his head repeatedly against it. The mirror had splintered, and before he was forcibly restrained by nurses, he had nearly succeeded in his second attempt to kill himself. Now, Max Loewe was strapped down in his bed, his arms bound to his body. Both of his wrists were heavily bandaged, as was his head. On either side of him, a male nurse stood guard.

Hildie Reading gave one of the nurses the flowers she had brought, and then tried to make conversation with Max Loewe, telling him she, too, was from Breslau, but:

"He could barely speak. He said his hopes were shattered. He had a horrible fear of being taken back to Germany and the concentration camps. It was terrible. They had destroyed him."

Babette Spanier awoke with a start. "Fritz, is that you? Did you hear the noise?"

There was no answer. Then she remembered her husband had taken the twins up on deck while she had an afternoon rest. It had been broken by the ship's engines beginning to pulsate six decks below. She scrambled off the bed to the porthole. Outside, nothing had changed. She looked at her watch: it showed 3 P.M.

The vibrations became louder, more insistent. She was puzzled, recalling no warning that the ship's engines were to start up. Suddenly, angry voices drowned the throbbing. She rushed to the porthole again. The shouting came from above, on A deck. Behind her, the cabin door swung open and her husband and the twins rushed in.

"They've gone mad up there," panted Dr. Spanier.

On A deck, Aaron Pozner experienced a similar reaction. The half dozen women passengers who had stood silently near the accommodation ladder since morning had begun to shout and scream as soon as the sound of the engines reached the deck.

The three Cuban policemen guarding the ladder looked uneasily at the women. Then, in a concerted rush, the women stormed the ladder, almost overwhelming the policemen.

In the clawing scramble, Clara Frank, a young married woman who was four months pregnant, was thrust against the rail by the other women, all desperate to escape from the ship they now believed was about to sail.

The policemen bunched together, sealing off the ladder, and drew their pistols.

"*Parar!*"

The women ignored a policeman's shout to stop.

"*Parar!*"

The policemen cocked their pistols. Heaving, sobbing, the women fell back. A couple of seamen rushed forward, lifting the unconscious woman, and carried her to the ship's hospital. Though Clara Frank did not yet know it, her baby had been seriously injured in the attempt to escape.

When Captain Schroeder reached the Ward Line pier, he was met by Luis Clasing and Hapag's lawyer in Havana, Dr. José Tamorga, a somber man who ushered them into a car and drove swiftly away before the reporters scented a development.

Tamorga briefed Schroeder on Bru's decree, and the captain ordered him to drive them to the palace. By the time they arrived, Schroeder had gradually worked himself up into a rage that carried them past the palace guards, the secretariat, and into the splendidly cool office of the president's plenipotentiary, Juan Estevez Maymir.

Schroeder demanded an immediate audience with Bru. Maymir regretted that was impossible. The captain offered to wait. The president's envoy replied that that was pointless. Controlling his anger, Schroeder described again the desperation of the passengers. Maymir made no response. The captain appealed for compassion for at least the women and children. The presidential aide's face remained impassive. Finally Schroeder erupted, threatening that Hapag would prosecute the Cuban government.

Maymir rose to his feet. For a long moment he looked at the three men and slowly shook his head in disbelief.

"Prosecute?" he echoed. "Hapag prosecute when it is they who have violated the law?"

He moved from behind his desk and stood in front of Schroeder. Speaking slowly, he said: "The decree is irrevocable. You will sail—or you will be forced out. That is the end of the matter."

"*Nein!*" Schroeder flushed. "I need more time!"

"Your time is over," replied Maymir.

"I need time to prepare for sea."

"How long?"

"Water must be taken on. Food, vegetables, fruit . . ."

"How long, Captain, how long?"

"A day, perhaps more."

Maymir abruptly left the room, and returned to say the ship's stay could be extended until 10 A.M. the next day, Friday, June 2. He then wished the three men good day.

No one spoke until they were in the car. Then Schroeder demanded to see Lawrence Berenson. He found the Sevilla-Biltmore besieged by reporters all awaiting Berenson's reaction to the decree, but the lawyer had left for his meeting with García Montes and López Castro. The reporters failed to recognize the captain of the *St. Louis*.

Schroeder asked to be driven to the German consulate. Clasing protested that it would be a waste of time, that they would be better employed supervising preparations for departure.

"*Verdammt!* Take me!" Schroeder shouted.

Dr. Kaempe, the chargé d'affaires, had a copy of the decree before him when Gustav Schroeder was shown into his office.

He listened carefully as the captain argued the case for exerting diplomatic pressure to ensure that the passengers disembarked. Kaempe said all such channels had been exhausted.

"These are Jews, Captain," Kaempe added. "Feeling here is against them."

"They are also people, Herr Doktor," retorted Schroeder. "And I care about people."

The diplomat bridled. Everybody cared about people, he replied, but there was nothing more he could do: "Take them back, Captain, and let someone else take over their responsibility."

Trembling with anger and nervous exhaustion, Schroeder stalked out of the consulate, and told Clasing to drive him to the pier: "I'm going back to my ship. I understand the people there better than I ever will those here."

The clash between the Cuban policemen and the women passengers had created a groundswell of resentment on the *St. Louis*. Now a large group of police, guns drawn, stood with their backs to the rail on A deck facing a hostile crowd. Between them first officer Ostermeyer and purser Mueller paced, pleading for restraint. From below came the pounding of the ship's engines.

When the captain stepped on deck, Ostermeyer quickly explained developments. Schroeder ordered the police to lower their weapons but they did not respond, perhaps not recognizing the little man in civilian clothes. Schroeder's tension and anger erupted again; this time no one was in doubt he was the captain. He stormed at a police sergeant that if his orders were not obeyed at once, he would have his crew disarm the Cubans and pitch them off the ship. The police obeyed.

Schroeder faced the passengers. He expressed deep regret that the incident had happened, but urged them to disperse; their presence would achieve nothing. A man pushed forward and asked whether it was true the ship was about to sail. Schroeder ignored him and briefly addressed all the passengers; their committee was the proper medium for information; it would inform them of any sailing date.

Alone in his cabin, sweating profusely, the captain, who now bore more responsibility for the immediate fate of the passengers than President Bru or Lawrence Berenson, sat and agonized with his conscience.

No matter how he reviewed it, the journey ashore had been a disaster. All his plans had collapsed. He had gambled on seeing the president and failed. He had hoped to shame Maymir into granting a worthwhile extension to provide time for Berenson to negotiate, and he had been rejected. His overture to Kaempe had proven fruitless.

Dejected and depressed, he felt "an acute sense of failure," a conviction that he had badly mishandled the voyage. He had failed always to make a clear assertion of his authority. He regretted his decision at the outset not to press Hapag harder for contingency plans for the crisis that now engulfed him. That had been a mistake. There were others: he had not recognized that the German news summaries offered a distinct warning of disaster; it had been a "mistake" allowing Clasing a free hand to conduct affairs ashore.

He paced the cabin, vowing that Clasing would be dismissed if he had anything to do with it.

But the heat of the room dulled such thoughts. He was weary. His behavior had already placed him in conflict with the Nazi party. He had received several warnings. Would he now find himself branded a "Jew-lover"? The thought, with its shadow of the Gestapo and the concentration camps, was a fearful one.

He was painfully aware of his family responsibilities. Added to those were the verities of his upbringing, his belief in Germany and in his officer's code. All these factors he now considered.

His instinct told him to cable Hapag asking whether he should return. But while that would absolve him from responsibility, it would not end the debate with his conscience. He knew he would never forgive himself if he did not keep his promise to the committee that he would make every effort to land the passengers outside Germany.

A knocking on the door cut into his thoughts. Radio officer Fritsch brought a radiogram from Hapag in Hamburg.

By the time he had deciphered it, Gustav Schroeder felt a sense of deliverance. He had been temporarily released from his timetable.

It was, he told the passenger committee who later assembled in his cabin, "a free hand to sail to any port that will take us."

They watched Schroeder draft a notice for passengers to be posted throughout the ship:

> THE CUBAN GOVERNMENT HAS ORDERED US TO LEAVE THE HARBOR. WE SHALL DEPART AT 10 A.M. FRIDAY MORNING. BUT OUR DEPARTURE DOES NOT MEAN DISCUSSIONS WITH THE CUBAN GOVERNMENT ARE ENDED. ONLY BY LEAVING HAVANA CAN MR. BERENSON AND HIS COLLEAGUES CONTINUE WORKING. THE SHIP WILL CONTINUE TO BE IN CONTACT WITH ALL JEWISH ORGANIZATIONS AND OTHER OFFICIAL BODIES. THEY WILL ALL CONTINUE TO TRY TO ARRANGE A LANDING OUTSIDE GERMANY. IN THE MEANTIME THE SHIP WILL REMAIN CLOSE TO THE AMERICAN COAST.

The committee studied the notice with care. Josef Joseph voiced a common thought: Did Schroeder have any information the United States would take them?

The captain replied: "Anything is now possible."

When the passengers saw the captain's notice about their departure, not all of them believed it.

Gustav Schroeder's early decision to remain aloof had caused most of the refugees to be suspicious of him, and his uniform was a constant reminder of others in uniform in Germany whom they feared and hated. This uncertainty about Captain Schroeder as a man, linking him with the unpleasant memories of what they had left behind, was to color the passengers' view of everything he did or said he would do. As a result, many did not believe him when he said he would "remain close to the American coast"; they were convinced that if they left Havana they would be heading back for Germany.

Some passengers, like Otto Bergmann, questioned the captain's notice even more fundamentally. He thought it "ridiculous.

We cannot leave. It is not true." But as Thursday evening wore on, more and more little boats pulled alongside the ship, and the occupants shouted up goodbyes to the refugees. Soon everyone on the *St. Louis* realized that the unbelievable was about to happen. In the boats, the emotion was equal to that on the ship. Many believed they would never see their loved ones again. Men and women were sobbing openly. Now and then one screamed. Outstretched arms almost beckoned passengers to jump.

Ten-year-old Marianne Bardeleben, still wearing the hair clips her father had sent her, stood by the rail with her mother. Mrs. Bardeleben could hardly hold back her tears; she pointed to her husband. Marianne waved, but she was still unsure which was her father in the sea of faces below.

Dr. Bardeleben was in the same boat as Hans Fischer. Staring up the black, towering sides of the *St. Louis*, past scores of heads peering down through portholes, Hans eventually spotted his son. The boy was with Wolfgang Feilchenfeld, who was carrying his year-old brother, while Mrs. Feilchenfeld stood nearby with her other two children.

Wolfgang saw his father in a rowboat holding up two pineapples; they were passed to a steward at the foot of the accommodation ladder. Later the pineapples would be cut up by one of the ship's chefs, arranged artistically with cherries, placed on the Feilchenfeld table, and remain in the memories of the four children as one of the most unforgettable moments of the voyage.

Liesl Joseph stood by the rail with her parents. Passengers frequently came up to her father seeking information and advice. Liesl "basked in his importance," unaware of the threat her mother and father were living under.

Lilli and Josef Joseph, using their considerable connections on shore, felt they could have arranged to leave the ship, but had decided against it. "There were dangerous people on board. Especially the ones who had been in concentration camps and who had promised the Gestapo they would never return to Germany. They said we would all leave the ship or no one would. They threatened to kill us if we tried to get off the boat."

Nevertheless, some of the passengers did make secret plans to escape that last night in harbor. Most involved simply dropping or being lowered from a porthole into the water, to be picked up by friendly Cubans. But when the time came, it was seen to be impossible. There were too many police launches and too many searchlights. In addition, at least one woman passenger realized she was too well endowed to squeeze through a porthole.

A steward suggested to Gertrud Scheuer, the shapely twenty-four-year-old friend of Assistant Purser Reich, a more promising proposal. He knew two young Cuban stevedores who had agreed they would smuggle Gertrud off in an empty container. But the steward was unable to introduce Gertrud to them; like all of the eighty stewards on the ship, the night before sailing he was carefully watched. Those not engaged in some necessary activity were confined to their quarters.

On deck, the passengers themselves were watched by the suicide patrols. They escorted anyone acting suspiciously to his or her cabin, and those who were hysterical were taken to the ship's doctor and sedated.

Dr. Glauner's supply of sleeping drugs nearly ran out.

Crowded together in the first-class cabin just after nine o'clock, the passenger committee listened attentively to Milton Goldsmith. The relief worker chose his words carefully, promising the group that after the ship sailed the Joint would work for "an early landing."

Josef Joseph asked why they could not go straight to the United States. Goldsmith said he thought that was out of the question. Dr. Weiss, note-taker of the meeting, pressed him on the point, but Goldsmith refused to elaborate.

Realizing it was necessary to end on a more positive note, Goldsmith promised they would be "kept fully informed of developments," and "need not fear a return to Germany." That too, he told them, was "out of the question."

As the meeting broke up, Herbert Manasse commented that it was a pity Lawrence Berenson had not yet seen fit to visit them.

"He has more important work," said Goldsmith. "He holds your future in his hands."

"Fifty thousand dollars is not enough."

García Montes's statement shook Berenson. It seemed to con-

tradict what the lawyer's other adviser, López Castro, had suggested.

Seated on the tiled verandah of the ranch house, the two
Cubans drew with slow deliberateness on their cigars and
carefully watched Lawrence Berenson for his reaction. Berenson's
face betrayed nothing. With studied indifference he sipped his
drink. Then, replacing his glass on the table, he looked at López
Castro.

"Are you sure it is necessary to put up any money at all?"

Through a small cloud of cigar smoke, the Cuban repeated
arguments now familiar to Berenson after hours of negotiations. A
bond, of suitable size, had to be posted on behalf of the refugees
before there was any chance of them being allowed on Cuban soil.
It could be cashed by the Cuban government if, and only if, the
refugees did not leave the country by a certain date—or if they
became a charge on the country during their stay.

Though nobody had mentioned it, Berenson believed it
represented Bru's solution to the situation; there was every possibility that it might also reflect Batista's wishes.

He had quickly accepted the proposal—with one important
proviso. He argued that it would be an act of good faith on the part
of the Cuban government to allow the passengers to land *before*
the bond was posted—"before the vultures get in"—or its amount
specified. His counterproposal had started hours of protracted,
polite, though stubborn, argument. Now, as the evening shadows
darkened the verandah, the discussions finally narrowed down to
the size of the bond.

Berenson believed that if they could agree to a figure, his other
demands would be acceded to; that the bond should also include
the passengers on the *Orduna* and *Flandre*, and that they should
all be allowed to land before the bond was posted.

As the matter was reduced to one of hard cash, Berenson felt
his confidence rise; he hugely enjoyed the cut-and-thrust of bar-
gaining over money. He believed he had managed the situation
adroitly, allowing himself to be forced to offer $50,000 as a bond,
but now, suddenly, as casually as he swatted an insect, García
Montes murmured the figure was not enough, that only $150,000
would be acceptable. This was three times what López Castro had
suggested.

"That figure is impossibly high," said Berenson.

"I think not," replied Montes.

López Castro replenished their drinks, raised his glass, and murmured, *"Salud."*

Three hours and several toasts later, the matter was still unresolved.

Finally, at midnight, Lawrence Berenson left the *finca*, taking with him the draft wording for the bond, with a blank space for its amount to be filled in.

As he drove away, Montes murmured with a shrug: "Fifty thousand, one hundred and fifty thousand. It's up to you."

It seemed inhuman to have to calculate the value of people in dollars, but to Berenson it was a necessity, and he hoped to negotiate the deal as cheaply as possible.

III

The Final Solution

FRIDAY, JUNE 2, 1939

Joseph C. Hyman, executive director of the Joint Distribution Committee, arrived at his office early on Friday morning, knowing it was the day the *St. Louis* was to leave Havana. He carried a copy of *The New York Times*. He was pleased to see that the *St. Louis* was once again front-page news. Under the heading: "CUBA ORDERS LINER AND REFUGEES TO GO," Ruby Hart Phillips, the newspaper's long-established and respected correspondent in Havana, had sent a comprehensive wireless report describing the situation.

There was little in the story that Hyman was not already aware of, having had frequent telephone conversations with Berenson. But a footnote to the article, datelined Washington and headed "Partial Solution Reported," gave the executive director cause for thought.

It stated that the Cuban government required a bond of $500 per refugee before they would be allowed to land. This was a much higher figure than Hyman had anticipated, and far exceeded the bond he hoped to raise through an insurance company. Nevertheless, Hyman should have realized, it was precisely the sum required of immigrants to Cuba who carried legal visas, and it was also a normal requirement for many other countries, including the United States itself.

The report from Washington also quoted America's most famous and powerful union leader, John L. Lewis. Following the public outcry in the United States, Lewis had cabled Batista asking that "in the name of humanity" the refugees be permitted to land. "I appeal to you because of your well-known feeling for the victims of German Nazism," Lewis went on. "If returned to Germany, these people will undoubtedly be sent to Nazi concentration camps."

Hyman wondered how many readers would understand what "concentration camps" really meant. A telephone call broke his meditation; it was Berenson from Havana. The lawyer spoke quickly and excitedly, outlining the plan he proposed to put to Bru. The bond would run for six years, and would be reduced proportionately as individuals left Cuba.

Hyman then referred to *The New York Times* report, pointing out that in hard cash, it meant raising a total of nearly half a million dollars for the *St. Louis* passengers. Berenson told the executive director he planned to negotiate a figure much less than that. Hyman replied that he hoped it would not be more than $125,000, as he had already mentioned that sum to the insurance company. He promised to cable the lawyer as soon as he arranged the bond, and gave his approval for the proposals to go forward to Bru.

In Havana, Berenson went off to deliver the draft to Antonio Bustamente, the Relief Committee lawyer, who would translate it into Spanish.

In New York, Hyman arranged a meeting with the insurance company, when, unknown to Berenson, he planned to ask if the bond could be raised to $200,000 "just in case."

Fifteen hundred miles south, in sweltering Havana harbor, the *St. Louis* prepared to sail. Its captain, crew, and passengers were convinced that nothing could now alter their situation, that no intercession—financial, political, or spiritual—could halt the departure proceedings.

From his vantage point high in the wheelhouse, Gustav Schroeder felt a great gloom settle over the liner. Forward, on the bridge, the silence was broken by a telegraph ring in the standby to the engine room. At that moment a launch tied up alongside the accommodation ladder and Milton Goldsmith clambered on board, forcing a path through the passengers thronging the decks. He hurried to the captain's day cabin.

In the social hall, the passenger commiteee struggled to placate a mass of agitated passengers. Some were shouting, a number were crying, a few prayed aloud. In the babble of sounds, a theme gradually emerged—a monotonous, frightening chant: "We must not sail. We must not die. We must not sail . . ."

The refrain carried out to the decks, sending a shiver through many of those lining the rails, too numbed to speak, shuffling their feet on decks vibrating ever louder from the increasing revolutions of the engines. For most of those at the rails, the arrival of Goldsmith and the chanting in the social hall did not matter. Their attention, their very existence, focused on the water immediately around the *St. Louis.*

It was empty.

A cordon of police launches now kept back all the motorboats, the rowboats, the dinghies, the catamarans, all the myriad little boats which every day had ferried out relatives and friends to wave and to shout encouragement to those on board the ship.

Even to men like Aaron Pozner, who had known nobody in those boats, their very presence had been a comfort. Now, that connection had been suddenly severed. And for Pozner, as for many other men who had endured in silence six days of torment, the absence of the small boats proved to be too much to bear. Tears trickled down his face, the first time he had cried in public since the day he had said goodbye to his wife and children.

Around him other men sobbed with grief.

Suddenly, a police launch left its station and raced toward the ship. As it arrived at the accommodation ladder, six figures, accompanied by Cuban policemen, scurried down the ladder and into the launch. It immediately sped toward the shore, carrying the last passengers to leave the *St. Louis.*

Their departure had been achieved by the use of personal outside influence and power—something that few others on the ship could have summoned.

The rescue had come through the direct intervention of the Annenberg publishing family in Philadelphia, a mysterious lawyer called Mr. Carson, and the Cuban ambassador in New York, Señor Pedro Fraga.

The exact sequence of events will now never be clear. But somehow Fraga was induced to authorize that Cuban visas be stamped in the passports of the lucky six while the ship was in Havana Harbor. Who they were, what their connnection with the Annenbergs was, is also something of a mystery. Carson arrived in a chartered aircraft to expedite the transfer of the group from Cuba to America.

The sight of the police launch spiriting the refugees away sent a shock wave coursing through the *St. Louis*, halting the keening in the social hall, the sobbing on deck, the very routine of departure. The passenger committee sought an explanation from Purser Mueller, failed to receive one, and burst in upon Captain Schroeder and Milton Goldsmith. The refugee director had come on board to urge the captain to remain close to Cuba, "even if it meant sailing around and around in a circle."

The two men turned, somewhat startled, as the committee bunched into the cabin, demanding that if six people had been whisked to safety, then the ship's departure should be postponed to see if new moves could be made to get the other passengers ashore.

"Gentlemen," said Gustav Schroeder. "I know nothing about these people who have gone. But one thing I do know. If I stay a moment longer than allowed, then the Cuban navy will force me out."

"Force?" echoed Josef Joseph. "How? By gunfire?"

"I would think that most unlikely," replied Schroeder evenly.

"But it would solve your problems, wouldn't it?" pressed Joseph. "If they damaged the ship, we would have to remain here, and even probably be taken ashore."

"An interesting hypothesis, but one I am not prepared to put to the test," retorted Schroeder.

Goldsmith shrugged, insisting there was nothing more the captain could do except leave on schedule. Then Gustav Schroeder reminded them that America was only a few hours' sailing away.

The captain had intended his remark to be no more than a morale booster, a reminder that the United States was close by. But to the desperate committee members his words raised a burst of questions. Did the captain plan to sail to the United States? Had he reasons to believe they would be admitted? Was some deal in progress of which they were unaware?

To all such questions Gustav Schroeder gave a negative answer, stressing that he had no positive information, that he had meant no more than he had said: the United States was a short cruise away. But the listeners were left with the definite belief that, if all else failed, the United States would probably accept them.

The committee men had been too preoccupied to study the American newspapers brought on board the previous day, which would have soured such optimism.

Roosevelt, contemplating running for an unprecedented third term, sensed too clearly the mood of the United States. With war once more brewing in Europe, the majority of Americans favored a strict isolationist policy, where refugees, however deserving, would at best be an unwelcome reminder of a world the United States wanted no part of. There were also other factors: U.S. business was again in a tailspin, swelling the unemployment figures by four million. The president was ready with appropriate phrases, attacking the "economic royalists" who were choking the Great American Dream. But in spite of progress to help the farmers and provide cheap public housing, Roosevelt's measures simply did not evoke the same confidence as in the early days of the New Deal. To allow a well-publicized shipload of refugees into such a situation would require a great deal more compassion on the part of the administration than had been shown so far.

Goldsmith's offer to address the entire passenger complement before the ship sailed was greeted warmly. The shy and modest relief director found himself invested with power never before accorded him. He planned to use it to full effect when speaking to the passengers.

In the purser's office, Robert Hoffman listened with impatience to Otto Schiendick's diatribe.

Hoffman had boarded the ship to express the customary farewell of the local Hapag office, and had been sharing a bottle of *Sekt* with Mueller when Schiendick arrived. The steward had peremptorily asked Mueller to leave, as he had "confidential party business to discuss," and then had launched into a brutal tirade against Leo Jockl.

Hoffman wondered if Schiendick had gone mad; he tipped back his chair and stared at the steward. In a voice meant to be angry but in reality only resigned, he asked: "You really wish me to contact Hamburg for the Gestapo to check on this man?"

"Yes."

Hoffman's tone became scathing. "All this because you suspect him of Jewish blood?"

"Suspicion can lead to the truth."

Hoffman realized he could not afford to upset the steward. He stood up. He would send the cable. But, he added, "I only hope you will display the same diligence safeguarding the material now in your possession as you have in this matter!"

With that, he walked out of the office.

Word of the meeting in the social hall was announced over the ship's loudspeaker. The room quickly became crowded. Many of the women were crying. A Cuban official stood by the entrance with the senior police officer on the ship.

At ten-thirty, the passenger committee filed in, followed by Goldsmith and Robert Hoffman. They were joined on the platform by the police officer and the Cuban official. There was no officer from the *St. Louis* present.

The ten men stood where only a week before the Cuban medical officer had "inspected" passengers as they passed in front of him, full of anticipation and excitement. As Josef Joseph surveyed the scene now, the contrast could not have been greater. A week ago, faces had been filled wiht hope; now it was hopelessness. Then, people had been crying with joy; now they cried from fear. Thirty passengers, including Max Loewe and Moritz Weiler, were no longer on the ship; 907 remained. They included Mrs. Loewe and Mrs. Weiler.

Milton Goldsmith, the American who had for months borne stoically the burden of criticism and helplessness in his Havana relief office, spoke first.

"Sisters and brothers," he began. "Do not give up hope. Be strong. Do not fear a return to Hamburg. The Joint committee here, in New York, and throughout the world, will work so that soon you can land outside Germany. Important people will contact the Cuban president as soon as you leave. Your committee will hear from the United States and us very often, possibly every two hours. The world is watching you. You are 'one family' now."

There was no applause as the speech ended, only a silence broken by sobbing. Then the Cuban police officer spoke.

"I am sorry, but I and my policemen have to do our duty, a hard duty. We wish, from our hearts, that you will soon land."

As the men left the platform, each smiled reassuringly, except for Robert Hoffman. The Abwehr agent led the group out, looking straight ahead, his face cold and unemotional. Hoffman walked directly to the accommodation ladder and down into one of the many official and police launches now alongside.

Milton Goldsmith waited until everyone lined up by the ladder was off, including the fifty policemen who had for so long been guarding the ship. He then shook hands with each member of the committee, and was the last person to leave the *St. Louis*.

Herbert Manasse looked at his watch. "Eleven o'clock. We're an hour late."

"Late for what?" said Josef Joseph. "We have nowhere to go."

First Officer Ostermeyer reported to the captain that the ship was ready for sailing.

"Ostermeyer," Schroeder replied, "the Cuban president reminds me of a man who invites guests to dinner, but on arrival, he keeps them waiting in the entrance hall, and then throws them out."

"I wonder," said Ostermeyer, "whether we will receive a second invitation."

At two minutes past eleven o'clock, Gustav Schroeder gave the order to stand to stations; the ship's engines increased their revolutions, from the bridge came "dead slow ahead," and the *St. Louis* began to move toward the open sea, observed by an estimated 100,000 onlookers on the shore.

The captain watched helmsman Kritsch responding to the course changes, almost anticipating the ringing telegraph on the port side of the bridge. Schroeder wondered how many bearing changes the young steersman would make in the next few days as the ship awaited the outcome of negotiations. It would depend, Schroeder believed, on "luck, Bru, and the American president." He had little faith in any of the three.

Below on the passenger decks, the mood was gloomier. The rails were lined with weeping people, or those who stood in silence as Havana steadily receded. The edginess communicated itself to crew detailed to stop any passengers jumping overboard: in their nervousness they plucked at several people leaning over the rails.

Aft, close to where Moritz Weiler and Max Loewe had gone

over the side, which had become a symbolic gathering place for
some of the more outspoken younger passengers, the rail had been
roped off.

Now, as the ship gathered way, a group of youths ducked
under the barrier and stood defiantly at the rail. A squad of seamen
turned to a deck officer; anxious to avoid trouble, he ordered the
ropes removed. A mocking cheer greeted this concession, and
somebody shouted: "We'll soon be running the ship—then we can
go where we like."

For Dr. Fritz Spanier those words held a chilling element of
truth. Ever since the women passengers had stormed the gangway
on the previous day, he had detected a growing feeling that some
of the wilder elements on board wanted to hijack the liner. Twice
this morning he had encountered small groups standing expectantly around, eyeing each other and whispering among themselves about "positive action." Shortly before the ship sailed, Fritz
Spanier overheard a trio of youths talking about storming the
engine room in a bid to cripple the ship.

Dr. Spanier firmly believed any such move would be
dangerous—and futile. He felt the plotters would be overpowered
long before they achieved their aim; worse, their actions would
alienate all sympathy among the crew, and, when the outside
world learned of the matter, it was likely the passengers would be
branded as pirates.

Yet now, as the *St. Louis* glided out of Havana harbor, he
spotted another group of youths, bunched together, looking
speculatively toward the bridge. Dr. Spanier walked toward them
in a determined way, and warned them that if they caused any
trouble he would see to it that "you will wish you had stayed in
Germany."

Discomfited, the youths walked away.

Aaron Pozner also watched them disperse with a feeling of
relief—but for reasons far different from those felt by Fritz
Spanier.

Since the confrontation between passengers and police on
deck the previous day, Pozner had concluded that passive resistance was not enough, that violence might now be the only answer,
that to seize the ship was the only hope left. He would be quite
willing to lead an assault on the crew to force them to sail
anywhere but Germany.

Pozner had also concluded it would be better to be branded as pirates, and possibly interned in some foreign jail, than to return to a Nazi concentration camp. Equally, he believed no immediate attempt should be made to capture the ship; that move should come only when all outside efforts had failed, when there was nothing to lose, when it would be better to risk death at sea than at the hands of the Gestapo.

As the youths walked away from Dr. Spanier, Aaron Pozner followed them, anxious to convince them of his arguments.

Below on B deck, in the *Tanzplatz*, Otto Schiendick and the Gestapo "firemen," the men charged specifically with ensuring the ship's safety, had once more defied Captain Schroeder by assembling in the nightclub to sing Nazi songs as the ship nosed her way out into the open sea, heading, they believed, for Hamburg.

Schiendick ordered a pause in the sing-song to read out a formidable list of the ship's complement whom he had booked for transgressing one Nazi edict or another. His roll call was headed by the captain and Purser Mueller. It included seven deckhands and five stewards accused of being too friendly with the passengers: Schiendick urged the Gestapo men to report any further infringements to him on the homeward journey so the ship could be purged of such deviants.

Finally, he revealed the inquiries being carried out on his instructions into Leo Jockl's background. The steward promised his companions that if his suspicions were confirmed, they would have "much fun." In the meantime they should continue to harass the passengers; he believed if they were goaded far enough some of them might be bold and foolish enough to retaliate. Then, Otto Schiendick promised, "they will soon remember who they are."

There were many passengers on deck who could never forget who they were. Everywhere they looked the reminder was there: the escorting flotilla of police launches, twenty-six in all, and beyond them the launches filled with press men and newsreel camera teams. From time to time a reporter bellowed out a question, hoping for a reaction or a quotable reply. Receiving no answers, several enterprising journalists invented their own replies, a touch of fiction that suited many of the eyewitness accounts of the *St. Louis* departure.

In the wake of the press launches came a sizable armada of

small craft, carrying relatives, minor Cuban officials, and a large number of people attracted by the possibility of further drama.

Three miles out, the limit of Cuban territorial waters, the police boats vectored back to shore; the press and public boats rolled gently in the swell, still hoping for a reaction from the *St. Louis*. None came.

Soon, only a handful of boats remained to keep the liner company.

In a Hapag launch were Robert Hoffman, Milton Goldsmith, and Lawrence Berenson; the refugee workers had persuaded Hoffman to take them along. At sea Berenson had maintained a breezy line of small talk, to which Goldsmith did not respond.

During Berenson's time in Havana, the relationship between the two men had grown cool. Berenson felt Goldsmith was out of his depth in the present situation. Goldsmith regarded the lawyer as altogether too brash for a crisis where he believed tact and a real understanding of the Cuban mentality to be essential. Now, as their launch turned away from the *St. Louis*, the attitudes of the two men were symbolized in their farewell salutes. Milton Goldsmith clasped his hands in prayer, Lawrence Berenson raised his hands in a boxer's victory salute. To those at the rails of the *St. Louis*, it was the gesture the third man in the boat gave which sickened them. Standing between the two refugee workers, Robert Hoffman raised his right hand in a stiff Nazi salute.

On the way back to Havana, Goldsmith's mood was somber; there were tears in his eyes. His attitude, Robert Hoffman noticed, contrasted strongly with Berenson's. The lawyer appeared relieved that the ship had left, but as Berenson began to tell Goldsmith of the proposals he would soon put before Bru, Hoffman became uneasy. The lawyer repeatedly told Goldsmith the *St. Louis* would return within forty-eight hours when he had settled "the money problems."

As Berenson's confidence gradually lifted Goldsmith's depression, it began to alarm Hoffman. He realized that if the ship returned, it could well put at risk the documents Otto Schiendick was taking to Hamburg; the U.S. secret agents could devise a plan to board the ship and retrieve them. Hoffman decided to try to throw Berenson off balance. Pointedly ignoring Goldsmith, the German agent asked the lawyer to join him for lunch, saying he had "information of great importance for your negotiations."

Berenson accepted.

On shore, the huge crowds, mostly Cuban sightseers, were gradually dispersing. For them, the star attraction of the past week had gone, and life could begin to return to normal.

Hoffman took Berenson to the Swiss Home Restaurant, where they were greeted warmly by Otto Ott, the dwarf. Ott motioned with his large cigar toward a secluded corner table. There Hoffman's spy poured Berenson a large rum and Coke.

Berenson asked what it was Hoffman had to tell him. Hoffman looked around, as if to make sure he was not being overheard, and then announced that he had a confidential message from the president.

"What most concerns him is money," began Hoffman.

"Money will be no problem," insisted Berenson.

"Señor Berenson, you underestimate what the president wants. He asks me to inform you that unless you are able to deliver a million dollars, then you should save your energy for more worthwhile ventures and return to the United States."

After careful questioning, Berenson decided that Hoffman's claims were a "come-on, that he was just another of those in Havana trying 'to get in on the act.' "

All afternoon and evening, the Joint negotiator was bombarded by other people claiming to represent Bru. Two of them were particularly troublesome, and, near midnight, Berenson finally agreed to meet them in his hotel bedroom.

The men were well-connected; Major Bernardo García, although known as a playboy, was also Cuba's chief of police; Colonel Manuel Benitez was the son and namesake of the former immigration director who had sold the illegal permits to the *St. Louis* passengers. In the "Sergeant's Revolution" of 1933, the young Benitez had been a renegade officer, siding with Batista, and had ever since been his staunch ally, often acting as Batista's personal aide.

Major García told Berenson he had been asked by President Bru to act as intermediary, and that all communications for the President must go through him.

Colonel Benitez apologized for his father's behavior over the *St. Louis,* expressing regret that the Cuban government "is unable to make good on the permits." The colonel claimed that the sum required to ensure the refugees' return was "between $400,000 and $500,000."

Berenson felt that this was yet another attempt to con him and that whatever they or Robert Hoffman or anyone else advised him, it would simply strengthen his resolve to conduct negotiations in his own way. Eventually, at 3 A.M., he told García and Benitez he was not prepared to discuss the matter further, and asked them to leave.

Unwittingly, the lawyer had missed an opportunity to gain two important, if decidedly slippery, allies. Major García had in fact been given authority by the president to handle all further negotiations.

Arrival in Havana. Photo: Paul Bendowski.

In Havana Harbor, friends and relatives shout up to the passengers on the *St. Louis*. Photo: *Stern*.

Cuban guards stop the passengers from leaving the ship in Havana Harbor.
Photo: European Pictorial Services.

Aboard the *St. Louis* in Havana Harbor. Photo: European Pictorial Services.

Cuban President Frederico Bru (left) and army chief Fulgencio Batista. Photo: UPI.

Arrival in Antwerp. Photo: *Stern*.

Der Abschied

Eine teuflische Komödie

Grinsende jüdische Emigranten an Bord eines Schiffes, das sie über den Ozean bringt. Es geht ihnen ausgezeichnet. Im Ausland aber markieren sie die „armen, unschuldig verfolgten" Juden.

According to *Der Stuermer*, the "happy Jews" as they departed on the *St. Louis*

Der Höhepunkt der Komödie

Die gleichen Jüdinnen und Juden, die sich während der Überfahrt skandalös frech benommen hatten, markieren bei der Landung in England die „unschuldigen Opfer der barbarischen Nazis".

and on their return to Europe. Photo: *Stern*.

Captain Schroeder makes his last visit to the bombed-out hulk of the *St. Louis* in Hamburg Harbor in 1947. The ship was later sold for scrap. Photos: *Stern.*

SATURDAY, JUNE 3, 1939

In Hamburg, Claus-Gottfried Holthusen telephoned Morris Troper in Paris. The Hapag director told Troper he had reluctantly decided that the *Orinoco*, sister ship of the *St. Louis*, having been kept hovering for days off Cherbourg, must return to Germany with its 200 refugees, all of whom had booked passage for Cuba.

"In view of the unresolved situation of the *St. Louis*, the risk is too great. The *Orinoco* is now on its way back to Hamburg," Holthusen told the European Joint director.

Troper had anticipated the decision, and iniquiries had already been made of the British and French governments as to whether, if the *Orinoco* was turned back, they would accept its passengers. Both countries had refused. Troper's main concern now was whether the passengers would be sent to the concentration camps, as *Der Stuermer* had advocated.

That real possibility also upset America's ambassador in London, the founder of the Kennedy dynasty, Joseph Kennedy. He was a man whose anti-British tendencies and defeatist attitude were already causing criticism in British government circles. Kennedy was on record as believing that in a forthcoming war with Germany, Britain "would be badly thrashed," a sentiment he continually impressed on Washington. He was also to state that he proposed to stay in London only thirty days after bombing began, "and not a moment longer." When the time came, he kept his word.

But even Kennedy's greatest critics admitted that he had one redeeming feature: an ability to bypass bureaucracy and, by dealing directly with those in authority, to produce results. This skill he brought to bear on the *Orinoco*.

239

In London, negotiations had reached a critical stage over Germany's plan for the wholesale resettlement of Jews. Sir Herbert Emerson, director of the International Committee on Political Refugees, was about to meet Hitler's representative for "final discussions."

Acting in concert with Emerson, Kennedy told the German ambassador in London that it would be "unfortunate if the discussions were marred by maltreatment of the *Orinoco* passengers" on their return to Germany. Kennedy's message reached Hitler; the Gestapo allowed the 200 refugees on the *Orinoco* to return to their homes unmolested.

Ambassador Kennedy had achieved his goal for the *Orinoco* passengers. And that same day, in Washington, his government was taking a decision about the *St. Louis* passengers.

Although they would not admit it publicly for a week, on this Saturday, June 3, the American government decided that, if the *St. Louis* passengers were not allowed into Cuba, they would be refused entry into America.

The decision to bar the refugees reflected widespread feeling in the United States toward immigrants. By June 1939, with some thirty million unemployed, opposition came from labor leaders, who claimed that work markets were being depressed by foreigners willing to accept minimum wages. Among the unemployed, as in the rest of the country, there existed a xenophobia which made the United States not so much a melting pot for racial and religious differences but rather a pit for racial and religious antagonisms. On the edge of this caldron perched the 100 per cent American, determined to return the nation to Anglo-Saxon purity. Despite having descended from immigrant stock, they now regarded themselves as native Americans, and were determined to exclude anyone of doubtful origin.

By 1939, the refugees of Europe had fallen into that category. While the average American decried Nazi policies, he was equally opposed to offering its victims a home. For some organizations, like the notorious Ku Klux Klan, which claimed a membership of 4.5 million "white, male persons, native-born gentile citizens of the United States of America," the European refugee posed a greater threat than the Negro. Imperial Wizard

Hiram W. Evans explained: "The Negro is not a menace to Americanism in the sense that the Jew or Roman Catholic is a menace." Increasingly, those two groups were to bear the brunt of the Klan's sectarian violence.

Such demagogues as the radio priest Father Charles Coughlin found willing response among the millions who saw refugees like those on the *St. Louis* as a further threat to the "purity" of the United States.

It was against that background that the State Department, itself filled with its share of prejudiced men, decided to exclude the *St. Louis* passengers. And Franklin Roosevelt, the "liberal" president, but always a president mindful of public opinion, did not overrule that decision.

The only hope now for the refugees drifting just outside Cuban waters was Lawrence Berenson.

In Havana, Berenson received a visit from Nestor Pou, consul of the Dominican Republic. He arrived with a cable from his government offering sanctuary for the *St. Louis* refugees at $500 a head. Pou explained that this was the "going price."

After some debate, he revealed that his government would not adhere strictly to the *per capita* figure of $500, but was "willing to listen to any sort of guarantee."

Berenson, understandably, felt he had "been here before," that Pou, for all his carefully couched diplomatic language, was "also on the make"; in short, the lawyer believed this was one further example of a Caribbean grafter trying to cash in. Instinct also told the lawyer it was better to deal with "the devil I knew," Bru, than enter into protracted discussions with Pou's government. But, careful to keep open options, Berenson informed Pou he would consult with the Joint in New York.

After the envoy left, Berenson informed Cecilia Razovsky that the Dominican offer would be a powerful factor in settling matters with Bru. For he now believed that when the Cuban president discovered another country was offering to take the refugees, Bru would be only too happy to settle for the bond Berenson would offer. It was, in the lawyer's view, a matter of "how you play these banana republic politicians."

Berenson asked Cecilia to tell Goldsmith about the Dominican offer, and then called on Antonio Bustamente, the Relief Committee lawyer who had translated the bond terms into Spanish. In the space still left blank for the amount of the bond, Berenson wrote in $50,000, the lowest figure anyone had suggested. He told Bustamente to get the papers to Bru "pronto."

Bustamente produced a handwritten document on palace notepaper, signed by the president, authorizing all negotiations be conducted through Chief of Police García—one of the men Berenson had shown the door to early on Saturday morning.

"This," said Bustamente firmly, flourishing the note, "is the only way open to us."

Berenson shrugged: as far as he was concerned any channel was only a formality; the deal was as good as settled. So confident was he that, with the help of Bustamente, he concluded arrangements for his visit to the Isle of Pines that afternoon to inspect its amenities for the refugees he expected to land there in a few days.

The visit to the island took on all the panoply of a state visit, with Berenson traveling in a motor cruiser crammed with Cuban dignitaries, army officers, and a detachment of soldiers.

Behind came supporting launches of press and newsreel teams.

Waiting to greet them was a smaller, but equally impressive entourage. At their head was the army chief of staff, the bemedaled, potbellied, jackbooted Fulgencio Batista. Smiling impassively, Batista grasped Berenson's hand, pumped it warmly for the benefit of the photographers, turned, and without so much as a word of explanation, led the lawyer on a swift tour of the island's compounds.

Hedged in by soldiers and officials, Berenson made repeated attempts to discuss the deeper implications of the *St. Louis* affair, but failed utterly to draw the army chief. Thirty minutes after stepping ashore, still dumbfounded, Lawrence Berenson was on his way back to Havana with Batista's parting words ringing in his ears: "This will do them very nicely, Señor Berenson."

It was the one and only time that the *éminence grise* of Cuba emerged from the shadows during the crisis. To Lawrence Berenson, this appearance by Batista, however brief, was the most significant omen he had received since arriving in Havana. The lawyer believed it a "positive sign" that Batista favored letting in the refugees, that it was "nothing less than a public declaration of support for our cause." And, he later told Cecilia Razovsky, it would clinch acceptance for his $50,000 bond. There was now no question of offering up to the $125,000 authorized in the latest cable from the Joint in New York.

As he and Cecilia Razovsky went for a celebration drink, Lawrence Berenson reiterated to reporters waiting in the lobby: "It's all over but the shouting."

The journalists preferred to wait and see before filing wrap-up stories.

Around the time Lawrence Berenson ordered cocktails, Gustav Schroeder was facing a new and serious worry, one that took precedence over the other anxieties he had experienced since leaving Havana.

Purser Mueller had finally confirmed, after a detailed analysis of the stores taken on board before sailing, that, at the present level of consumption, there would be a food and water shortage in about twelve days. The effect if they did not land their passengers before then, Schroeder told Mueller and First Officer Ostermeyer, could be disastrous. Faced with such shortages, the passengers might well stage an open revolt.

The three men already knew the seeds were there after Dr. Spanier had reported that some of the male passengers were talking of hijacking the ship. The news had placed the captain in a dilemma. He could not arrest, or confine on suspicion, numbers of passengers; such action could trigger a mass uprising in which, by sheer weight of numbers, his crew would be overpowered. Equally, he could not ignore the warning. Instead, with the knowledge of the passenger committee, he had compromised by increasing the crew security patrols on board and building up a file of possible troublemakers. Included on his list was Aaron Pozner.

Another worry was the total absence of radio communication. For over twelve hours the *St. Louis* had sailed in ever-widening circles off the Cuban coast, hoping for a message recalling her. Then, in the early hours of Saturday, Gustav Schroeder ordered the ship to steer slowly northward toward Florida. At the back of his mind was still the vague hope of intervention by the United States, and he had reasoned that, should that come, he wanted to be well placed to run for the nearest American port.

After his last discussion with the committee on the possibility of an American solution, when they had read more into his remarks than he ever intended, he had decided to keep such thoughts to himself. To the committee's queries about the course change, he answered that the weather would be cooler the farther north they were, providing some respite for the passengers, who were still suffering from the heat.

Level-headed though the committee was, Schroeder also felt he should not mention to them the suggestion Ostermeyer had made about introducing rationing.

Gustav Schroeder vetoed the idea as potentially dangerous: "If we cut down their food and water, some might even think we're trying to starve them, and that could lead to a riot."

At 4:50 P.M. a cable from Luis Clasing was brought to the captain's day cabin. It read:

INFORMED BY BERENSON VIA GOLDSMITH DOMINICAN REPUBLIC WILLING TAKE YOUR PASSENGERS.

Five minutes later a second cable arrived, this one from the Hapag office in New York:

THERE IS STILL HOPE OF LANDING IN CUBA.

Gustav Schroeder summoned the committee, wondering as he did so how the two new members would react. Both Solly Guttmann and Ernst Vendig were first-class passengers who had become outspoken critics of the committee. When news of their feelings had reached the captain, he promptly suggested that they be co-opted onto the committee—a shrewd move which silenced their public carping.

The newcomers, like the other members, regarded the cables as "hopeful." A suitable notice was drafted for their fellow passengers to read. Though no mention was made in the notice about the Dominican Republic specifically, scores of passengers assumed it was the country involved, and were sure they would land there.

By early evening, the ship was near Miami, still heading north, away from The Dominican Republic and Cuba, on a course that if maintained would bring the *St. Louis* to that point in the ocean where it must either continue northward, reverse course, or swing east—northeast—toward Europe.

Armed with a pair of dividers and an atlas he had borrowed from the ship's library, Otto Schiendick calculated that at its present speed the ship should reach that point in a few hours.

In Havana, reporters cornered Luis Clasing and were surprised to hear the *St. Louis* was "following her course back to Hamburg." To those who asked about rumors that the ship was off Florida, Clasing replied they were "absurd and false."

Clasing's statements were a curious fabrication, no doubt invented to rid him of the unwelcome attention he and his office had endured during the days the ship was in the harbor.

The reporters returned to the Sevilla-Biltmore for a follow-up comment from Berenson, but the lawyer had told the hotel reception he was not to be disturbed. Alone in his room, Berenson confidently awaited a reaction from President Bru to the proposal given to Major García that afternoon. Soon after 11 P.M., it came. Antonio Bustamente telephoned to say that the president, while accepting in principle the idea of a bond, rejected $50,000 as too low a figure. He added that Bru wished to discuss the matter with Berenson at his country seat the next day, Sunday, at noon.

Berenson was not unduly pertrubed by Bru's reaction, but surprisingly, although it was nearly midnight, he decided to communicate it to the American ambassador, Butler Wright.

The ambassador was not pleased to be interrupted at the party he was attending, the more so as Berenson insisted on talking "for nearly an hour about the *St. Louis* situation." Nevertheless, as Wright made clear in a subsequent report to Washington, the lawyer was as optimistic as ever, for the ambassador quoted Berenson as saying:

"The president is going to accept the plan as outlined, with certain unimportant modifications, one being that the bond is raised to $150,000."

SUNDAY, JUNE 4, 1939

On Sunday morning, the passengers on the *St. Louis* were relieved to see that they were still near the American coast, and even closer to Miami than the night before. Now the city could be seen without binoculars.

The sight was comforting; the refugees knew where they were, for the miniature Hapag flag pinpointing their position on the map outside Purser Mueller's office was not believed. Most passengers thought Mueller placed the flag wherever he considered it would please them most.

But more important for the passengers than the ship's position was the direction in which it was traveling. Only one passenger on the ship was able to describe their course with any certainty: ten-year-old Wolfgang Feilchenfeld. Wolfgang had won a compass at the children's party held just before arrival in Havana, and after leaving the harbor, he had become a center of attraction. Sitting unconcernedly at the stern of the ship on B deck, playing chess with his friend Hans Fischer, as the two boys had been when the *St. Louis* had departed Havana and had continued to do ever since, Wolfgang confidently told inquirers on Sunday morning that they were now heading "south southwest, toward Cuba."

Looking toward Miami, Rosemarie Bergmann said to her husband: "So near and yet so far." The remark prompted Otto to state again his view that the passenger committee was a "forum for polite talk, not action." He wanted to offer his services but Rosemarie restrained him. Instead she drew his attention to the deep-sea fishing yachts from Florida that from time to time came close to the *St. Louis*. Many, she pointed out, were taking photographs of the passengers; she wondered if they would be sold to the newspapers.

In midmorning, a much larger ship joined the fishing fleet. It was U.S. Coast Guard cutter 244, from the naval base at Fort Lauderdale. Most passengers believed it was there "to protect us, to pick up anyone who jumped overboard." Only a few thought the cutter's presence was to ensure that the *St. Louis* did not enter American waters.

The sight of the approaching vessel caused Otto Schiendick to panic. He moved to the radio room, where he ordered the duty operator to tune in to the coastguard boat's frequency. The man was about to comply when First Officer Ostermeyer arrived and ordered the steward out.

Schiendick darted back on deck and saw that the cutter was now cruising close to the ship, a fact which undoubtedly unnerved him further. He doubtless wondered if it was part of a move by U.S. intelligence to apprehend him. For a moment, Schiendick probably considered whether he should follow Abwehr practice and destroy the material if the ship was boarded. The quickest way to do that would be to dump it overboard.

As if anticipating the steward's thoughts, the cutter circled the *St. Louis,* and Otto Schiendick clearly saw its officers scanning the decks through binoculars.

Then, one of them waved. Soon everyone on the *St. Louis* was waving back. Schiendick's fears faded. The Abwehr agent managed a nervous smile, and along with all the others, he hesitantly raised his arm in a gesture of greeting.

At noon on Sunday Lawrence Berenson and Antonio Bustamente entered the large, comfortably furnished office which President Frederico Bru used during weekends at his palatial country estate, Parraga. It was to be a meeting of enormous importance to the *St. Louis* passengers.

The president motioned the two men to sit, and then immediately asked whether Berenson could meet his demands.

The lawyer said he could. As the president had requested, the bond could run for nine years instead of six. Males over twenty-one years of age would be the first to leave the country. Berenson thought it "likely" the bond could be raised form $50,000 to $150,000.

Accounts differ about the critical discussion which followed.

According to Bru, he went on to remind Berenson that the $150,000 bond was to guarantee the passengers' sustenance on the Isle of Pines or elsewhere, and that, *in addition*, he required that the normal $500 in cash to be deposited in the Cuban treasury for each immigrant; it would be returned as they left the country. Further, Bru maintained that at the meeting he had insisted that his demands must be met in full within forty-eight hours or the matter would be closed. Finally, Bru later stated, Berenson had agreed to all his qualifications.

Berenson's recollection of what was said differed fundamentally. He claimed the president made no mention of a deadline, and insisted he had said only that "the *St. Louis* can be brought back in forty-eight hours." Regarding the money, Berenson maintained that it was left "open to negotiation after speaking to my principals in New York."

What is known is that Berenson was shaken badly by the president's demands but that even so, Antonio Bustamente advised him to accept them. Equally clear, Berenson was left with no doubt that President Frederico Bru wanted $500 per refugee in cash—nearly half a million dollars—plus the $150,000 bond.

After the meeting, Berenson returned to his hotel to seek the advice of the Joint in New York.

Joseph Hyman, executive director of the Joint Distribution Committee in New York, did not react as strongly to Bru's new demands as Lawrence Berenson had feared. The director stated that he was "prepared to deposit up to $250,000 if there were proper safeguards, plus a bond for the further amount required." He would send the cash to Cuba "only as a last resort," and requested the lawyer, "if possible, to eliminate children from the deposit."

Berenson was satisfied. He was now in a position to offer the president real money, as well as the bond that had been requested earlier. The lawyer then asked Hyman whether, apart from the Dominican Republic, any other countries had offered refuge. Avoiding mention of the United States, the director replied that although many approaches had been made, so far Venezuela, Ecuador, Chile, Colombia, Paraguay, and Argentina had all said no. He thought the Dominican Republic need not be considered: "All our efforts should be directed toward Cuba."

That Sunday evening, Berenson once again contacted American Ambassador Butler Wright. At 9:30 P.M., he and the ambassador met at Consul General Coert du Bois's home. There, Berenson told them of Bru's demand "for an immediate deposit in the Cuban treasury of nearly $500,000"—much more than the maximum Hyman had offered—and indicated that this might be avoided altogether if the American diplomats made a personal appeal to Fulgencio Batista, requesting the army chief to instruct the president to waive the cash deposit demand.

The diplomats were not prepared to be drawn by Berenson. Instead, du Bois commented unhelpfully to the lawyer that his "house of cards, so carefully built up, appears to have fallen down."

At midnight, as the discussion ended, the ambassador told Berenson that the Dominican Republic was his "ace in the hole, and it seems the time has come for you to play it."

The Joint negotiator thought otherwise. He returned to the Sevilla-Biltmore, and began to work out his new offer to Bru.

It was not an easy matter.

Berenson lacked any adviser whom he could trust, having received conflicting advice from, amongst others, Robert Hoffman, Major García, Colonel Benitez, López Castro, García Montes, Antonio Bustamente, and the American diplomats. Batista had seemed to indicate that a solution was possible, but had given no indication how it was to be achieved.

With only the instructions he had received from New York as his guide, Berenson began drafting his revised proposals.

The lawyer estimated, wrongly, that there were 933 passengers on the *St. Louis*, 26 more than there in fact were, and after "eliminating 162 children and 25 tourists who will go to the U.S.," he calculated that the sum of $500 each would come to $373,000.

Working on the same premise of discounting the children, he calculated that the refugees on the *Flandre* and *Orduna* would cost a further $70,000, making a grand total of $443,000.

Berenson then described how the $443,000 was to be paid. Bearing in mind that Hyman had said he could send up to $250,000, Berenson wrote:

From New York	$200,000
From Havana Committee	50,000
From passengers	40,000
Total in cash	$290,000
Difference	153,000
Total	$443,000

As with all computations made by a good accountant, everything neatly balanced. Berenson's usual confidence returned. Remembering Hyman's message that he would send the cash "only as a last resort," the lawyer added a rider: any excess funds provided by relatives of the passengers would be used to reduce the amount of money coming from New York.

Early the next morning, Monday, June 5, after a night of little sleep, Berenson confidently delivered the proposals to Bustamente, who translated them and gave them to Major Bernardo García precisely at 2 P.M., for forwarding to Bru.

In Washington, an hour later, a telephone conversation took place between Henry Morgenthau, Jr., secretary of the treasury, and Cordell Hull, secretary of state, two of the most influential members of President Roosevelt's government.

The sixty-eight-year-old Hull considered himself something of an expert on Cuba, having as a young man raised a regiment of Tennessee Volunteers and accompanied them to fight in the Republic. But the millionaire Morgenthau did not think that experience of much help in the present crisis, and considered Hull's State Department "simply not equipped psychologically, or administratively, to handle the refugee job." Nevertheless, he knew State was the department concerned, and at 3:17 that Monday afternoon he called up Hull.

A flavor of the somewhat ambiguous conversation which followed, and the relationship between the two secretaries, is provided by the transcript of the telephone call.

M: Hello, Cordell.

H: Yes, sir.

M: How are you?

H: Fine!

M: Cordell, some of my good friends have called me about this terrible tragedy with those 900 refugees.

H: Yes.

M: And there have been so many things back and forth.

H: Yeah.

M: Guaranteeing money and so forth.

H: Yeah.

M: You see?

H: Yeah. Well I talked with the president about twenty minutes ago . . .

M: Yes?

H: And this morning I talked to old man James Carson, who is in Havana.

M: Yes?

H: He brought up the question they might go out to the—the islands—our islands down there. What the devil are they . . .

M: Virgin Islands?

H: Yeah. I took that up at once and found we couldn't unless they had a definite home where they were coming from, and in a situation to return to.

M: I see.

H: I think the Jewish organizations . . . will work it out if the financing will be made certain . . . They've got a real chance of doing it, that's what I'm trying to say.

M: I see.

H: We'll do what we can, you understand, but they need a man there who knows how to dicker with them on the financing . . .

M: I see.

H: This is a matter primarily between the Cuban government and these people.

M: I see.

H: And not this government.

M: I see. Well, would you mind if I called you again tomorrow?

H: Yes, sir. I'm keeping up with it the best I can.

M: And I can call you again?

H: Yes, sir. Anytime.

M: Thank you.

H: Yeah.

M: Thank you.

The conversation could hardly have been the most illuminating for Morgenthau. Even so, it provided more information than most inquiries made of the American government.

President Roosevelt did not reply to or even acknowledge the two telegrams sent to him by the passenger committee on the *St. Louis*. Other telegrams were handed down by Roosevelt's personal secretary to the State Department to answer; they often left them unanswered for over a week, and then simply stated that it was "a matter for the Cuban government."

American newspapers attempted to arouse public sympathy by editorials such as the one in the Philadelphia *Record*:

"Granted that the refugee problem is complex and difficult, there must be a better solution for a civilized people than sending out police boats to pick up those who jump in the water."

Although this was typical of many editorials appearing on this Monday, June 5, neither the *Record* nor any other American newspaper advocated that the *St. Louis*'s passengers should be given immediate, unrestricted admission to the United States.

And the official view was explicitly stated by immigration inspector Walter Thomas of Miami: "The *St. Louis* will not be allowed to dock here, or at *any* U.S. port."

At three-thirty Monday afternoon, President Frederico Bru repeated his terms for a settlement to the press in Havana. The president stated he was willing for the refugees to return, and to be housed on the Isle of Pines, as long as acceptable guarantees were given that "they will not become public charges, and that their food and lodging while in Cuba is paid for." Bru added the offer was valid until noon the next day, Tuesday, June 6, and concluded:

"I feel deeply the plight of the refugees, but the post that I occupy has painful duties, which oblige me to disregard the impulses of my heart and follow the stern dictates of duty."

Questioned by reporters, Lawrence Berenson described Bru's statement as an "inspired declaration of a humanitarian and a great statesman."

Thirty minutes after the president's announcement, Major Bernardo García delivered to him Berenson's revised proposals.

That same Monday afternoon, Gustav Schroeder closeted himself in the radio room with Ostermeyer, his first officer. Weeks of tension had brought the two men closer together, and now, both were firmly convinced that Hapag was impeding and confusing matters. Their anger was aroused by company cables from Hamburg, Havana, and New York which were contradictory, and, in the captain's opinion, verged on irresponsible meddling.

A message from Claus-Gottfried Holthusen said the company was scouring the western hemisphere for a suitable port, and warned Schroeder to prepare to sail "anywhere at short notice." Luis Clasing cabled that plans to land the refugees in the Dominican Republic "will only go ahead if they all disembark." From New York had come a message that the Hapag office there was ready to process the passengers "if they land."

Gustav Schroeder thrust the cables aside, growling that this spate of company interest was even less helpful than Hapag's periodic silences. He turned to a sheaf of cables from newspapers and radio and newsreel companies. The one from the Associated Press read: "KINDLY INFORM US YOUR INTENTIONS IN VIEW WORLD INTEREST YOUR SITUATION."

Those last words stayed Schroeder's impulse to ignore the media's request for information. If public opinion could be aroused it could materially improve their chances of landing the refugees in Cuba; publicity might mitigate the unremitting wave of abuse beamed daily in Nazi broadcasts whose tone had become more vehement since the ship departed Havana.

Gustav Schroeder replied to the Associated Press, giving the ship's latest position, speed, and course. His cable concluded:

MY INTENTION IS TO DO ALL POSSIBLE TO ALLEVIATE MOUNTING CONCERN OF MY PASSENGERS WHOSE ONLY WISH IS TO FIND A HOME.

Similar replies were sent to other wire and newsreel services and radio stations, though the captain declined requests from

American networks to allow their reporters on board. Tropical Radio in Miami then announced that some newspapers had chartered aircraft, and shortly afterward several planes swooped and circled over the *St. Louis*.

On board, this unprecedented interest buoyed hopes. Babette Spanier probably spoke for all the passengers when she told her husband: "With this going on we must land somewhere."

The possible choice of landing places widened further with a cable from New York philanthropist Bernard Sandler:

URGE YOU SAIL INTO INTERNATIONAL ZONE NEAR BEDLOES ISLAND IN NEW YORK HARBOR AND STAY THERE WHILE I AND GROUP OF OTHER AMERICAN BUSINESSMEN MEET ALL YOUR COSTS WHILE AT THE SAME TIME MAKING APPEAL TO CONGRESS FOR ASYLUM ALL YOUR PAS-SENGERS.

Gustav Schroeder was nonplused by the offer. It sounded attractive, but, as he told Ostermeyer: "I can't just sail into New York Harbor on the authority of a cable from a man I've never heard of."

He cabled Sandler:

PLEASE CONFIRM AND FINALIZE ALL DETAILS WITH HAPAG NY.

On board ship this Monday, Sandler's offer, when it was posted by the committee, increased still further the mood of optimism.

Schroeder and Ostermeyer left the radio room and went to the captain's cabin. Leo Jockl, who served them coffee, noted that "they were definitely in better spirits than before."

Later that afternoon, Otto Schiendick entered the radio room. He ordered the radio operator to show him the morning's traffic log. When the man hesitated, Schiendick said refusal to cooperate with the party *Leiter* would have serious consequences. The operator handed him the log.

Its recital of press dispatches, Sandler's offer, and Hapag cables, must have confirmed Schiendick's worst fears: the *St. Louis* was not en route back to Hamburg; the ship could well land in New York or another port with potentially disastrous results for his Abwehr mission.

That is the most likely explanation for the steward's next

action: he drafted a message addressed to a secret Abwehr "letter box" in Hamburg, told the operator to send it at once, and walked out of the room.

The message read:

USE ALL INFLUENCE TO BRING SHIP BACK
TO GERMANY IMMEDIATELY.

Astounded, believing the steward had gone mad, the radio man took the message to the bridge.

When the captain read it, he too thought Schiendick had taken leave of his senses, or else the steward was indulging in some sinister practical joke. He then reasoned that unless the steward had gone completely berserk, he would never have dared try to send such a message if he was not totally confident of being supported in his action by someone very well placed in Germany.

Later that afternoon, the captain faced Schiendick in his day cabin, but with more caution than he would have preferred. Schiendick stated that as ship's *Leiter* he had the right to send the message. Schroeder pointed out that the steward's influence did not extend beyond the crew. Schiendick hesitated, and then revealed his Abwehr connection and enough of his mission to make the captain realize he was telling the truth.

Schroeder was shocked and angry at what he heard. He saw now that not only were his passengers pawns of Nazi propaganda, but his ship had been used by the German secret service. He was powerless to prevent that, but there was one thing he could do. As he dismissed Schiendick, he told him:

"Your cable will not be sent. As far as I am concerned, you are still only a steward with certain political responsibilities. They do not include telling me when or where my ship goes."

At four-fifty that afternoon the ship's radio picked up a news flash from a Miami radio station; it quoted President Bru as saying the passengers could disembark on the Isle of Pines. The news flash confirmed a cable from Havana received a short time before.

Schroeder promptly turned the *St. Louis* south again, heading the ship back to Cuba. At 5 P.M. he informed the passenger committee of the reason for his decision, and earned himself a spontaneous burst of applause. Excited questions followed, but the captain could not answer whether the Isle of Pines would be a temporary or a permanent home, nor could he describe what facilities the island offered.

The committee posted the news at ten prominent points throughout the ship, and by 5:30 P.M. a groundswell of relief and excitement spread throughout the *St. Louis*. Most people felt, as Babette Spanier did: "we are no longer wandering Jews."

She suggested to her husband that they bring their suitcases on deck so that they could disembark as soon as the ship arrived at the island. Others had the same thought, and by 7 P.M. the decks were cluttered with luggage.

Aaron Pozner felt only tired relief. He would "do anything" on the island to earn enough money to send for his family. He could abandon the desperate plan to hijack the ship. He, and his fellow plotters, some dozen able-bodied young men, had proposed to storm the bridge in the early hours of the following day, hold the duty watch as hostages, and force the captain to run the ship onto the American coast. Though they had all recognized it as a foolhardy scheme with little chance of success, Pozner had argued that even if they failed, it would make "the world realize how desperate we are." But he feared nevertheless that failure could compel the captain to make full speed for Germany. Once there, the plotters would be doomed.

When Rabbi Weil brought the widow Weiler the news, her first thought was that there might be a synagogue on the island where she could commemorate her husband. The rabbi promised that somehow one would be provided.

Now their future seemed settled, a number of the younger passengers went to the after deck, where couples danced, and some of the men indulged in playful roughhousing. This joyful mood carried on into the evening meal. Leo Jockl had not seen such high spirits in the first-class restaurant since the gala dinner just before arrival in Havana. The air of conviviality brought smiles from Purser Mueller and his assistant, Hans Reich, when they toured the social hall after dinner. How long, they were repeatedly asked, would it take to reach the Isle of Pines?

"Not long," was Reich's unfailing response. "But won't you be sorry to leave us?" More than one pretty young passenger said they would be.

By 10 P.M. First Officer Ostermeyer had revised his estimated time of arrival at the island; he now calculated that with her present speed of twelve knots, the *St. Louis* would arrive soon after 9 A.M. the following day.

"An early breakfast and then they can go on their way," Ostermeyer told Schroeder. "And we can go home."

"I hope so," replied the captain. "I really do hope so."

With that he retired to bed.

Josef Joseph and his fellow committee members had spent part of the evening combing the ship's library for information about the Isle of Pines. Later they pooled their knowledge: all they had gleaned was that the island was thirty-five miles wide, with tropical vegetation, and had been a penal colony, information which brought a wry smile.

Dr. Max Weiss, who had uttered a restraining note when the ship had first approached Havana Harbor, again urged caution: "Let's get our feet on the ground before we celebrate." Once more he was a lone voice. His colleagues pointed out that in the "most unlikely event" of a new failure, there were still offers from Sandler and the Dominican Republic.

"Cuba, Dominican Republic, New York. It doesn't matter in the end so long as it isn't Germany," insisted Josef Joseph.

By midnight the last of the passengers were in bed and the ship was left to the security patrols.

TUESDAY, JUNE 6, 1939

At 5 A.M. Tuesday, the cleaners swept, dusted, and polished their way through the public rooms, followed by stewards laying up for breakfast. At 6 A.M. the radio room received its first message of the day. It came from Havana.

ISLE OF PINES NOT CONFIRMED.

Schroeder studied the cable. If disembarkation was "not confirmed," it did not mean it was canceled. Still, "not confirmed," could be the precursor to cancellation. For fifteen minutes he debated what action to take. At 6:30 A.M. he ordered the ship to reduce speed.

To an Associated Press cable which arrived soon afterward requesting the latest information, Gustav Schroeder replied:

SHIP REMAINING BETWEEN CUBA AND FLORIDA PENDING CLARIFICATION.

At 7 A.M. the captain assembled the passenger committee in his quarters and showed them the cable. The shocked silence was broken by Josef Joseph's question: "What about the Dominican Republic and New York?" There was no new information. Herbert Manasse asked what they should tell the passengers.

"Nothing for the moment," Schroeder said. "Let us wait and see what develops. In the meantime, he suggested, the committee should continue to cable influential figures to intervene. No one could think of a suitable name. Then Ernst Vendig, a new member of the committee, suggested the mayor of St. Louis; the town, after all, had the same name as the ship and might be moved to take an interest.

That Tuesday morning, Lawrence Berenson arrived at the Havana office of Antonio Bustamente just before ten o'clock, the hour when Major Bernardo García had promised to telephone with President Bru's reaction to the revised proposals submitted to him the previous afternoon. At ten-thirty, having heard nothing, Bustamente telephoned the palace and was told the president was still in conference with García and his secretary of the treasury.

There is no record of what was said during that meeting. No doubt Bru was aware his public announcement stating that the refugees could return to the Isle of Pines had not been favorably received by the general public; Havana newspaper morning editions were distinctly critical of the offer.

Waiting with Bustamente, as time passed, Berenson's optimism began to wane. Just after noon, as Bustamente was reminding Berenson that was the hour Bru had said the offer would expire, the telephone rang. It was García. Bustamente watched Berenson's face gradually go pale as he listened. After a long pause, Berenson spoke: "Major García, I don't believe it. The president promised. I must see him immediately." Then the line went dead.

"A statement has just been put out from the palace," Berenson told Bustamente. "It says the government has terminated the matter. The president refuses to see me."

The telephone rang again; the press wanted Berenson's reaction. The lawyer told them: "The declaration has come entirely unexpectedly and I have no explanation for it." He then tried to contact Coert du Bois, eventually locating him at the American Club at 1:30 P.M. Soon after, the two men met in the consul general's office.

Berenson was disconsolate, and du Bois gave him little reason to feel otherwise.

"In my opinion," du Bois said, "you and your coreligionists in New York had better prepare for the worst. You have removed this matter off the plane of humanitarianism and onto the plane of horse trading."

In Washington, unaware of the latest development in Havana, Henry Morgenthau again telephoned Secretary of State Cordell Hull:

> M: Cordell?
> H: Yes, sir.
> M: How are you?
> H: Good!
> M: I'm calling you about this *St. Louis*, the German boat.
> H: Yeah.
> M: My friends in New York say they are having some trouble, the Cubans demanding cash.
> H: The situation, you see, is that the—the folks in New York don't want any money to get in the hands of the Cubans, and the Cubans do.
> M: Uh-huh.
> H: My men . . . are working down there . . . with the—the man who represented the New York people.
> M: That's right.
> H: I forget his name.
> M: Well—there's nothing that I could do, or that they should do?
> H: Nothing I see right now. If I find out anything I'll let you know.
> M: Thank you so much.
> H: Yeah.
> M: Thank you.
> H: Yeah.
> M: Goodbye.

Soon after, an assistant handed to Cordell Hull a cable from Coert du Bois setting out President Bru's midday announcement.

A further announcement was made at 6 P.M. The Cuban government stated:

"Agreement was reached two days ago with Señor Berenson to land the exiles on the Isle of Pines after he had deposited $500 in cash per person, with a subsidiary guarantee with regard to their food and lodging. He was given forty-eight hours to meet these requirements. Yesterday Señor Berenson made an alternative proposal, offering $443,000 for the *St. Louis* passengers, plus 150 additional refugees on the *Orduna* and *Flandre*, the sum to include expenses for food and lodging. The Cuban government could not accept the proposal, and having passed excessively the time allowed, the government terminates the matter."

The next day, the Joint in New York would cable President Bru directly, offering to fulfill his each and every condition. By then it would be too late.

But, on this Tuesday evening, after telling Cecilia Razovsky and Lawrence Berenson that he proposed to inform the *St. Louis* of Bru's decision, Milton Goldsmith looked to Berenson for approval. Lawrence Berenson, now tired, humiliated, and beaten, could merely nod.

Captain Schroeder received Goldsmith's cable at 8 P.M. He kept its contents to himself. At 11:30 P.M., he received a second cable, this time from Claus-Gottfried Holthusen in Hamburg. Again the captain kept the contents to himself.

But as a result of that second cable, at 11:40 P.M., Gustav Schroeder walked from his cabin to the bridge, and ordered helmsman Heinz Kritsch to bring the ship onto a heading of east northeast, a change of course which would take the *St. Louis* back to Germany.

WEDNESDAY, JUNE 7, 1939

The message Holthusen had sent Captain Schroeder ordered:

RETURN HAMBURG IMMEDIATELY.

Even before he had heard from Clasing of Bru's decision, the Hapag director had been under considerable pressure to recall the ship. He had estimated that the *St. Louis* would need to leave for Germany on this Wednesday night at the latest in order to disembark its passengers there and sail to New York in time to meet its scheduled summer cruises. Further, Captain Schroeder had informed him that the constant changes of course and maneuvering had reduced his fuel to such an extent that he could "hold out for little longer than a week before being forced into port to refuel."

Holthusen had heard from the Hapag office in New York that reservations for the *St. Louis*'s Caribbean cruises were in danger of falling off, due to adverse publicity; some American newspapers placed Hapag's advertisements for the pleasure cruises on the same page that reported the plight of the refugees on the "pleasure liner."

Hapag was never a company to court publicity, and now Holthusen hoped that with the return of the ship the matter would fade from the headlines. Instead, newspaper coverage increased. In Germany, President Bru's rejection of the passengers, coupled, by inference, with that of President Roosevelt's, gave Goebbels' propaganda machine a field day. How could the world criticize Germany for its treatment of Jews, Goebbels asked, when the world could see how other countries rejected them? It was not a question easily answered.

262

For internal consumption, Goebbels took a different tack, stoking hatred against the returning refugees. German radio stations announced:

"Since no one will accept the shabby Jews on the *St. Louis,* we will have to take them back and support them."

It was not difficult to guess where they were to be "supported": in the concentration camps. The relatives of the *St. Louis* passengers, most of them elderly parents who had stayed behind in Germany, knowing this, suffered with the refugees on the ship as it traveled homeward.

Elise Loewe's mother in Breslau, knowing nothing of her son-in-law's attempted suicide, feared for his life on his return. She knew he was on the Gestapo's wanted list before he left, and believed there was no doubt the Gestapo would take him away when the *St. Louis* reached Hamburg. The same fear gripped Rachel Pozner in Nuremberg, Lilli Joseph's sister and mother in Berlin, and Josef Joseph's sister in Duesseldorf.

In London, the press, while mentioning Bru's decision, devoted more space to the crucial talks about to take place with Hitler's representative on the plan for the resettlement of all remaining Jews in Germany.

Paul Baerwald, the highly respected chairman of the Joint Distribution Committee, had arrived from New York for the discussions, and was staying at the Savoy Hotel. On this Wednesday, he read with resignation the newspaper reports of what had happened in Cuba. A cable arriving from Joseph Hyman, Baerwald's executive director in New York, suggested that Baerwald "test" the attitude of the British and French governments toward giving the *St. Louis* passengers asylum.

During the afternoon, the chairman spoke to various of his contacts in London on the possible British position. Sir Herbert Emerson, director of the International Committee on Political Refugees, about to embark on the most delicate of all negotiations affecting "not just a few hundred, but hundreds of thousands of refugees," thought it "a most inappropriate moment to raise the matter."

In the late afternoon, Baerwald cabled his colleagues in New York telling them the response to his first tentative inquiries "did not seem promising."

At about the same time, on the *St. Louis*, Captain Schroeder called the passenger committee to his cabin, and told them the ship was returning to Europe. "I have left it as late as possible," he said, "in the hope the position would change, but I can no longer keep it from you."

Some of the committee had already guessed the worst, noting the ship's direction, but after so many hopeful signs in the past, they could not at first bring themselves to believe what the captain had said. Josef Joseph asked Schroeder how he could ignore the offer of the island off New York, and the Dominican Republic.

"That is why I delayed telling you until now," the Captain replied. "I have just had a cable from Hapag in New York saying that both these possibilities are now extremely remote." Answering the unspoken question, he went on: "I do not believe you will disembark in Germany. I believe you should now pin your hopes on Great Britain."

A terrible, personal realization touched each member of the passenger committee. They dared not say it openly, even to each other. Some could not bear even to mention it to their wives and children. It was inhuman, degrading, and endured in private, but it cut deeply into one of the most basic of all human needs: the need to be wanted. Instead, they had been rejected. Even the New World did not want them; now they must rely again on the Old. The committee suffered in silence, knowing it was not just an anonymous group of people who had been turned down, but that they, individually, each one, had had the open door shut in their faces; through them, their entire race had been judged, and found wanting. If some other country accepted them, they now believed it would be on sufferance.

Joseph advised they should not yet inform the passengers. Dr. Weiss agreed: "We need time for our own strength to return."

The captain watched them leave. He knew, as they did, that the only certain gate that remained open to welcome the passengers on the *St. Louis* was the gate to a concentration camp.

THURSDAY, JUNE 8, 1939

The next day, Thursday, in New York, the executive committee of the Joint met to review matters. On Wednesday, they had received an offer from the quarantine station at Balboa, in the Panama Canal Zone, to house the refugees at a cost of $1.50 per day for those over twelve years of age, half price for children. The offer had been declined by the Joint because "negotiations in Cuba are continuing."

Now, there were two new offers to consider: the president of Honduras said his country was willing to take the passengers, but did not specify terms; Bernard Sandler, evidently unsuccessful in his bid to persuade Congress to accept the refugees, stated that he could provide a ship for them to transfer to if $50,000 was forthcoming. It was reported that singer Eddie Cantor had offered the money. Both suggestions were refused by the Joint. Then they examined the earlier offer of the Dominican Republic. After careful consideration, it too was rejected: the country did not have the facilities to accommodate them, the $500 deposit for each passenger was not thought to be returnable, the deposit applied only to Jews and might therefore set a precedent to be followed by other countries.

Having disposed of that matter, the Joint executive committee turned its attention to more "positive" action. A cable was sent to their chairman in London, Paul Baerwald, criticizing the British government's failure to cooperate. In light of their own country's decision to keep out the refugees, and subsequent events, it seemed singularly inappropriate.

As the Joint executive committee was meeting in New York, on the *St. Louis* the ship's loudspeakers summoned all passengers

to the social hall for an announcement of extraordinary important. Dr. Fritz Spanier, like many others, suspected what it would
be. Their fears were swiftly confirmed by Josef Joseph's stark
announcement that they were heading back to Europe.

An audible gasp swept the room. A voice cried out: "You
mean we are going back to Germany!"

"Not necessarily. But we must stay calm."

Joseph's appeal was lost in voluble protests from a group of
young men. One of them, Aaron Pozner, was thrust forward as
their spokesman. In an impassioned voice, he argued that many
men on board had been in concentration camps, and only
released on the strict condition that they left Germany forever.
His words rang through the social hall: "For us to return means
one thing—returning to those camps. That could also be the future of every man, woman and child on this ship!"

His statement brought an anguished chorus. Babette Spanier
tearfully begged her husband to promise her their twin daughters
would not face that fate. Embracing his wife and children, Fritz
Spanier found no words of reassurance.

Shalote Hecht turned to her nephew, Otto Bergmann, and
vowed fiercely: "If the worst happens we'll stay together. After
all, they can only kill us once."

Recha Weiler, leaning on the arm of Rabbi Weil, murmured
quietly she was only glad her husband's death had spared him
from the fate now facing them.

Little Judith Feilchenfeld asked: "Momma, if they put us in a
camp will they let Papa come and see us?" Alice Feilchenfeld held
back her tears and gently told her daughter she was not to think
such things. Judith's eldest brother, Wolfgang, looked at his compass and said it was pointing east northeast. For the first time in
several days, nobody paid any attention to the boy's news.

Elise Loewe felt her children's arms slip protectively around
her, and Ruth whispered: "Somebody will think of something."

For their sake, she did not say what she had thought for many
days: that the future held no personal interest for her from that
moment her husband, Max, had plunged overboard in Havana
Harbor.

Around the Loewes, the low-keyed chant first heard when the

ship had sailed from Havana took on a new life as scores repeated: "We must not die . . . we will not return . . . we must not die."

Herbert Manasse, the youngest member of the committee, demanded silence. The sound of his strong, confident voice stilled the crowd.

"Ladies and gentlemen," Manasse said, "the news *is* bad. That we *all* realize. But Europe is still many days away. That gives the Joint, and all our other friends, time to make new moves to help us. In the meantime this sort of behavior will do nothing to alter or help our situation. The committee will welcome practical suggestions—but we cannot tolerate rash behavior."

One of the men elbowed his way to the rostrum where Manasse stood. He had, he said, a suggestion: a number of the best swimmers should volunteer to jump overboard at selected intervals; the ship would be forced to stop and pick them up; in that way they could delay almost indefinitely their return to Europe.

Manasse quashed the idea: "That is an example of the sort of suggestion we will *not* act upon. It is foolhardy and futile!"

The man stormed out of the social hall, followed closely by Pozner and the rest of his group.

That morning, like the passengers, steward Leo Jockl also faced a threat to his future.

It had arrived in a coded cable addressed to Gustav Schroeder, from Hapag, Hamburg:

POLICE REQUEST FULL DETAILS OF YOUR PERSONAL KNOWLEDGE STEWARD JOCKL'S FAMILY BACKGROUND AS THEY HAVE REPORTS HE IS OF JEWISH ANTECEDENTS. MATTER REGARDED MOST SERIOUSLY AS POLICE SAY COMPLAINT BASED ON SOUND SOURCES. IF NECESSARY CONSULT ORTSGRUPPENLEITER SCHIENDICK TO CLARIFY JOCKL BACKGROUND AND RADIO ALL INFORMATION IMMEDIATELY.

The request sickened the captain; for him it was further proof that the company he had served so proudly was now "acting as a messenger service for the Nazis." His determination to resign at the end of the voyage grew even stronger.

Schroeder guessed, correctly, that somewhere behind the cable was the hand of Otto Schiendick. But a confrontation would probably simply bring the response that the steward had a

right to be involved in such a matter; undoubtedly Schiendick
would relish the prospect of interrogating Jockl.

Yet the cable could not be ignored; that would certainly raise
the curiosity of the Gestapo. The captain sent for Jockl, showed
him the message, and watched with compassion as the steward
read it. Then, with a sigh, Schroeder drafted a reply and handed it
to his steward:

FULLEST QUESTIONING REVEALS STEWARD JOCKL LOYAL TO PARTY
AND COUNTRY. NO EVIDENCE OF SEMITIC BACKGROUND.

The two men looked silently at each other. Then the captain
began to encode the message. He paused only once to say to the
steward: "God help us both if they discover the truth."

That same morning Otto Schiendick told Purser Mueller that,
in his capacity as *Ortsgruppenleiter,* he was banning all further
"social intercourse" between crew and passengers. Mueller retorted that Schiendick needed the captain's permission for such an
action. "In such party matters I do not have to consult the captain," the steward replied.

Shortly afterward the ship's loudspeakers announced the ban.

At lunchtime, passengers learned of another development.
The menus, formerly individually printed for each meal and
offering a choice of food, were now on single mimeographed
sheets. All three meals were typed on the page, and there was no
longer a choice. Stewards explained: "We face a food shortage due
to our hurried departure from Havana."

That evening the ship's orchestra played to a virtually deserted dance floor; the cinema was almost empty. A mood of
lethargy steadily tightened its grip on the *St. Louis* as hour by
hour, knot by knot, Germany came closer.

FRIDAY, JUNE 9, 1939

The next day, Friday, the first formal meeting took place at the Home Office in London to discuss the *St. Louis*. After pressure from Paul Baerwald, chairman of the Joint, allied to that of American ambassador Joseph Kennedy, the British government had agreed the matter could be raised at a "low level" by a representative of the German-Jewish Aid Committee with a junior member of the Home Office staff, Mr. Cooper. Baerwald's earlier impression as he had reported it to New York was confirmed: the Home Office's initial attitude was "not promising."

Cooper thought it "significant" that the Joint itself had not "been prepared to secure the refugees' admission to Cuba on the terms offered." Why, therefore, should Britain, a country with no real knowledge of the passengers, put itself out when, in Havana, the responsible American relief organization had been unable "to lend a helping hand."

It was an embarrassing question for the British relief worker to answer. He also found it impossible to tell Cooper whether the passengers "were of a desirable, or undesirable, class." The Home Office official believed they "might well be, in fact, something in the nature of a general jail delivery at the insistence of the Gestapo who had forced the voyage on the Hamburg-American Line."

What Cooper did not state, but later included in his report of the meeting, was his "feeling" that if the British government were to "accede to the request at the instance of the Aid Committee, the ruse once practiced and proved successful would be repeated ad infinitum."

The two men agreed it was of paramount importance that Sir

Herbert Emerson's discussions on the plan for orderly emigration from Germany were not upset. As they parted, they also agreed it would be "altogether wrong to come to any decision with regard to these people while the vessel is on the high seas; if steps were taken to ensure their admission to the United Kingdom, it should only be done after their return to Germany, when individual cases could be investigated."

The words would have chilled the passengers on the *St. Louis*, but, fortunately, they had no knowledge of the meeting. Nor, again fortunately, did they know what was said when the executive committee of the Joint met in New York the same day to bring themselves up to date on developments.

Morris Troper in Paris had cabled again that if the passengers were returned to Germany, the entire shipload would be sent to the concentration camps. However, it was his impression that if the British government were prepared to offer help, the French might also. Troper reported that Baron Robert de Rothschild was attempting to persuade the authorities to make available a French colonial island off South America, or, failing that, perhaps Tangiers in North Africa.

There was little the executive committee could usefully do. They sent a cable to Troper requesting that they "be assured no single possibility of escape should fail to be given utmost consideration." The Joint decided to hold another meeting, three days later, on Monday, at 4 P.M., "inconvenient and troublesome as it is," because, the acting chairman wrote, "I want the record to show our unremitting efforts."

By midday of that Friday, June 9, unable to afford the luxury of any postponement of action, the *St. Louis* passenger committee had made the radio room their virtual headquarters, as the latest salvo of appeals was sent to Prime Minister Neville Chamberlain in London, the governments of France, Belgium, and Holland, and religious and civic leaders throughout Europe. Extra care had been taken to make the messages brief as well as poignant, for Hapag had refused to grant the committee further free cabling facilities.

Money to pay for the radiograms had been raised by passengers, who pawned their jewelry, cameras, and even their clothes with crew members. Now, with no more cash available, all on board knew those cables contained their last hopes of intercession.

The cable to Prime Minister Chamberlain was typical:

907 PASSENGERS ON S.S. ST. LOUIS HALF WOMEN AND CHILDREN REFUSED LANDING IN CUBA IN SPITE OF PERMITS AND NOW ON RETURN VOYAGE TO HAMBURG BEG TO BE SAVED BY BEING GRANTED ASYLUM IN ENGLAND OR AT LEAST DISEMBARKATION AT SOUTHAMPTON AS RETURN TO HAMBURG IMPOSSIBLE AND ACTS OF DESPERATION WOULD BE UNAVOIDABLE.

But around the time it was transmitted, the final stages of one act of desperation were already under way. Singly, at intervals, one young man followed another down a corridor on D deck to cabin 373, where Aaron Pozner greeted them. When they were assembled, twelve in all, they stood with heads bowed as Pozner prayed for divine help for the violent action they planned.

Close by in the crew's quarters, violence, verbal but no less wounding, was also in the air as Otto Schiendick briefed the Gestapo "firemen" before they fanned out in pairs through the passenger decks to carry out the steward's orders. By midafternoon a number of passengers had been told by the "firemen": "These are your last free days. Enjoy them. After you return to Hamburg you won't be heard of again." The refugees, apart from Rabbi Weil, were too terrified to make any protest. And, when he remonstrated, he was warned: "In Dachau they'll shave off your beard if you open your mouth."

The majority of the crew continued to behave in an exemplary manner, and there were many acts of generosity. Stewards and cabin boys smuggled in the last of the fresh fruit from the kitchens and placed them in children's cots; the Spanier twins were each slipped five Reichsmarks by their table steward; Carl Lenneberg, who had run out of money for pipe tobacco, found a one-pound tin left for him by his table steward; Assistant Purser Hans Reich took a bottle of *Sekt* to a couple of pretty girls in their cabin.

Leo Jockl had obtained a special gift for Aaron Pozner, a couple of slices of smoked salmon on black bread. There had been no opportunity or time since Havana for the steward to visit Pozner. But, unexpectedly, on this Friday afternoon Jockl found himself free. He hurried to Pozner's cabin, anxious to know how the teacher was bearing up. There was no reply to Jockl's knocking; impulsively he opened the door, and found the cabin empty, but showing signs of recent occupation by several persons. Jockl knew Pozner was a nonsmoker and usually a tidy man; his visitors had shown no such fastidiousness in grinding out their cigarette butts on the carpet. The steward clearly recalled that Pozner had no friends on board. The more he thought about it, the stronger his feeling grew that Aaron Pozner was involved in something out of character. He put the sandwiches on the bed and left.

Later, when Jockl brought tea to the captain, he mentioned his suspicions. Schroeder consulted a list on his desk, stabbing a finger against a name halfway down the paper. Aaron Pozner, he said, was one of the passengers he had been warned might try to sabotage the ship.

"Find him, Jockl, and bring him to me before he does anything foolish," ordered the captain.

At that moment, Aaron Pozner and the other plotters were waiting in the nearest public room to the bridge, the gymnasium. At 4:30 P.M., they slipped out of the gymnasium and entered the bridge area. First Officer Ostermeyer looked up from a map as the man appeared in the chart room. Before he could move, two of them bundled him through the bridge.

Helmsman Kritsch gasped at the sight. As he moved to ring the ship's emergency system—designed to warn of fire at sea—he was sent flying into a corner. In minutes the rest of the watch was overpowered. Pozner ordered Ostermeyer to send for the captain.

When Captain Schroeder appeared he was surrounded by Pozner and two other men. The captain demanded to know what they hoped to achieve.

"To save our lives," said Pozner, "by taking over the ship and sailing it to any country other than Germany."

Schroeder looked carefully at the slightly built, tense young teacher, and in a flat and resigned voice, began:

"The other passengers will not support you. You have not seized the engine room. My crew will overpower you. All you are doing is laying yourself open to a charge of piracy."

The group looked uneasily at each other. One said defiantly

that they would hold the captain and those on the bridge as hostages.

"I will give no order, no matter what you do, that will take my ship off its set course," insisted Schroeder, "and without that order you can do nothing."

The captain walked over to Kritsch and guided him back to the wheel, painfully aware of how frightened the helmsman was. He then said to Pozner:

"You have done enough damage already for me to prefer serious charges. If I do, I can assure you that you certainly will be taken back to Germany. And you know what that means. I understand and sympathize with your desperation. But you have behaved in a criminal manner. However, I am willing to overlook that in all the circumstances if you leave this bridge, having given me an understanding that you will take no further such action. You have exactly one minute to accept this offer."

He deliberately turned his back on the group, who began to whisper among themselves.

"Captain, we cannot return to Germany," pleaded Pozner.

Schroeder turned and saw the fear in the young man's face. At that moment First Officer Ostermeyer began to struggle with his captors. The captain sharply ordered him to desist, then, in a softer voice, he told the group he would do everything possible to land the passengers in England. That promise ended any further resistance. The men gave solemn pledges about their future good conduct, and filed off the bridge.

The captain saw that the crisis had deeply affected all the watch, particularly helmsman Kritsch; even the usually cool Ostermeyer was making a visible effort to control himself.

"The incident is over," said Schroeder firmly. "There is no cause for further worry."

Nodding for Ostermeyer to follow, the captain left the bridge, aware that he, too, was now showing signs of reaction. He knew that the attempted hijacking might be the prelude to similar acts unless he acted swiftly and surely. Pausing only to pour himself and Ostermeyer large brandies in his day cabin, he made rapid plans. There was no time to convene the committee; in any case, they would be powerless to quell further trouble. Nor could he muster the crew to guard the bridge and engine room; that might well lead to a violent reaction from other headstrong passengers.

Schroeder decided it was time to follow up a suggestion made to him a number of times in the past.

"I must talk to the passengers myself," he told Ostermeyer. It would be the first time the captain had done so on the voyage; he believed that would be a factor in his favor. "When I speak they will believe me," he said to his first officer.

At 5 P.M., some 600 passengers—the absentees were mostly children—assembled in the social hall to hear the captain. As he stood beneath the huge portrait of Hitler, Schroeder experienced a great "sense of hopelessness. It was as if the whole *St. Louis* had been cast out of this world and must now leave this inhospitable planet. It was this feeling which gave me complete understanding for the desperate position of my passengers and led me to the correct words to say."

His speech was brief; whatever happened they would not be returned to Germany.

The sheer confidence in his voice brought the reaction he desired—"an almost physical wave of relief was felt when I finished speaking." His words carried far more conviction than he really felt, but no one knew that.

Schroeder left the social hall to plan his most crucial move. Later, he would not be able to recall how long the idea had been in his mind, or what placed it there. But his promise to Pozner's group to land the refugees in England had given impetus to his schemes.

That evening he summoned the first officer, the purser, and the chief engineer to his cabin, and swore each of them to secrecy over his intentions. Schroeder decided not to inform the passenger committee until the last possible moment about the course of action he proposed: he felt they migh leak his intentions to some of the other passengers.

Instead, he sent for Dr. Fritz Spanier. The captain had come increasingly to trust the doctor's medical judgments of how passengers would react to a given situation. The doctor listened without interruption as Schroeder unfolded his scheme. The advice Spanier then proffered was short and simple.

"Don't tell the committee. Don't give anybody any warning.

That includes the crew. When it happens, treat it as a real emergency. The risk of panic will be higher, but in the circumstances that will be beneficial."

The "circumstances" Dr. Spanier and the three ship's officers had approved was the captain's plan to run the *St. Louis* close to Beachy Head on the Sussex coast of England, set the ship on fire, and evacuate the passengers ashore.

SATURDAY, JUNE 10, 1939

On June 10, four weeks to the day after the *St. Louis* had set sail from Hamburg, Morris Troper in Paris spoke by telephone to Max Gottschalk in Brussels. Gottschalk was president of the Refugee Committee, and already knew of the *St. Louis*'s plight. He promised Troper he would "do what I can." What he did set the seal on the future of everyone on board the ship.

At ten-thirty, Gottschalk spoke to Belgian Minister of Justice Paul Emile Janson. Janson in turn promised to bring the matter to the attention of Prime Minister Hubert Pierlot. In less than an hour after it was raised, Belgium made the decision which Cuba and A   ica had debated for days, even weeks, and finally refused to make: King Leopold III and Prime Minister Pierlot agreed that 200 of the passengers could land in Belgium.

Morris Troper heard the news from Max Gottschalk just after noon. The Joint director decided not to tell the *St. Louis* until it was officially confirmed. By then, it would be too late to stop yet another tragedy aboard the ship.

On Saturday morning, helmsman Heinz Kritsch failed to report for duty. He had last been seen by Leo Jockl near the halyard on the after deck. A search party found him in a locker room—hanging from a beam.

Captain Schroeder was too overcome to speak when he heard of the helmsman's suicide. He had been genuinely fond of the young sailor, sharing with him a passion for ornithology and a pride in seamanship. The captain committed his thoughts about Kritsch's death to his private diary, an entry that shows the deep feelings it aroused in him:

"God knows why he did it. His death is an irreplaceable loss for both the line and myself, for there was no more reliable man than he. Thoughts about the terrible finality of death depress me for the third time on this journey. First Weiler, then Berg, now Kritsch."

Shortly before midnight this Saturday, the captain read the burial service and saluted as Kritsch's shroud was dropped over the side to sink beneath the surging bow wave of the *St. Louis*.

SUNDAY, JUNE 11, 1939

On Sunday, in Paris, Morris Troper continued to press representations to other governments. Belgium had provided the necessary initial breakthrough, and now France, Holland, and Great
Britain were actively considering the question.

Troper knew the matter was still urgent, for he had been told
by an emissary from Berlin, a Jewish relief worker with suspiciously close and reliable ties with the Gestapo, that the German secret police intended to intern the *St. Louis* passengers if
more than half of them were returned to Hamburg.

The Gestapo also claimed that the ship had been ordered by
them to proceed slowly until noon on Monday; after that, unless
$50,000 was provided for purchase oil, it would be instructed to
head immediately for its home port. Troper told the intermediary
to "inform the Gestapo no such money would be forthcoming."

In London, American ambassador Joseph Kennedy met with
the chairman of the Joint, Paul Baerwald, and received a letter
from him guaranteeing that any of the *St. Louis* passengers who
were permitted to disembark in Britain would be maintained and
cared for by the Jewish relief agency. Kennedy promised to
arrange that the letter was put before the proper authorities in
the hope that "the British government will receive some or all
these people here."

MONDAY, JUNE 12, 1939

The next morning, Monday, June 12, Morris Troper heard from Holland that Queen Wilhelmina and the Dutch government had agreed to give temporary asylum to 194 of the refugees. With this knowledge, Troper cabled the *St. Louis.*

EVERY CONCEIVABLE POSSIBILITY TO FIND HAVEN BEING EXPLORED WITH SOME PROSPECTS WHICH WE HOPE WILL BECOME DEFINITE NEXT THIRTY-SIX HOURS.

At about the same time in London, the passenger committee's cable was delivered to Prime Minister Neville Chamberlain. After reading it, Chamberlain approved a high-level meeting to be held that afternoon at 3 P.M., to be chaired by the British prime minister's permanent undersecretary at the Home Office, Sir Alexander Maxwell. Among those present were Sir Herbert Emerson, chairman of the International Committee on Political Refugees, Paul Baerwald, chairman of the Joint Distribution Committee, and their various advisors.

Cooper, the junior official who had earlier reported his doubts about letting the refugees in, now repeated his argument that they should be returned to Germany before any promises were made. He told the meeting:

"It is probable that a proportion of the passengers are undesirable. It would be easier to reject such individuals while they were on German soil than to refuse them admission to this country and enforce their return to Germany."

Sir Alexander Maxwell overruled Cooper's objections. Instead, he stated that he would recommend to the British government that they accept up to 350 of the *St. Louis* passengers. The British government agreed.

That evening, at 6:30 P.M., the French government officially announced that it would take 250 of the refugees.

On the *St. Louis* that Monday night, none of these decisions was yet known. Even so, Troper's cable with its promise of definite news "in thirty-six hours" had changed everything: Captain Schroeder shelved his plan to set fire to the ship; the refugees no longer worried that, with the water shortage and the ship's laundry unable to accept their clothes, even their dress was now beginning to show the effects of the voyage.

That night, many went to the ship's cinema. Ever since Havana, it had been running and rerunning the same films. Even Liesl Joseph, who had often sneaked out of her berth when her parents were asleep to go to the films, had become bored with seeing the same ones over and over again. But tonight, Purser Mueller provided a film which had not been seen before, *Ihr Liebhusar,* a comedy starring Magda Schneider.

The showing was well attended. One particular line caused an outburst of laughter: "Traveling by sea makes one nervous."

The tension on the *St. Louis* had been broken.

TUESDAY, JUNE 13, 1939

On Tuesday, the world learned that the "wandering refugees" would not be returning to Germany. In Berlin, Propaganda Minister Joseph Goebbels ordered that the British and French governments in particular should be heavily criticized in the German press for "selling out to the Jews."

In Paris, Morris Troper cabled the ship:

FINAL ARRANGEMENTS FOR DISEMBARKATION ALL PASSENGERS COMPLETE. GOVERNMENTS OF BELGIUM, HOLLAND, FRANCE, AND ENGLAND COOPERATED MAGNIFICENTLY WITH AMERICAN JOINT DISTRIBUTION COMMITTEE TO EFFECT THIS POSSIBILITY.

The passenger committee replied that their "gratitude is an immense as the ocean on which we have been traveling since May 13." They decided to inform all the passengers the next morning after breakfast in the social hall.

WEDNESDAY, JUNE 14, 1939

At 10 A.M., in the presence of Captain Schroeder, the telegram from Troper was read aloud. From every corner of the large room came cheering and sobs of joy. Josef Joseph asked for silence, and then expressed the gratitude of everyone present to Schroeder and his crew. The captain smiled but did not speak.

That night, a celebration party was held in the jam-packed social hall. There were singers, magicians, classical pianists, and comedians. Most of the jokes had to do with holiday cruises to Cuba. But the biggest laugh was raised by one of the refugees simply reading from a Hapag brochure. The handout stated:

"The *St. Louis* is a ship on which one travels securely, and lives in comfort. There is everything one can wish for that makes life on board a pleasure."

THURSDAY, JUNE 15, 1939

In Paris, the French national chief of police, exercising considerable restraint, told the press that he "regretted our American friends, to whose country the majority of the refugees were eventually going, stopping at Cuba only en route, were not able to direct them to one of their ports instead of sending them back to Europe."

FRIDAY, JUNE 16,
to SATURDAY, JUNE 17, 1939

Morris Troper left Paris on Friday and spent the night in Antwerp. The next morning, at 4 A.M., he and his party, along with representatives from all the countries concerned, traveled by car to the Dutch port of Flushing at the head of the estuary leading to Antwerp in Belgium. There, at nine o'clock, a tug took them out to the *St. Louis*.

On the *St. Louis*, Thursday and Friday had been spent on the ship packing and preparing lists itemizing which of the four countries each passenger preferred to go to.

On board the ship, now, the passengers lined the rails to catch their first glimpse of "the man who had saved our lives." A reception line of small children waited to greet Troper. At its head was Liesl Joseph, chosen because she was the daughter of the passenger committee chairman, but also because Liesl was that day celebrating her eleventh birthday.

As Morris Troper stepped onto the ship, Liesl moved forward, and made her prepared speech:

"We thank you with all our hearts. I am sorry that flowers do not grow on ships; otherwise we would have given you the largest and most beautiful bouquet ever."

The sea odyssey was almost over. But for many passengers on the *St. Louis*, it was, at best, only the end of the beginning.

As the *St. Louis* steamed slowly toward Antwerp, Morris Troper and the relief workers from France, Belgium, the Netherlands, and the United Kingdom began sorting out which of the passengers were to go where. Though they did not know it, they were, in effect, sitting in judgment on who would live and who would die.

After the welcoming ceremony, Captain Schroeder had
stepped forward and told Troper, "The entire ship's complement
is at your service." He suggested that Troper and the relief
workers use the social hall as their office, ordered Purser Mueller
and his staff to make the necessary arrangements, and then returned to the bridge to guide the *St. Louis* up the Schelde estuary
to Antwerp.

The social hall, where in Havana the Cuban doctor had inspected the passengers before their expected disembarkation,
where afterward so many momentous announcements had been
made, now was the setting for the final decisions about the fate of
each individual *St. Louis* passenger.

At the center table sat Morris Troper and his assistant
Emanuel Rosen, both Americans. To their right were the tables of
the Belgian and Dutch representatives. To the left, those of the
British and French. Hovering in the background was the passenger committee, offering help and advice. In all there were
twenty-six officials present; the only member of the ship's company continuously on hand was Assistant Purser Hans Reich. In
front of each table was a long line of anxious passengers, all
talking at once and hoping to influence the representatives of the
country of their choice. Behind the tables, overlooking the entire
scene, as usual, was the portrait of Adolf Hitler.

Morris Troper made only one promise to the assembled passengers: he and his coworkers would do their best to keep families
together. The first two hours were spent deciding who would be
sent to Great Britain. Although the representatives of the four
countries gave an outward appearance of friendly compromise
and reasonableness, beneath the surface there was tension. From
time to time it appeared, especially between the British and the
French, Emanuel Rosen noticed, that they barely concealed their
competition for those passengers who had the lowest numbers on
the U.S. quota list and could therefore be expected to leave after
minimum of delay.

The Dutch representative, Alfred Moser, had orders to accept
only those with a U.S. registration card, preferably with a low
number, because, he explained:

"We already had so many refugees and refugee camps, and
now another two hundred! So we tried to get people we could, so

to speak, get rid of quickly, in order to comply with the wishes of the Dutch government. But in any case, it was no real solution. Only a delay in the fatal solution."

Not all the passengers on the *St. Louis* held U.S. quota numbers. Those who did not were barred from Holland.

Soon after two o'clock, Captain Schroeder nosed his ship alongside Antwerp Harbor's pier 18. For the first time since leaving Hamburg, the *St. Louis* had been allowed to tie up at a quayside. Police and customs officials flocked onto the ship, but, as in Havana, friends and relations on the shore, and the press, were not allowed on board.

Just before the ship berthed, there had been ugly scenes near pier 18 when Antwerp's Nazi-inspired National Youth Organization staged a demonstration protesting the arrival of the refugees. Handbills had been distributed containing the message: "We too want to help the Jews. If they call at our offices each will receive gratis a length of rope and a long nail."

The handbills were confiscated and their distributors dispersed by the Belgian police. Passengers on the *St. Louis* knew nothing of the demonstration, nor did they see the parade of the black-shirted Fascists which passed through the main streets of Antwerp just at the time the ship arrived. In this case, the police did not intervene.

During the afternoon, the atmosphere in the social hall became more feverish as passengers learned that, in many cases, they were not to be allowed to go to the country of their choosing. Sometimes there were even arguments within families: Rosemarie and Otto Bergmann wanted badly to go to Britain, but the domineering aunt, Shalote Hecht, had her heart set on France, and as the young couple had promised to look after her on the voyage, they felt obliged to do as she wished.

Even so, Rosemarie Bergmann had other worries on her mind, as she made clear to Emanuel Rosen.

"She amazed everyone," he recalled, "because in the midst of the excitement and confusion, she asked what would become of her dog, which Hapag had forwarded to Havana separately, and please could I do something about it?" Rosen could not. Oshey, Rosemarie's fox terrier, would have to fend for herself without the benefit of the relief worker's efforts.

In the calm of his day cabin, Captain Schroeder reflected on the trip and his future. He had received instructions from the head office not to return to Germany from Antwerp before proceeding directly to New York, to begin the season of summer cruises to the Caribbean. In the circumstances, he decided not to resign until he could hand in his resignation personally to Holthusen when he returned to Hamburg in the autumn. Having made that decision, the man who had done as much as anyone and more than most to save the lives of his passengers now, typically, began to write individual, private letters to each member of the passenger committee thanking them for what they had done for him.

At five o'clock in the afternoon, Morris Troper announced by loudspeaker the names of the 214 passengers selected to go to Belgium. They were given a last dinner on the *St. Louis,* and at seven o'clock began filing off the ship, the envy of many fellow passengers for being able to leave so soon.

Among the first down the gangway were George and Carl Lenneberg, the brothers who had prevented reporters from interviewing Elise Loewe after her husband's attempted suicide in Havana Harbor. They wanted to go to Britain but had been chosen for Belgium. The brothers reflected that they had traveled 10,000 miles since leaving Hamburg without setting foot on land, and now as they stepped ashore, they were only 300 miles from where their journey had begun.

One mishap occurred as the passengers disembarked. The woman the children had christened "Big Bertha" fell heavily and broke her leg. She was taken to hospital by the Belgian Red Cross. She was, at least, spared the indignity that awaited the others on their journey to Brussels.

The special train waiting to take them away was on a siding, shielded from the street by iron barriers. The train's appearance reminded the refugees of their status: all the coaches were third class, with wooden seats; the manner in which it had been prepared reminded them of the suspicion with which they were still viewed: all the windows were barred and nailed firmly shut. Once the passengers were on the train, they were locked inside. The police who accompanied them, and watched their every move on the way to Brussels, told the refugees the precautions had been taken for their own safety. Those who had been selected for

Belgium would spend Saturday night in various hotels in the capital, before being moved on the next day.

By nine o'clock in the evening, a little before the Belgian passengers arrived in Brussels, the relief workers on the *St. Louis* had completed the final reckoning. A French consular official boarded and gave those who would be bound for France a card stamped "Refugees from the *St. Louis.*"

Otto Bergmann received his, and observed later in his diary: "In order to get permission to enter France we had to come to Antwerp in Belgium. And to get to Belgium, we had to travel to Cuba."

SUNDAY, JUNE 18, 1939

On Sunday, the 181 passengers who were to travel to Holland were awakened at 5 A.M., and given breakfast an hour later as the little steamer which was to take them to Rotterdam, the *Jan van Arckel,* came alongside the *St. Louis.* Although it would have been quicker, and more convenient, for them to travel by land, the Belgian authorities had decreed that only those destined for Belgium could actually land at Antwerp.

Before boarding the *Jan van Arckel,* Gertrud Scheuer, the popular girl who was friendly with Assistant Purser Reich, had a proposition put to her by one of the crew. He offered to hide her in a cleaning cupboard, to feed and look after her, and then to smuggle her off when the ship docked in New York. Although she did not want to go to the Netherlands, she turned down the offer, believing, "he might throw me overboard or something if I didn't do what he asked."

Accompanied by Alfred Moser, the Dutch contingent left at nine-thirty in the morning and began the journey through the complicated waterway system to Rotterdam. In front of and behind the *Jan van Arckel* was an escort of river-police boats, reminiscent of the departure from Havana; along both sides of the narrow canals, the now famous refugees were waved at and called to by hundreds of well-wishers.

They arrived at Rotterdam at five o'clock in the afternoon, and were immediately interned in the quarantine station of Heijplaat, where many hundreds of other German refugees already languished, all awaiting somewhere to go. Most would remain in the camp for weeks, and few would ultimately survive. Up to fifty people were crowded into some of the long, barracklike rooms.

Outside, the camp was surrounded by barbed wire, and watched by guard dogs.

Back on the *St. Louis,* the remaining passengers, feeling very strange in the ship that for so long was packed to capacity and now was half empty, had an early lunch in preparation for boarding the *Rhakotis*—the Hapag passenger/cargo vessel which they had been told had been specially prepared to take them to France and England.

In fact, the *Rhakotis* was an eleven-year-old freighter, with first-class cabins for 28 and tourist cabins for 24. Soon it would carry 512 people. In three days, Hapag had hastily converted the ship, filling its two large cargo holds with rows of doubledecker steel bunks, and long tables for eating on in the center. The women would be segregated from the men and sleep communally in the forward hold, the men aft. There was nowhere to change. The too-few lavatories had been set up on deck.

Boarding began about two o'clock Sunday afternoon. Purser Mueller and his staff handed out a box containing sandwiches and sweets to each passenger as the last of them finally took their leave of the *St. Louis.* By midafternoon, all had boarded the *Rhakotis,* and the cargo vessel was towed upstream, where it was to spend the night; for security reasons, the Belgians did not allow it to remain alongside the *St. Louis* after four o'clock. For the rest of the day and into the early evening, the passengers' luggage was taken from the *St. Louis* and put on the quay, awaiting collection in the morning by the *Rhakotis.*

The last message Captain Schroeder received before sailing for New York was from Hapag director Claus-Gottfried Holthusen in Hamburg. In part, it read:

> The Board of the Hamburg-America Line wishes to express its thanks to you for bringing back the *St. Louis* safely. The purser's report gives a perceptive picture of your journey, and we give you our fullest sympathy. We congratulate you for the way you dealt with your crew and passengers, and hope that on your journey to New York, you will find new strength to fulfill the pleasure cruises.

Just after midnight, on the very day the *St. Louis* had always been scheduled to leave Europe for New York, the ship began slowly to pull away from pier 18. On the *Rhakotis*, passengers silently watched her go with, according to Rosemarie Bergmann, "one dry and one wet eye." The *St. Louis* crew lined the rails, and as they passed the *Rhakotis* they shouted: "Good luck to the Jews." It was a moving moment, and one even the most bitter of the refugees would never forget.

Most of Captain Schroeder's crew had decided to stay with him, partly fearing a return to Germany, where they would almost certainly have been severely criticized for their generally compassionate treatment of the Jewish passengers. One of the few who did sign off at Antwerp carried a Cuban walking stick, a sheaf of magazines, and a pocket full of pens—Abwehr agent and ship's *Ortsgruppenleiter* Otto Schiendick. Captain Schroeder was not sorry to lose him.

The air in the overcrowded converted cargo holds had soon become stale and unbearable. Many of the refugees on the *Rhakotis* chose to spend the night in the open air on deck, sleeping on mattresses and deck chairs. The few cabins which were not allocated to the extra crew were used by the more fortunate passengers. Each member of the passenger committee and his family had one, as did Rosemarie Bergmann's mother and Aunt Shalote; two stewardesses gave up their berths so the elderly ladies could have a restful night.

MONDAY, JUNE 19, 1939

On Monday, the passengers were awakened as the *Rhakotis* moved in to the quay, berthing at pier 18, which the *St. Louis* had vacated the night before.

Although conditions on board left much to be desired, spirits remained high. Passengers commented on the superior quality of the food: "We had fresh eggs for the first time in three weeks." The meals were served on the long tables in the holds: "We practically had breakfast in bed."

At two o'clock in the afternoon, Morris Troper came to the ship. He shook hands with each member of the passenger committee, and then the American who had succeeded where his own country had failed was applauded and waved goodbye to as he left by car for Paris. An hour later, the *Rhakotis* departed for Boulogne, traveling close to the Belgian and French coasts. Soon it began to rain heavily, driving the passengers down into the cargo holds. In the confined atmosphere, Otto Bergmann confided to his diary: "I fear it is still possible for a cable to recall us to Germany."

TUESDAY, JUNE 20, 1939

The *Rhakotis* arrived in Boulogne at four-thirty on Tuesday morning, and was ordered, as the *St. Louis* had been so many weeks before at Cherbourg, to anchor out in the harbor. At ten o'clock, the purser and stewards on the *Rhakotis* gave a packed lunch to each of the 224 passengers to disembark in France.

As they boarded a small tender for the trip ashore, Raoul Lambert, the Secretary-General of the Comité d'Assistance aux Refugies, welcomed them with the words: "I greet you on Free French soil." Lambert himself would soon die in a Nazi concentration camp.

On shore, the French porters refused to accept tips for carrying the passengers' luggage.

The refugees would spend Tuesday night in hotels around Boulogne before being moved the next day.

The remaining 288 refugees, the largest contingent, departed from Boulogne for Great Britain Tuesday evening just as, in New York, the Joint was releasing an official communique stating that the "*St. Louis* rescue operation is not to be taken as a precedent, and would not be repeated in the future."

WEDNESDAY, JUNE 21, 1939

The passengers were greeded in Southampton at noon on Wednesday—midsummer night, the longest day—by a spectacular display. The harbor was gaily decorated, sirens wailed, the firefighting boats sent sprays of water dramatically high into the air. It was not until they had landed that the refugees learned it was actually a rehearsal for the arrival of King George VI and Queen Elizabeth, due in Southampton the next day. They too had been on a trip to the "New World."

As the passengers stepped ashore, at least one of them, Fritz Gotthelf, the Berliner who had been a member of the suicide patrol, "knelt down, and kissed the earth." At two o'clock, they left by train and arrived at London's Waterloo station—platform 13—at 3:45 P.M. There some sixty of the single, able-bodied men were immediately dispatched to the famous "Kitchener Camp" at Richborough, which was to become a temporary home for nearly 5000 men awaiting emigration to the U.S.A., Palestine, or South America. The rest of the passengers were housed in small hotels and private houses.

After precisely forty days and forty nights of wandering on the high seas, the last passengers from the *St. Louis* had found their Promised Land.

Epilogue

For many of the refugees on the *St. Louis,* their rescue proved to be the beginning of the end.

The 288 who went to England were the luckiest, although at first it must not have appeared so to them. Soon after war was declared, early in September 1939, as German nationals, they were all classified as enemy aliens, and the men interned.

At Kitchener's camp at Richborough, an Aliens Tribunal was set up to examine the internees. Of the 3500 men then there, the loyalty to Britain of only one was found to be doubtful. The first Alien Companies of the Pioneer Corps—initially organized as a noncombat military force—were raised and trained. More than half the refugees in the camp volunteered, although they knew that if they were caught by the Germans they might be tried as traitors and shot.

In 1940, the first Alien Pioneer Company went to France, under the leadership of Major F. J. Brister, the man who had represented Britain on the *St. Louis* in Antwerp Harbor, and who now had in his command men from the ship he had chosen for Britain when the allocation of passengers was made. During the retreat to Dunkirk, they were given arms and, according to all reports, fought bravely. Later they were dispersed among regular British army regiments. Some even went into a special unit of commandos composed exclusively of refugees, mostly German Jews, whose burning hatred of the Nazis made them formidable fighters. Half of them died.

Elise Loewe and her two children were among the *St. Louis* passengers fortunate enough to be chosen for England, the country Max Loewe had thought too close to Germany when he decided originally to take his family to Cuba. In England, Elise

Loewe still did not know the fate of her husband in Havana after his suicide attempt, but in 1940 he was released from the Cuban hospital and somehow made his way to London to be reunited with his family. There, in 1942, aged only fifty-one, he died of a heart ailment probably stemming from his suicide attempts in Havana. In 1947, Elise Loewe took her children to the United States, where they reside today.

The head of the passenger committee, Josef Joseph, and his wife Lilli and daughter Liesl were, after landing in Britain, guests on the estate of the millionaire Rowntree family in York. Though they were offered a stay there for the duration of the war, Joseph was anxious to emigrate to the United States, and after three months they moved to London. In May 1940, just a year after boarding the *St. Louis,* Joseph was interned on the Isle of Man as an enemy alien. In September, the family was allowed to book passage for New York, and Lilli and Liesl left London in the middle of an air raid, to travel in a blacked-out train filled with refugees to Glasgow where all the families were to meet their husbands, traveling from internment on a separate train.

When they arrived in Glasgow, it too was having an air raid. After many delays and anxious moments caused by the bombing the families were united, along with 350 British children being evacuated to America. Vastly overcrowded, unarmed, without convoy or escort for two days the ship was shadowed by a U-boat, but it was not torpedoed and arrived safely.

Josef Joseph later died in America. Lilli remarried, and today, in her seventies and still beautiful, she lives in a suburb of New York, where she trustingly loaned us original handwritten passenger committee notes and the drafts of their telegrams to world leaders, as well as much else to do with the *St. Louis.* She and her daughter Liesl were fortunate to survive. Both of Lilli's sisters, their husbands and children, her mother, and her husband's sisters died in German concentration camps.

In France, after the first night in Boulogne, most of the *St. Louis* refugees went either to Laval or Le Mans, arriving after midnight.

Herbert Manasse, the youngest member of the passenger committee, continued to carry responsibility for certain *St. Louis* passengers, leading and looking after the group who went to Laval. When France was occupied, he attempted to escape with his wife and two young children to Italy, but they were caught and sent to Auschwitz, where the entire family was gassed.

Rosemarie and Otto Bergmann, the newly married couple who had promised to chaperon eighty-year-old Shalote Hecht for the two weeks of the voyage, found themselves instead taking care of her for almost two years.

Soon after war was declared, Otto was interned in France as an ememy alien. Rosemarie, with her ailing mother and aunt Shalote, moved into a hotel room in Vichy, paid for by money sent from friends in the United States. There the young woman looked after her "two old ladies" for thirteen months until Otto bribed his way out of internment in October 1940, made his way to Marseilles, and at the U.S. consulate, managed to get his group on the American quota. At Bordeaux, he got a temporary visa for the Dominican Republic, allowing them to wait there until their U.S. quota number came up.

Aunt Shalote refused to leave France, choosing instead to go to friends in Nice, where she died three months later.

In the meantime, Otto and Rosemarie Bergmann and Rosemarie's mother began the long journey to freedom. First they traveled to the south coast and near Perpignan, hired two French fishermen to row them by night to Spain. They made the journey without being discovered and continued on to Lisbon.

In Lisbon, Emanuel Rosen, the man who had helped Morris Troper on the _St. Louis,_ and who had not been able to offer Rosemarie advice regarding her dog Oshey, had set up an office of the Joint when the Paris office was closed. Between 1940 and 1942, Manny Rosen guided many hundreds of refugees through Spain to North Africa and Portugal, among them passengers he had met on the _St. Louis._

The Bergmanns and Rosemarie's mother made their way to Portugal. From there they got a ship to New York, where they stayed only long enough to transfer to another ship for Santo Domingo. In Santo Domingo, they were, at last, reunited with their dog Oshey, who, according to Rosemarie, was "skinny as a chicken. It had pined for us ever since Havana. It, too, had suffered because of the Nazis."

The group was finally allowed into the United States in 1941; six months after arriving, Rosemarie's mother died.

Marianne Bardeleben, the ten-year-old who had been barely able to recognize her father in one of the little boats in Havana Harbor, found herself, the day war was declared, alone and frightened in a cheap lodginghouse room somewhere in France—she did not know where—with only her nine-year-old friend from the *St. Louis*, Ruth Fischer, for company. Their mothers had gone to Paris to get bona fide visas for Cuba, where their fathers still were, and were unable to return to the children for a week. Travel had virtually come to a halt. The girls were alone in a strange country whose language they could not speak.

Four months later, on Christmas Eve, both families left Le Havre on the liner *De Grasse* in a convoy of nearly 100 ships bound for the United States. Most of the ships in the convoy were sunk in the English Channel by U-boats, but the *De Grasse* got through.

During the trip, the ringworm which Marianne had contracted while living in the louse-ridden room in France grew worse. The ship's doctor promptly shaved her head. It was covered with open sores. When they arrived at New York, because of the ringworm Marianne and her mother were confined to Ellis Island. Marianne described it:

"A sort of prison. I was put in the hospital and remember finding a dead mouse in my slipper one morning. I was still only ten. Every day they shaved my head and put red iodine on it. The pain was excruciating. I could only speak German. No one talked to me. No doctor, no nurse, no one. My mother wasn't allowed to visit me. They put me in a Boy Scout uniform, short pants, and took me out into the snow for exercise. At ten years of age, with my open sore shaved head painted red, in my Boy Scout uniform, the humiliation was terrible."

Marianne and her mother left Ellis Island when their American visitors permits expired and they were forced to leave the United States.

"Then, only then," Marianne recalled, "the doctor spoke to me. In German! He could speak German, but all the time I had been in the hospital he had never said a word to me. I thought he was crueler than the Nazis."

In Havana, Cuban officials once again told them they could not enter the country to join her father, this time because of Marianne's head wound. The child was overcome with guilt; she believed all the family's troubles were her fault. Her mother assured her they would both commit suicide if they were not allowed in. The next day, they were admitted. Marianne's father had bribed officials.

In 1942, when their quota number finally came up, they returned to New York. But even then, Marianne's sense of humiliation was not over. Because her English was still not perfect, she was put in the first grade, a twelve-year-old with children half her age. For her, the humiliation was complete.

In Belgium, the Joint paid for the upkeep of the *St. Louis* refugees. Among them was passenger committee member Ernst Vendig, his wife and their three children. After Belgium was overrun, he was interned, escaped, collected his family, and made his way to freedom by crossing the Swiss Alps on foot.

Carl and George Lenneberg, who had been in Dachau before joining the *St. Louis*, made their escape in April 1940, just before the Germans arrived. They got out via Dunkirk, as did so many others.

The father, mother, aunt, and uncle of Hildie Reading, the girl who had boarded the *St. Louis* in Havana and given her parents $1700, also tried to escape through Dunkirk. They failed. Her uncle was caught and sent to a concentration camp, where he died.

Hildie Reading's mother, father, and aunt returned to Belgium and went underground. They lived in an abandoned store, its front boarded up, its back looking onto a cemetery. There they stayed for five years. Only one Belgian family knew where they were, and with the $1700 Hildie had given them, they paid the family to keep quiet, and bought food. Without the money, they might not have survived.

Alice Feilchenfeld and her four children spent the entire war in Brussels. Although the dollars she received weekly from the Joint were enough to pay for a decent apartment, she chose to live in a rooming house in a poor district because, she recalled, "there the Germans didn't seem to trouble us much, and the poor non-

Jewish Belgians did not 'squeal' on anyone. Not like some of the rich people did." For a time, Alice Feilchenfeld and her children lived in their top floor room by day, and by night they hid in a morgue beside a hospital filled with German soldiers.

When the Germans arrived, the Joint left. From then on, the Belgian government made regular welfare payments to the Jews, never divulging their names or addresses to the Germans. In 1946, Alice Feilchenfeld took her children to America, where they rejoined their father, from whom they had been separated since late 1938. Today, she lives in the New Utrecht area of Brooklyn, with memories of looking after her four children for seven years, alone, bravely, most of the time in hiding—an example of courage for her daughter Judith, who lives nearby; now grown up, and with her own family of nine children.

In Holland, Gertrud Scheuer also spent the war in hiding, part of the time in a house near the one in which Anne Frank was writing her famous diary. She survived and now lives in a Baltimore suburb. She had worked as a maid, moving from family to family, always one step ahead of the Germans.

She was in the minority. Most of the refugees in the Netherlands were to die in the gas chambers, after first passing through Holland's notorious transit camp, Westerbork. Westerbork was planned and built by the Dutch government before the outbreak of war to house German refugees. It opened in October 1939, and among its first inmates were the Dutch contingent from the *St. Louis*.

The 250-acre camp was completely isolated, set on a windswept plain in an area little better than a peat bog, and from the beginning, conditions were deplorable. The place was a haven for disease-carrying flies and vermin of all kinds; when it rained, it became a swamp. Even so, when the Gestapo took over Westerbork in 1942 from the Dutch, staying in the camp would be safer than leaving, though the refugees did not know it.

But they were not allowed to stay. For two years, every Tuesday, week in, week out, the cattle trucks at Westerbork were loaded with their human freight and trundled off to the gas ovens of Germany and Poland. Westerbork became another word for purgatory.

Alfred Moser, the Dutch relief worker who had shepherded his

St. Louis flock to Antwerp, was interned in Westerbork. From there, he was taken to Belsen, but he miraculously survived. On the basis of a fake Paraguayan passport purchased for him by a friend in Switzerland, Moser was taken by train with some 300 other Jews from Belsen, to Berlin, and then to Switzerland. Many of his fellows had typhoid and died on the way before the Swiss Red Cross could save them.

Aaron Pozner was also interned in Westerbork. Before he was taken by cattle train to Auschwitz, he gave his diary to a friend, and it survived. Aaron Pozner, along with the hundred thousand others who passed through Westerbork, did not. The fate of his family is not known.

Fritz Spanier, his wife Babette, and their twin daughters went to Westerbork.

The girls had looked forward to their time in Holland on the *St. Louis* in Antwerp. Dr. Spanier told them it was a beautiful country of tulips and daffodils. Years later, they found their experiences in Westerbork too painful to recall, remembering only "the bloodhounds and the rats."

They survived because of the extraordinary power Fritz Spanier wielded in Westerbork. At one point he was even able to have his wife and the children removed from one of the cattle trains bound for Auschwitz; S.S. guards obeyed his order to unbar the door and let his family out.

Dr. Spanier became the chief medical doctor of Westerbork, in charge of a large hospital with 1725 beds, 120 physicians, and a general staff of over 1000. He had a mysterious influence over the camp commandant, and did not even bother to stand in his presence, something no one else dared. He held the power of life and death over his fellow refugees, because those he accepted into his hospital, or whom he told the camp commandant were too ill to travel, generally were not put on the trains to the concentration camps.

In 1944, Dr. Spanier called together five of his doctors and told them they had been ordered to sterilize all the Jewish women in Westerbork who were married to non-Jews. Once sterilized, so the Gestapo said, they would not be subject to deportation. If the doctors refused to carry out the order, it would mean either deportation or death.

One of the doctors, a woman, did refuse to carry out the sterilization order, and her decision caused it to be reexamined. Surprisingly, the order was withdrawn. The refugees who chose sterilization instead of deportation had the operation performed by Jewish or Dutch doctors outside Westerbork, and for a time received special privileges. But in the end, they too were sent to the concentration camps.

Dr. Spanier was later accused of abusing his power in Westerbork, of helping those who had the "right connections," of being too friendly with the S.S. If he was, perhaps he remembered that in a way he and his family owed their life to the young S.S. officer who had originally driven them to Hamburg to board the St. Louis. Whatever the truth, Dr. Spanier's hospital in Westerbork was a model of efficiency, though in fact it only kept people alive for the gas chambers.

Fritz Spanier and his family stayed in Westerbork throughout the war. When Holland was liberated, Dr. Spanier returned immediately to Germany, to the terrible extermination camp of Belsen. There he worked with survivors, especially the young, and became almost as well known as he had been in Westerbork. Later, having decided once again to make his home in Germany, he opened an office in Duesseldorf. He died in 1967.

Today, the Spanier twins are both married and live in the United States with their families. Renee and Ines still find it too upsetting to recall what they experienced in the Dutch transit camp.

Their mother lives alone in a modest apartment in Cologne, West Germany, wasted by time and experience, leaving only her eyes to remind one of those news photographs on the St. Louis when her bright stare had looked out of scores of front pages. For several hours, virtually without interruption, she told us of events surrounding the voyage, with that attention to detail that makes a born raconteuse. She conjured up the *feeling* of 1939, that harsh time when no Jew would have dared enter the Dom Hotel, where she talked to us. Did we realize, she asked, that on the balcony of the very room next door to where we sat, the balcony of suite 108, Hitler had delivered some of his most virulent anti-Semitic propaganda?

It sounded an improbable story until we checked with the

Dom's head porter. He could still clearly remember Hitler standing on the balcony and haranguing 50,000 people below in the
Grossplatz of the cathedral.

Babette Spanier urged us to call on Dr. Spanier's second wife,
Njuta. We found her near the Hofgarten in Dusseldorf, a small,
tidy woman whose only bond with Babette Spanier is that they
both loved the same man.

Njuta Spanier's memories are kept alive by fading newspaper
reports of the *St. Louis* saga; she also has a collection of letters,
documents, and snapshots, all of which have a curious, two-
dimensional effect, heightened by the knowledge that although
she had not been on the ship, for years afterward she had acted as
a sounding board for Dr. Spanier, faithfully storing in her mind all
that he had told her about the event.

From a corner of the apartment a caged parrot suddenly
screeched, interrupting our discussion. Njuta Spanier explained
that her late husband had taught the bird to speak "so that his
voice would live on for me after he was gone."

In Cuba it was not easy for a middle-aged man with no money
to learn a new language, study for American medical examina-
tions, and cook for, keep amused, bathe, and clothe two young
girls—all on a few dollars a week. Dr. Max Aber looked after his
daughters, Renatta and Evelyne, as best he could and by 1941 he
was in America, a practicing doctor.

In 1973, at the age of seventy-eight looking much younger than
his years, still attending to patients in Cape Cod, Dr. Aber
described the Cuban newspaper report of 1939 that he was a
"millionaire" as a "prognosis not altogether incorrect."

No one can say with certainty how many of the *St. Louis*
passengers eventually perished. One estimate states that of the
907 who were returned to Europe only 240 lived. Those who died
became part of the "final solution"—a total of six million Jews who
perished as a result of Hitler's policies.

If those from the *St. Louis* survived the war and the concen-
tration camps in the same proportion as did their fellows, then in
France, 180 would have lived out of the 224 who went there; in
Belgium, 152 out of 214; in Holland, only 60 out of 181. Most of the

288 who went to Britain lived. What is certain is that if Cuba or the United States had opened their doors, almost no one from the ship need have died.

A disproportionate number of those featured in this book survived, for it was largely from personal interviews with them or their families and from accounts written by them at the time that we were able to piece together *Voyage of the Damned*.

Today, scattered throughout the world, mostly uncertain of each other's existence, the survivors tend to have one thing in common: a love of life and an enthusiasm for living it every day to the full. Having been near death, escaping through a miracle of chance, they realize how precious and precarious life is. They also have an uncommon respect and affection for the people and countries that gave them the chance to live.

Most members of the crew of the *St. Louis* served in the German armed forces in the war, among them Leo Jockl. In 1941, plumper, his receding hairline more pronounced, he joined the German navy. By then he had fallen in love with a beautiful Aryan girl, Gerda Kickbush, whose father was a high-ranking Nazi official in Berlin. He soon told her of his background, and she insisted that it made no difference to their love. But her family was not so tolerant.

Gerda's mother denounced Jockl to Nazi party headquarters in Berlin. Soon afterward Gerda found she was pregnant. Unable to marry because of the infamous Nuremberg Laws forbidding unions between Jews and gentiles, ostracized by her family, Gerda stood by her man. They lived a cat-and-mouse existence with the Gestapo.

In January 1944, Jockl was drafted into a road gang of "half Jews." Their role was to act as human minesweepers for German troops trying to stop the Allied invasion of the Fatherland. At three minutes past 2 P.M. on November 17, 1944, near Aachen, an American fighter strafed the road gang, killing Leo.

Today his widow—they were one of the first couples to be "married posthumously" in postwar West Germany—lives in West Berlin with her son Frank and her memories and mementos. Among them is a letter a *St. Louis* passenger wrote to Leo: "I think my whole life will never be enough to thank you for what you did for us." Gerda Jockl believes it is the finest epitaph she would ever want for her husband.

Otto Schiendick has many epitaphs among surviving crewmen who remember and disliked him. Men like former steward Paul Zochert, pastry cook Christian Muhlbacher, stewards Hermann Kempe and Pieter Schmitt. Paul Bendowski, the ship's photographer and his wife, Irene, who was the ladies' hairdresser on the *St. Louis,* told us that Schiendick was "as nasty as they come—and a bully, too."

Around 1940, Schiendick worked in the overseas Message Center, the nerve center of the German secret service, a massive underground concrete cavern below the tree-shaded suburb of Wohldorf in Hamburg. In early 1945, British troops occupied the city as the Germans were demolishing the center. Among the sabotage squad was Otto Schiendick. As he scrambled clear of the ruins, a British patrol shot him dead.

Purser Mueller and First Officer Ostermeyer survived the war only to fall into Russian hands. The last they were heard of by other crewmen, they were living quietly in East Germany; their material was made available to us by sources that must remain anonymous.

Captain Gustav Schroeder survived.

After taking the *St. Louis* from Antwerp to New York in June 1939, he carried out the planned summer cruises to the Caribbean. He was forbidden by the German embassy to refer in public or in private to the refugee trip. Cruise passengers reported him charming and the ship gracious, although the crew was "jittery" after the Cuban voyage.

On August 26, 1939, the *St. Louis* was scheduled to depart New York for Bermuda, but its passengers were abruptly told the trip had been canceled. The next day, the ship sailed empty, departing her pier at Forty-sixth Street at 8 P.M., and was at sea when war was declared on September 3.

Captain Schroeder ran the British blockade and reached safety in Murmansk, Russia. There, all but the engineers on the *St. Louis* traveled by train to Leningrad, and on to Germany. After a stay of four months in Murmansk, still under Schroeder's command, the *St. Louis* made a dash for Hamburg, arriving on New Year's Day, 1940, the last of the Hapag ships on the North American run to reach home port. Schroeder took a desk job, never to return to sea again.

The *St. Louis* was badly damaged by the Royal Air Force in 1944, and at war's end lay as a burned-out hulk in Hamburg Harbor. For a time, after part of it was renovated, the ship was used as a floating hotel. In 1950, it was sold for scrap and broken up.

The *Rhakotis,* the freighter that had taken the passengers to France and England, was sunk by a British cruiser in 1943.

After the war, Schroeder tried to make a living as a writer, sometimes using parts of his diary of the voyage in his books. However, they were not very successful financially, and some of his refugee passengers helped by sending him food and clothing. They also came to his assistance when, under the de-Nazification process, he was put on trial; their testimony helped to acquit him. In 1957, two years before his death, Gustav Schroeder received a citation and medal from the West German government for the part he played in saving the lives of his passengers on the voyage to Cuba.

Appendices

SPECIAL THANKS

Those that follow were either spoken to by telephone, corresponded with, or interviewed in person.

Crew:
Bendowski, Irene
Bendowski, Paul
Kempe, Hermann
Muhlbacher, Christian
Schimon, Josef
Schmitt, Pieter
Zochert, Paul

Passengers:
Alan, Rolf
Altschul, Hans
Aron, Alfred
Aron, Sofi
Brauer, Kaethe
Buff, Fred
Falk, Eugene
Frieberg, Regina
Freund, Charlotte
Fridberg, Ruth
Friedman, Lillian
Geismar, Sonja
Goldberg, William
Goldman, Renee (née Spanier)

Greilsamer, Erich
Herz, Theresa
Hurtig, Herta
Jacobson, Greta
Jacoby, Ines (née Spanier)
Jacoby-Byk, Regina
Jungerman, Harry
Kadden, Leah
Kahn, Arthur
Karliner, Herbert
Karliner, Walter
Kassel, Fritz
Langnas, Leon
Lavatch, Herma
Leyser, Fred
Lichtenstein, Norbert
Mahler, Vera
Marcus, Ilse
Oster, Alice
Oyres, Herbert
Phillipi, Margarete
Pommer, Martin
Prager, Margarete
Rosenback, Harry

Safier, Jakob
Schwager, Reni
Schwartz, Hilda
Shilling, Maria
Sichel, Beatrice (née Bonné)
Sondheimer, Alse
Sternberg, Alice
Strauss, Fred
Strauss, Joseph
Wallerstein, Anton
Weil, Ernst
Zellner, Ruth

Others:
Adler, Inge
Aldoughby, Swy
Altmann, Hilde
Annenberg, Walter
Babish, Reuben
Band, Harold
Barrocas, Jack
Ben-Johoshna, Margot
Bieber, Konrad
Blackburn, Pitch

307

Brady, Kathryn
Clyma, Frances
Eckstein, Nelly
Egelert, Karl
Estedes, José
Felton, Anton
Field, Harold
Friedlander, Albert
Froehlich, Henry
Gantz, Sarita
Gilbert, Martin
Goetz, Harald
Goldstein, Charlotte
Gottschalk, Max
Guttfeld, Martin
Hamel, Otto
Heald, David

Heilbronner, Marie
Jacob, Johannes
Jacoby, Golda
Jellin, Fred
Jockl, Gerda
Kallman, Charlotte
Karetsky, David
Karetsky, Geraldine
Kramarsky, Lola
Kraner, Joachim
Kruger, Inge
Lenz, Gunther
Leopold, S.
Lewin, Henri
Luftig, Lillian
Man, John
Marx, Sidonie

Miron, Chia
Montagu, Ivor
Moser, Alfred
Neuberg, Gertrude
Pearlman, Moshe
Piton, Mary
Prinz, Arthur
Rosen, Emanuel
Samson, Rita
Sanders, Frank
Schiller, Harriet
Schuster, Max
Seligman, Jenny
Simon, Arthur
Slee, Mac
Spanier, Njuta
Weigall, Michael

ACKNOWLEDGMENTS

Individuals:
Adler-Rudel, Schalom
Adni, Daniel
Alberti, Frederic
Douglas, Sid
Elon, Amos
Erdman, Fred
Fraenkel, Heinrich

Fredericks, Joan
Harms, Gustav
Japhet, Ernest
Kochan, Lionel
Levin, Marlin
Litvinoff, Barnet
MacDonald, Malcolm
Maier, Beatrice

May, Phineas
Morse, Joan
Neter, Hans
Oppenheimer, Max
Patai, Saul
Schild, Warner
Schwab, Henry
Summerfeld, Eva

ORGANIZATIONS, SOCIETIES, INSTITUTIONS

Two deserve special mention. Hapag-Lloyd, successors to the Hamburg-American Line, regretted that they could not be more helpful. At headquarters in Hamburg we were told, the "*St. Louis* documents are missing; we presume that during World War II things got lost." The files in Hapag's New York office were confiscated in 1941 by the F.B.I., and subsequently destroyed.

The F.B.I., too, was friendly, but they regretted that their job was "to collect information, not dispense it."

On the other hand, persons named below in parentheses were particularly cooperative.

Alliance Israelite Universelle, Paris
American Friends Service Committee, Inc., Philadelphia
American Jewish Committee, Paris (Zachariah Shuster); New York (Morton Yarmon); Blaustein Library (Harry Alderman)
American Jewish Congress, New York
American Jewish Joint Distribution Committee, Inc., New York (Herbert Katzki, Rose Klepfisz)
American Joint Distribution Committee, Geneva and Paris
Association Consistoriale Israelite de Paris
Association of Jewish Refugees in Great Britain, London (W. Rosenstock)
AUFBAU, New York
Berliner Allgemeine, Duesseldorf (Lilli Marx)
British Broadcasting Corporation, London
British Museum, London and Colindale
Bund des Antifashisten VVN, Frankfurt
Central British Fund for Jewish Relief and Habilitation (Joan Stiebel)
Central Zionist Archives, Jerusalem
Centre de Documentation Israel et le Moyen Orient, Paris
Centre de Documentation Juive Contemporaine, Paris
Centre de Recherches et Etudes Historiques de World War II, Brussels (M. Bok)
Columbia University, Lehman Papers, New York (William Liebmann)
Comité d'Action Sociale Israelite de Paris
Consistoire Central Israelite de France et d'Algerie, Paris (Marice Moch)
Department of the Navy, Naval History Division, Washington, D.C. (Mrs. Lloyd Allard)
Dokumentationszentrum, Vienna (Simon Wiesenthal)
Embassy of Belgium, London
Embassy of Cuba, London
Embassy of France, London
Embassy of Israel, London and Washington
Embassy of the Netherlands, London
Embassy of the United Kingdom, Washington

Embassy of the United States, London
Embassy of West Germany, London
Federal Bureau of Investigation, Washington
Franklin D. Roosevelt Library, Hyde Park, New York
General Register and Record Office of Shipping and Seamen, Cardiff
Hapag-Lloyd A.G., Hamburg
Hebrew University, Institute of Contemporary Jewry, Jerusalem
Herzfeld and Rubin, New York
Institute for Advanced Studies in Contemporary History, Weiner
Library, London (Mrs. G. Johnson)
Institute of Jewish Affairs, London
Jabotinsky Institute in Israel, Tel Aviv
Jedioth Chadoshot, Haifa
Jerusalem Post
Jewish Agency, Jerusalem
Jewish Chronicle, The, London (William Frankel)
Jewish Historical Society of England, London
Jewish Observer and Middle East Review, London
Jewish Refugees Committee, London
Jews' College Library, London
Jews Temporary Shelter, London
Joods Historisch Museum, Amsterdam
Leo Baeck Institute, London (Arnold Howell); New York (Fred
Grubel); and Jerusalem
Library du Centre National des Hautes Études Juives, Brussels (M.
Reicher)
Library of Congress, National Archives, Washington (State Depart-
ment Bureau of Public Affairs Historical Office, Security Room, Modern
Military Section, John Taylor)
Lloyd's Intelligence Unit, Historical Research Section, London (T.
M. Dinan)
Lloyd's Register of Shipping, London
Maariv, Tel Aviv
Ministerie Van Buitenlandse Zaken', S-Gravenhage
Ministry for Foreign Affairs, Information Division, Jerusalem
Ministry of Defense, Admiralty Historical Branch, London
National Maritime Museum, London
New York Public Library, Jewish Division and Refugee Section
New York Times, The

Office of Alien Property, Department of Justice, Washington

Paris-Match

Public Records Office, London

Rijksinstituut voor Oorlogsdocumentatie, Amsterdam (L. de Jong)

Royal Institute of International Affairs, London

Service for Foreign Born, National Council of Jewish Women, New York

Stern, New York (Yvonne Luter); Hamburg (Heidi Repp-Gwlo)

United HIAS Service, New York

United Restitution Organization, New York

United States Committee for Refugees, New York

United States Secret Service, Washington

University of Southampton

Weizmann Archives, Rehovot (Julian Meltzer)

World Jewish Congress, London

Yad Vashem Remembrance Authority, Jerusalem

YIVO Institute for Jewish Research, New York (Zosa Szajkowski)

Bibliography

BOOKS:

This list is of a general nature, most of the books referring to refugees and allied matters; few refer directly or in detail to the voyage of the *St. Louis*.

Batista, Fulgencio, *The Growth and Decline of the Cuban Republic*, Devin-Adair, New York, 1964.

Bemis, Samuel Flagg, *Diplomatic History of the United States*, Jonathan Cape, London, 1937.

Bennet, Marion T., *American Immigration Policies*, Public Affairs Press, Washington, 1963.

Bentwich, Norman, *They Found Refuge*, Cresset Press, London, 1956.

Bermant, Chaim, *The Cousinhood*, Eyre and Spottiswoode, London, 1971.

Birley, Robert, *Speeches and Documents in American History*, Oxford University Press, London, 1942.

Black Book, The, Jewish Black Book Committee, New York, 1946.

Bowle, John, *Viscount Samuel*, Gollancz, London, 1957.

Bullock, Alan, *Hitler*, Bantam, New York, 1961.

Burns, James M., *Roosevelt*, Harcourt, Brace and World, New York, 1956.

Cecil, Lamar, *Albert Ballin*, Princeton University Press, 1967.

Chandler, Edgar H.S., *The High Tower of Refuge*, Odhams Press, London, 1959.

Chester, Edmund A., *A Sergeant Named Batista*, Henry Holt & Co., New York, 1954.

Dilks, David, *Sir Alexander Cadogan*, Cassell, London, 1971.

Elon, Amos, *The Israelis*, Holt, Rinehart and Winston, New York, 1971.

Encyclopaedia Judaica, Keter Publishing House Ltd., Jerusalem, 1971.

Epstein, Isidore, *Judaism,* Penguin, London, 1968.

Feingold, Henry L., *The Politics of Rescue,* Rutgers University Press, New Brunswick, New Jersey, 1970.

Graetz, H., *History of the Jews,* David Nutt, London, 1891.

Grossman, Kurt R., *Emigration—Geschichte der Hitler—Fluchtlinge 1933-1945,* Europaische Verlagsanstalt, Frankfurt am Main, 1969.

Gunther, John, *Roosevelt in Retrospect,* Harper & Bros., New York, 1950.

Haas, Jacob de, *The Encyclopaedia of Jewish Knowledge,* W. and G. Foyle, Ltd., London, 1934.

Habe, Hans, *The Mission,* Harrap & Co., London, 1967.

Hausner, Gideon, *Justice in Jerusalem,* Nelson, London, 1967.

Herlin, Hans, *Kein gelobtes Land,* Nannen Verlag, Hamburg, 1961.

Herzl, Theodor (S. d'Avigdor, trans.) *The Jewish State,* H. Pordes, London, 1967.

Hilberg, Raul, *The Destruction of the European Jews,* Quadrangle Books, Chicago, 1967.

Hirschmann, Ira, *Life Line to a Promised Land,* Vanguard Press, New York, 1946.

Hodgson, Stuart, *Lord Halifax,* Christophers, London, 1941.

Levin, Nora, *The Holocaust,* Thos. Y. Cromwell Co., New York, 1968.

Long, Breckinridge, *The War Diary of Breckinridge Long,* University of Nebraska Press, Lincoln, 1966.

Morse, Arthur, *While Six Million Died,* Random House, New York, 1968.

Paneth, Philip, *Eichmann—Technician of Death,* Robert Speller & Sons, New York, 1960.

Pearlman, Moshe, *The Capture and Trial of Adolph Eichmann,* Simon and Schuster, New York, 1963.

Phillips, R. H., *Cuba: Island of Paradox,* McDowell Obolensky, New York, 1959.

Pool, David de Sola, *Why I Am a Jew,* Thomas Nelson & Sons, Edinburgh, 1957.

Presser, J. (Arnold Pomerans, trans.), *Ashes in the Wind,* Souvenir Press, London, 1968.

Proudfoot, Malcolm J., *European Refugees,* Faber and Faber, London, 1956.

Reitlinger, Gerald, *The Final Solution,* Vallentine Mitchell, London, 1968.

Ritter, Gerhard (R. T. Clark, trans.), *The German Resistance*, Geo. Allen and Unwin, London, 1958.

Robinson, Jacob, *And the Crooked Shall Be Made Straight*, Macmillan, New York, 1965

———, and Friedman, Philip, *Guide to Jewish History under Nazi Impact*, YIVO Institute, New York, 1960.

Roosevelt, Eleanor, *This I Remember*, Harper & Bros., New York, 1949.

Roosevelt, Franklin, *The Public Papers and Addresses of Franklin D. Roosevelt*, Random House, New York, 1950.

Russell, Lord, *The Trial of Adolph Eichmann*, Heinemann, London, 1962.

Sapir, Boris, *The Jewish Community of Cuba*, JTSP Press, New York, 1948.

Schroeder, Gustav, *Fernweh und Heimweh*, Rutten and Loenig Verlag, Potsdam, 1943.

———, *Heimatlos auf Hoher See*, Beckerdruck, Berlin, 1949.

Sharf, Andrew, *The British Press and Jews under Nazi Rule*, Oxford University Press, London, 1964.

Shirer, William L., *The Rise and Fall of the Third Reich*, Secker and Warburg, London, 1960.

Simpson, John Hope, *The Refugee Problem*, Oxford University Press, London, 1939.

Stein, Leonard, *The Balfour Declaration*, Vallentine Mitchell, London, 1961.

Sykes; Christopher, *Cross Roads to Israel*, London, 1965.

Tartakower, Arieh, and Grossmann, Kurt, *The Jewish Refugee*, Institute of Jewish Affairs, New York, 1944.

Thomas, Hugh, *Cuba*, Eyre and Spottiswoode, London, 1971.

Uris, Leon, *Exodus*, Corgi, London, 1971.

Weisgal, Meyer, *So Far*, Weidenfeld and Nicolson, London, 1971.

White, Lyman Cromwell, *300,000 New Americans*, Harper and Bros., New York, 1956.

Wischnitzer, Mark, *To Dwell in Safety*, Jewish Pub. Society of America, Philadelphia, 1948.

———,*Visas to Freedom: The History of HIAS*, World Publishing Co., New York, 1956.

Wise, Stephen S., *Challenging Years*, Putnam, New York, 1949.

Wyman, David S., *Paper Walls*, University of Massachusetts Press, 1969.

PERIODICALS, PAPERS, DIARIES, FILES, ETC.

This list is not comprehensive, and does not include any of the hundreds of magazines and newspapers consulted, published in America, Great Britain, Belgium, Holland, France, Germany and Cuba, some of which are mentioned specifically in the text. Reports in the British and American press were the most accurate, in particular the *London* and *New York Times;* those in the Jewish and German were almost always highly suspect; the Cuban papers were, as ever, inaccurate but entertaining.

Brochure, S.S. *St. Louis.* Hamburg-Amerika Linie, Hamburg, 1937.

Periodical, Contemporary Jewish Record, vol. II, no. 4, July–August, American Jewish Committee, New York, 1939.

Periodical, Central Council for Jewish Refugees, Report, London 1939.

Yearbook, American Jewish, vol. 41, pp. 387–88, Jewish Pub. Society of America, Philadelphia, 1939.

Yearbook, Willing's Press Guide, London, 1939.

Files, President Roosevelt's Official and Personal, Franklin D. Roosevelt Library, Hyde Park, N.Y. Also Morgenthau Diaries, and Files of War Refugee Board.

Files, Official and Personal Papers of James Grover McDonald, Chairman President's Advisory Committee on Political Refugees, 1938–45, Columbia University, New York.

Files, Official and Personal Papers of Herbert H. Lehman, governor of New York, 1933–42, Columbia University, New York.

Files, American Jewish Joint Distribution Committee, *St. Louis,* New York City.

Files, YIVO, 1939, New York City.

Files, American Jewish Committee, 1939, New York City.

Files, Diplomatic Records, Group 59, no. 837.55J, National Archives, Washington.
Also Modern Military Records, Group 165

Files, Naval History, Group C-10-e, Register 22889, and Group C-10-j, Register 20764-A, Operational Archives, Washington.

Files, Foreign Office Despatches, most under file FO 371/24101, Public Record Office, London.

Pamphlet, "Paper Concerning the Treatment of German Nationals in Germany 1938–1939," His Majesty's Stationery Office, CMD 6120, 1939.

Letters, Heinz Grunstein, 1939.

Letter, Charlotte Sachs, 1939.

Letter, Herman Schliessor, 1939.

Letter, Gertrude Meijer, 1939.

Letter, Oscar Schwartz, 1939.

Letter, Hans Cramer, 1939.

Diary, Rose Bergmann, 1939.

Diary, Otto Bergmann, 1939.

Diary, Aaron Pozner, 1939.

Diary, Carl Lenneberg, 1939.

Diary, Werner Feig, 1939.

Report, *St. Louis* passenger committee, 1939.

Notices, posted on *St. Louis*, 1939.

Telegrams, to and from *St. Louis*, 1939.

Letter, Gustav Schroeder, 1950.

Bulletin, Wiener Library, vol. IX, nos. 3–4, May–August, Refugee Internment in Britain 1939–1940, by H. Jaeger, London, 1955.

Yearbook, Leo Baeck Institute, no. 1, pp. 373–90. "A survey of Jewish Emigration from Germany," by W. Rosenstock, London, 1956.

Periodical, *Yad Vashem Studies*, no. 1, pp. 125–52. "The Rescue of Latin American States," by Nathan Eck, Jerusalem, 1957.

Diary, Anne Frank (B. M. Mooyaart, trans.), Vallentine Mitchell, London, 1958.

Periodical, *Yad Vashem Studies*, vol. II, pp. 205–18. "The Role of the Gestapo in Obstructing and Promoting Jewish Emigration" by Arthur Prinz, Jerusalem, 1958.

Bulletin, AJR Information, vol. XIX, no. 7, July, Association of Jewish Refugees, London, 1964.

Periodical, *Mainstream*, vol. XII, no. 3, March, Theodor Herzl Foundation, New York, 1966.

Periodical, *Jewish Quarterly*, vol. 14, no. 4 (52), Winter Jewish Literary Publications, London, 1967.

Booklet, "Short History of the Hamburg-Amerika Linie," Hamburg, 1968.

Atlas, *Jewish History*, Martin Gilbert, Weidenfeld and Nicolson, London, 1969.

Periodical, *American Jewish Historical Quarterly*, vol. 61, no. 2, pp. 144–56. "The *St. Louis* Tragedy" by Irwin Gellman, December 1971.

Yearbook, Leo Baeck Institute, no. 16, pp. 63–95. "The Immigration and Acculturation of the German Jew in the United States of America," by H. A. Strauss, London, 1971.

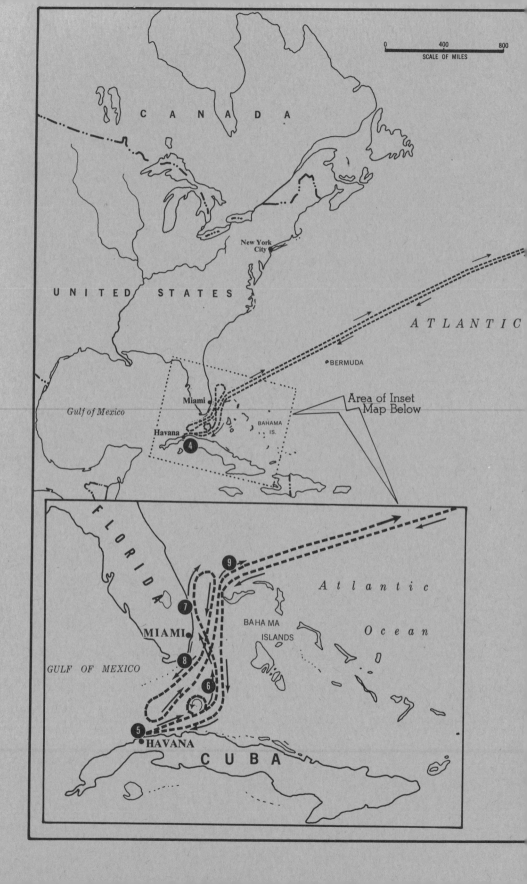

SCALE OF MILES
0   400   800

CANADA

New York
City

UNITED STATES

ATLANTIC

Gulf of Mexico

Miami

BERMUDA

Havana

BAHAMA
IS.

④

Area of Inset
Map Below

FLORIDA

⑨

Atlantic

⑦

Ocean

MIAMI

BAHAMA
ISLANDS

⑧

GULF OF MEXICO

⑥

⑤

HAVANA

CUBA